SONGS FOR EUROPE
THE UNITED KINGDOM AT THE EUROVISION SONG CONTEST

VOLUME TWO: THE 1970s

SONGS FOR EUROPE
THE UNITED KINGDOM AT THE EUROVISION SONG CONTEST

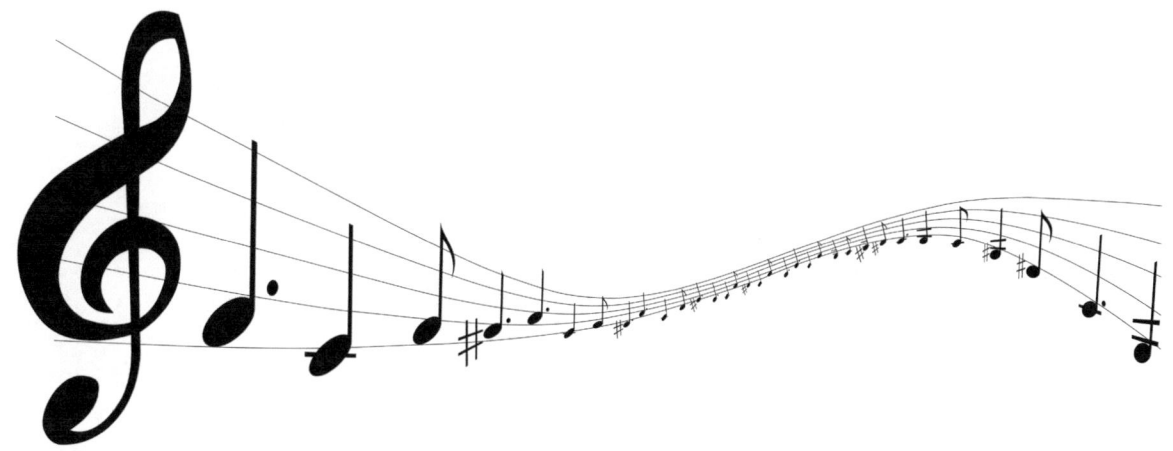

VOLUME TWO: THE 1970s
GORDON ROXBURGH

First published in the UK in 2014 by
Telos Publishing Ltd
www.telos.co.uk

Telos Publishing Ltd values feedback. Please e-mail us with any comments you may have about this book to: feedback@telos.co.uk

ISBN: 978-1-84583-093-9

Songs for Europe: The United Kingdom at the Eurovision Song Contest: Volume Two: The 1970s © 2014 Gordon Roxburgh

The moral right of the author has been asserted.

Internal design, typesetting and layout by Arnold T Blumberg
www.atbpublishing.com

Printed in the UK by Berforts Group Ltd

British Library Cataloguing in Publication Data.
A catalogue record for this book is available from the British Library.

This book is sold subject to the condition that it shall not by way of trade or otherwise, be lent, resold, hired out or otherwise circulated without the publisher's prior written consent in any form of binding or cover other than that in which it is published and without a similar condition including this condition being imposed on the subsequent purchaser.

DEDICATION

This book is especially dedicated to Richard Walter, with whom I have been firm friends ever since we first met back in 1978. He was kind enough to ask me to be his best man at his wedding to the lovely Sheena, and this dedication is in some small part to return that compliment.

CREDITS

The author would like to thank the following for their assistance and contributions to this book:
Stanley Appel, Richard Astbury, Valerie Avon, Mark Ayres, Cheryl Baker, Sietse Bakker, Colin Berry, Wayne Bickerton, Terry Bradford, Ken Bruce, Tim Clark, Nic Culverwell, Clem Curtis, Hazell Dean, Lynsey de Paul, Stephanie De-Sykes, Neil Dickinson, Guy Fletcher, Paul Griggs, Alan Hawkshaw, Tony Hiller, James Hodge, Terry Hughes, Michael Hurll, Nick Ingham, Tony James, Ray Johnson, Helen Wyn Jones, Eleanor Keenan, Paul Layton, Martin Lee, Tony Macauley, Bill Martin, Nichola Martin, Ernest Maxin, Dominic May, James Meredith, David Mindel, Mitch Murray, Pete Murray, Mike Redway, Roger Lee Reynolds, Ron Roker, Paul Rumbol, Louisa Sanderson, Lee Sheriden, Jill Shirley, Norman Smeddles, Aaron Smith, Steve Spice, Nicky Stevens, Sandra Stevens, Paul Vanezis, Lydia Vine, Jeff Walden and staff at the BBC Written Archives Centre, Peter Walsh, Richard West-Soley, Carl Wiser, Johnny Worth, Dougie Wright and Nola York.

BIBLIOGRAPHY

In the course of researching this book, the following publications and websites have been consulted:

Billboard; *Daily Express*; *Daily Mail*; *Daily Mirror*; *Daily Record*; *Diary Of A Musician* – Paul Griggs; *Eurovision Network News*; *Look-In*; *New Musical Express* (*NME*); *Radio Times*; *Record Mirror*; *The Sun*; *Vision*; *What This Katie Did* – Katie Boyle; *Which One's Cliff?* – Cliff Richard & Bill Latham.

www.andtheconductoris.eu
www.cliffrichardsongs.com
www.eurovision.tv

www.songfacts.com
www.songs4europe.com

AUTHOR'S NOTES

Where song durations are given in the text of this book, these have been taken mainly from the BBC's Programme as Broadcast (PasB) paperwork, especially where the original programmes no longer exist. However, for those programmes that do exist, a comparison has been made between the duration given in the paperwork and the actual duration. Sometimes these have proved to be wildly different, though in most cases they agree to within seconds. Any minor differences have been ignored. Where timings have differed greatly, I have included the actual duration from the transmitted version. This is of most interest where a song is down on the paperwork as having lasted 3'00" or over, as this has generally been the *Contest*'s limit on song duration. Any song that BBC paperwork lists as having lasted over 3'00" has been double checked. Not necessarily all songs of less than 3'00" on the paperwork have been double checked, so it is possible that some listed durations may differ from actual durations.

Start times and durations of programmes have been taken from the PasBs in most cases, otherwise times published in *Radio Times* have been used. Viewing figures have been taken from the BBC's own paperwork where known.

Where possible I have tried to identify for each song who wrote the lyrics and who composed the music. If it is not known who did what, or all contributors had a hand in both areas, the term has been simplified to *Composed by*. With English language versions of *Eurovision* entries, I have generally only referred to where the lyricist(s) have been identified as being British. (Exceptions have been made when referring to the lyricist(s) of English versions of the winning songs.)

I have included some information on record releases. It is by no means an exhaustive list, and generally I have included only cases where the song has been recorded by the original artist, rather than cover versions.

SONGS FOR EUROPE VOLUME TWO

Exceptions have been made where the original artist didn't record the song at all, or if a cover version did well in the charts, or a high profile artist recorded it.

If anyone has any further information on copies of missing programmes (either on film or on audio), record releases omitted or missing voting data, the author and publishers would appreciate being passed this for any future editions of this book.

COMMONLY USED ABBREVIATIONS

A&R – Artists and Repertoire (the division of a record label that scouts for new talent and oversees artistic development of recording artists)
BASCA – British Academy of Songwriters, Composers and Authors
BBC – British Broadcasting Corporation
BFBS – British Forces Broadcasting Service
BPI – British Phonographic Industry
DJ – Disc Jockey
EBU – European Broadcasting Union
ITN – Independent Television News
ITV – Independent Television
MPA – Music Publishers Association
NME – New Musical Express
OOV – Out of Vision (where a performer is not seen on screen)
PRS – Performing Rights Society
RI – Reaction Index (a figure used by the BBC Audience Research as an approval rating for a programme, on a scale from 1-100)

INTRODUCTION

The end of the 1960s had been a highly successful period for the United Kingdom in the *Eurovision Song Contest*, with two victories in 1967 and 1969, and a near miss by a single point in 1968. Consequently the contest was continuing to attract well-known artists to represent the country.

Chart success for any British entry was virtually guaranteed, and the sales potential was huge, both at home and abroad; and unsurprisingly artists generally recorded their songs in several European languages to further boost their exposure and disc sales.

Prolific and successful composers were also only too keen to enter the contest, as they saw the opportunities that it opened to them. Even the prospect of writing a runner-up was extremely financially attractive, as the record of the winning entry would include the second-place song on the B-side.

The television audience for the contest had steadily grown throughout the decade as an increasing number of people had acquired television sets and network coverage of BBC1 had widened. By the end of the 1960s, over 20 million people would tune in to watch each international final. It was becoming one of the television events of the year.

Colour television had also arrived, starting in 1967 when BBC2 began the first colour transmissions in Europe. So it was in 1968 that the BBC had the honour of producing the first *Eurovision Song Contest* made for colour television. However only a very small number of people were able to afford colour television sets, and not all parts of the UK could even receive the colour signal. Therefore the BBC1 live broadcasts of both the 1968 and 1969 contests were only in black and white, although the 1968 final had a deferred colour transmission the following day.

On 15 November 1969, colour television was extended from BBC2 to BBC1, which meant that from then on viewers would be able to watch the *Eurovision Song Contest* broadcasts live in colour. The contest was entering a new era.

Welcome to the 1970s.

1970 UNITED KINGDOM

It was announced in August 1969 that for the 1970 competition BBC Head of Light Entertainment Tom Sloan had chosen Mary Hopkin to be the nation's representative. Hopkin had previously won the ITV talent show *Opportunity Knocks*; in fact she had appeared for ten consecutive weeks, winning week after week, and had been one of the first artists to sign up to the Beatles' record label, Apple Records, securing the contract even before her initial win was announced. Her single 'Those Were The Days', which she recorded in five different languages, had seen off 1967 winner Sandie Shaw's version of the same song in the UK charts, as it reached the top position. An appearance in the *San Remo Contest* in 1969 along with top ten singles 'Goodbye' and 'Temma Harbour' made her a natural choice for the *Eurovision Song Contest*. At just 19 years old, she was already used to performing in competitions; and around the time of recording the *A Song for Europe* show, she was appearing at the London Palladium in the pantomime *Dick Whittington* with Tommy Steele.

Just over 200 songs had originally been submitted for the 1970 contest, and the MPA whittled them down to 15.

'I'm pretty sure Peter Callander and I entered "Turn On The Sun" for Mary Hopkin,' says composer Mitch Murray, 'which ended up with Nana Mouskouri recording it'. A Robin Gibb and Vic Lewis composition, 'Lavender Water', also failed to reach the final.

At this stage Hopkin was able to add three songs that she had commissioned herself. A selection committee of seven people, chaired by Sloan, then reduced the entries down to the final six songs. These were previewed on BBC1's weekly *It's Cliff Richard* show from Saturday 24 January to Saturday 28 February, with one song on each show. *Radio Times* promoted the contest in its 22 January edition. A colour photograph of Cliff Richard and Mary Hopkin graced the cover, and inside there was a one-page feature, mostly comprising an article on

SONGS FOR EUROPE VOLUME TWO

Richard, with one column on the contest.

At the time, Hopkin told *Radio Times*, 'I'm very pleased with the songs. The writers have taken my kind of singing into account and I'm going to do my very best with all of them. I'm not nervous yet, and I am looking forward to going to Holland. Actually with *Dick Whittington*, and all the preparations for the contest, I probably won't have time to get nervous. It won't be the end of the world if I don't win … but I would like to be remembered for making people happy with my singing'.

The 5 March edition of *Radio Times* carried a one page feature on the composers behind the six entries in the Final.

All the songs were recorded on Sunday 18 January, for the show to be broadcast on 7 March.

A SONG FOR EUROPE 1970
Saturday 7 March at 18.15.12 (Duration 34'26")
Presented by Cliff Richard

Mary Hopkin was accompanied by backing singers John Evans and Brian Bennett. A 35-piece orchestra also took part in the programme, conducted by John Cameron and Johnny Arthey. The backing singers and the orchestra were OOV (out of vision). Richard took on the presenting duties, providing the introduction to the programme and the links between the songs.

There was a brief musical introduction with about 10" of Hopkin's biggest hit song 'Those Were The Days'. Then, over some specially shot titles, comprising the *Eurovision* logo, a still photograph of Hopkin, and flying dove silhouettes with various European flags within them, appeared the words *A Song for Europe*, with the orchestra playing a 21" fanfare composed by Norrie Paramor.

1970 UNITED KINGDOM

| Song One | 'Three Ships' (2'23") | Sung by Mary Hopkin (with Brian Bennett and John Evans OOV). | Composed by Doug Flett and Guy Fletcher. | Conducted by John Cameron. |

Guy Fletcher and Doug Flett had come third in the 1968 contest with 'Wonderful World' with Cliff Richard, but they hadn't put forward a song in 1969. 'We didn't come up with one that we thought was right for [that year's singer] Lulu,' explains Fletcher. They would enter a song to the contest only if they thought it was right. 'You know when you have got the song to put in, and you know when you haven't, so there was no point in putting in one if it was all wrong'. Fletcher remembers that Mary Hopkin wasn't particularly enthusiastic about the contest, in fact: 'She didn't have any enthusiasm about anything, I recorded with her at Abbey Road on the song "Temma Harbour" – I sang with her – and she wasn't enthusiastic about that either. ["Three Ships"] just wasn't a satisfactory entry as far as I'm concerned.'

The 24 January edition of *It's Cliff Richard* in which the song was previewed was watched by 30.0 % of British adults (equating to 15.15 million viewers) and scored a Reaction Index (RI) of 66.

| Song Two | 'Early In The Morning Of Your Life' (2'52") | Sung by Mary Hopkin (with Brian Bennett and John Evans OOV). | Composed by Alan Hawkshaw and Ray Cameron. | Conducted by John Cameron. |

SONGS FOR EUROPE VOLUME TWO

The songwriting team of Alan Hawkshaw and Ray Cameron had come fifth the previous year with 'Are You Ready For Love?'

Looking back on the experience, Hawkshaw comments, 'Most songwriters got around to entering the *Eurovision Song Contest*, as winning guaranteed a hit record, and the financial rewards that went with it, and it was an exciting thing to do. But the songs had to be very basic, commercial in the very extreme.'

The BBC archives have retained a broadcast-quality copy of the *It's Cliff Richard* show from 31 January, in which Hopkin performs 'Early In The Morning Of Your Life'. The programme was watched by 28.7% (14.49 million).

Song Three	'I'm Going To Fall In Love Again' (2'03")	Sung by Mary Hopkin.	Composed by Cyril Ornadel and Hal Shaper.	Conducted by Johnny Arthey.

Two veterans of the contest teamed up for 'I'm Going To Fall In Love Again', and for both it would be their final credited contribution to the contest. Cyril Ornadel had been responsible for the music for the 1966 *A Song for Europe* winner, 'A Man Without Love'. Ornadel was born in London in 1924 and went on to study music at the Royal College of Music. He wrote the music for the Matt Monro song 'Portrait Of My Love' (with lyrics by Norman Newell). He was known mainly for musical theatre, having composed *Pickwick* along with Leslie Bricusse, and *Great Expectations* and *Treasure Island* along with his co-composer on this occasion Hal Shaper. He went on to write music for the television series' *Edward the Seventh* and *Sapphire and Steel*. He went to live in Israel, and in 2007 his autobiography *Reach for the Moon* was published. Cyril Ornadel died in June 2011.

South African-born Shaper had written with Peter Foss a song called 'My Impression of You', which failed to qualify for the *Festival of British Popular Songs* in 1957. In 1961 under the pseudonym John Harris he co-wrote 'A Place In The Country' for the contest. Shaper went on to achieve huge success in 1962 with the Matt Monro song 'Softly As I Leave You', for which he provided an English lyric. In the 1963 *A Song for Europe* he had composed, along with Steve Race, the runner-up, 'If You Ever Leave Me', and in the following year's competition his entry 'Beautiful, Beautiful' had finished in third place when performed by Matt Monro.

Shaper composed music for many films, including 'Its A Long Road' from *First Blood, Free as the Wind* and the theme music from *Papillon*. His songs were recorded by many world-famous artists, including Petula Clark, Nana Mouskouri, Barbra Streisand and Elton John to name just a few. In 1992 he returned to South Africa and worked hard to help unite the nation. He continued to write from there, and amongst his later works were the lyrics for Elaine Page's *Piaf* album. Shaper died in January 2004.

The 7 February edition of *It's Cliff Richard* in which the song was previewed was watched by 27.30 % (13.79 million) and scored an RI of 66.

Song Four	'You've Everything You Need' (2'26")	Sung by Mary Hopkin (with Brian Bennett and John Evans OOV).	Composed by Roger Reynolds and Anthony Dyball.	Conducted by Johnny Arthey.

Anthony Dyball and Roger Reynolds had been members of a group called the Planets that had reached the finals of a television talent show. Although they hadn't won, they had managed to secure a recording contract, but chart success had eluded them, and they had found themselves moving towards the cabaret end of the market. They had then changed their name to the Barry Lee Show, after one of the band members, as he incorporated impressions within the act. Reynolds and Dyball had regularly written songs for the group, sometimes individually and as a team. However they always took joint credit for all the songs, no matter who had actually done the work. In fact 'You've Everything You Need' was written entirely by Reynolds, as he explained:

'We were on the Engelbert Humperdink tour around April 1969, on the bill with Mary Hopkin, who closed the first half. Also on the bill were Ted Rodgers and Jerry Stevens. While on the tour, I had this song; in fact I first played it to Engelbert, in his dressing room, just on my guitar. For some reason I thought he might be interested in it, but he said "Why don't you play it to Mary?" So I went to play it to Mary, and she loved it, but I never thought any more about it. We were only on the tour for about ten days and nothing happened until about five or six months later. Our agent rang to say that Mary Hopkin was doing the *Eurovision Song Contest*; "She's doing six songs, and is allowed to add some of her choice. She would like to do your song, would you like it to be included with your permission?" Of course, yes, how could you refuse that? Anthony and I went down for the recording of the final show; in fact the whole group went down. The only image I have is that my auntie took a photo off the TV set when we were on; a blurry image with our names on it. It was all great and fantastic, but then we just had to wait. I always thought "Knock, Knock (Who's There?)" was the most commercial entry, but I thought ours was a little bit different from the usual, and Mary enjoyed singing it.'

Reynolds recalls trying two or three more times to enter the contest in subsequent years, but without success. He notes that the whole thing changed a few years later when entrants would need to come up with the whole package – the song and the act to perform it – whereas he had been quite happy just to submit a demo tape.

Reynolds and Dyball, along with Dyball's brother Michael, continued to perform their comedy impression act, as the Brothers Lee, and were regulars on shows such as *Seaside Special* and especially *The Generation Game*, where all three would do impressions of Max Wall, Tommy Cooper, Ked Dodd and Groucho Marx, which made them ideal for the show's format. Michael Dyball retired from the act in 1991 through ill health, while in the mid-'90s Reynolds moved on to pursue his interest in running snooker venues. Anthony Dyball continued on for a few more years with the act, before he too retired.

1970 UNITED KINGDOM

The 14 February edition of *It's Cliff Richard* in which the song was previewed was watched by 28.20 % (14.24 million).

| Song Five | 'Can I Believe'(2'33") | Sung by Mary Hopkin (with Brian Bennett and John Evans OOV). | Composed by Val Avon and Harold Spiro. | Conducted by John Cameron. |

Val Avon was a member of the Avons, a trio that had come close to singing in the 1960 *Eurovision Song Contest British Final* with 'Pickin' Petals', which was ultimately sung by Pearl Carr and Teddy Johnson. The group had started to put harmonies together and then found they just went into writing songs, eventually recording some of these as B-sides to their own singles. One of their first writing successes came with the Shadows' January 1963 number one instrumental hit 'Dance On', which, with a lyric added, became a chart hit for Kathy Kirby in September of the same year.

After the Avons spilt up, Val Avon went to work for Pye records as a plugger; and, as she puts it, her artistic side took over and she started to put groups together, writing songs for them and recording them:

'I worked for Belwin Mills music publisher, where I was also promoting other people's songs. I would go around with these long lists of songs, with some of my own in between – you couldn't say which were yours, for obvious reasons – and they would see which artists they suited. It was so much easier in those days; you'd just go to the A&R men and they would have lists of artists looking for material, and you submitted songs that way.'

Avon then met up with Harold Spiro and they just seemed to gel together as songwriters. 'He was very talented,' she adds.

Spiro was born in 1925. He grew up inspired by the music halls, where he met Tony Hiller, with whom he enjoyed

SONGS FOR EUROPE VOLUME TWO

a lifetime friendship. It was Hiller who gave him his first publishing deal. Later on, together with Phil Waineman, he wrote for Mike and Bernie Winters and worked with the group that later became glam-rock hit-makers the Sweet.

When it came to the division of words and music, Avon says, 'I'm not a very good piano player, but I play chords, and as a singer I'd play the chords and sing. Sometimes words would just come out with the tune, so I tended to write both. Harold was the same, but he played the piano much better than I did. He would start something off, and then we would get together, and sometimes it was just a case of coming up with a title line, a good idea, and going from there.'

The pair weren't writing specifically for *Eurovision*, but songs had to be instantly memorable to get into the charts, as there weren't so many airplays in those days. 1970 was their first attempt however at *A Song for Europe*.

'We were thrilled to bits to get through,' says Avon. 'We did think the song was absolutely right for Mary Hopkin, we thought we might stand a chance, but didn't think we would win. Ours was a folky type song, classy and melodic.'

Regarding Mary Hopkin's dislike of the contest, Avon remarked, 'We didn't spend a lot of time with Mary Hopkin, but knowing what little I did of her, she was very fussy about what she recorded. I would have thought she would hate to do something like "Knock, Knock (Who's There?)"'

The 21 February edition of *It's Cliff Richard* in which the song was previewed was watched by 26.70 % (13.48 million) and scored an RI of 66.

| Song Six | 'Knock, Knock (Who's There?)' (2'27") | Sung by Mary Hopkin (with Brian Bennett and John Evans OOV). | Composed by Geoff Stephens and John Carter. | Conducted by Johnny Arthey. |

1970 UNITED KINGDOM

John Carter was born John Shakespeare in Birmingham in 1942. He met his future songwriting partner Ken Hawker at school, and together they formed a skiffle band in the 1950s. In the '60s they used the pseudonyms John Carter and Ken Lewis for their songwriting, and as an outlet created their own band, Carter-Lewis and the Southerners. However, early success eluded them. It wasn't until they formed the Ivy League along with fellow session singer Perry Ford, that they scored some hits, including 'Tossing And Turning', which had been the most successful song chart-wise from *The British Song Festival* in 1965. Herman's Hermits also took one of their songs, 'Can't You Hear My Heartbeat', to number one in the US Billboard Hot 100.

Carter quickly got tired of touring with the Ivy League and left the group in 1966, the same year he got married to Gill, who wrote lyrics for some of his songs. He then concentrated on songwriting, supplying hits for Brenda Lee and Peter and Gordon. He met Geoff Stephens, and they wrote 'My World Fell Down' for the Ivy League. Carter also sang lead vocals on the hit single 'Winchester Cathedral', credited to the New Vaudeville Band. His own version of 'Knock, Knock (Who's There?)' was subsequently released on CD.

Stephens, born in 1934, had a variety of jobs, including schoolteacher and air traffic controller, but he began his days writing song and sketches for musical revues. It was in 1964 when with Les Reed he had his first big break, with a top ten hit 'Tell Me When' for the Applejacks. He then went on to discover and manage Donovan, producing his first hit and album.

Working together, Stephens and Carter had already achieved hits for Manfred Mann and Ken Dodd, and had written the song 'There's A Kind Of Hush', which was originally written for the New Vaudeville Band but became a big hit for Hermans' Hermits and was subsequently covered by many other artists.

The 28 February edition of *It's Cliff Richard* in which the song was previewed was watched by 26.50 % (13.38 million) and scored an RI of 69. An Audience Research Report was also commissioned for this edition, and from the sample of 200 viewers a minority did not care for 'Knock, Knock (Who's There?)' at all. Others described it as 'passable, but not a contest winner', with several in fact feeling that this year had not produced one sure-fire contender at all. A few found Hopkin rather 'wooden' and an 'expressionless performer' whose songs 'all tended to sound alike'. Most however thought she sang beautifully and many found this a catchy and enjoyable tune. It was the best of the six, in the opinion of a substantial number, 'with a chance in the [international] contest if chosen'. Some thought the background for Hopkin a bit sparse.

THE CONDUCTORS

Two conductors divided up the task of arranging the six songs for Mary Hopkin. These were Johnny Arthey, who had already been associated with the contest, having arranged Anne Shelton's 'My Continental Love' in 1963, and John Cameron.

Cameron had started his career in earnest while as Vice President of the Footlights at Cambridge University. He was soon writing arrangements for artists including Donovan, for whom he became musical director. He worked extensively in television, and was the musical director and arranger for three series of *Once More With Felix* starring Julie Felix, the *Bobby Gentry Show* and the *In Concert* series for Stanley Dorfman, working with artists such as Randy Newman and James Taylor. A song he wrote, 'If I Thought You'd Ever Change Your Mind', was a hit for Cilla Black, and also for Agnetha Fältskog many years later, both versions reaching number 11 in the UK charts.

Once all six songs had been performed, they were all played again – as had been the tradition in recent years – to give the public a further opportunity to familiarise themselves with the entries. The closing date for the postcard vote was Thursday 12 March.

Cliff Richard then closed the show singing 'Congratulations', backed by the Breakaways, with Norrie Paramor conducting the orchestra. The programme is no longer held in the BBC archives, although an off-air audio recording exists of most of it. Off-air recordings also exist of the songs from the previews on the weekly editions of *It's Cliff Richard*.

1970 UNITED KINGDOM

The final of *A Song for Europe* was watched by 27.70 % (13.99 million) and scored an RI of 70. The programme had been much enjoyed, according to the BBC's Audience Research Report of 200 viewers, with many of them feeling that this year's selection was a distinct cut above average. Each song had its supporters within the sample, but 'Knock, Knock (Who's There?)' was most often preferred, having 'a good melody and lively rhythm', and was felt to stand the best chance of winning the international final, due to take place in Amsterdam. The second most popular choice was 'I'm Gonna Fall In Love Again', while 'Early In The Morning Of Your Life' was the least fancied.

Some felt it had been unnecessary to go through the songs twice. Hopkin was generally considered to have put them over well, though some thought that while she had a pleasant enough voice, she was somewhat lifeless and lacking in personality. There was little 'light and shade' in her singing, according to some, and her range was limited. On the other hand, her unspoilt charm had an appeal in many quarters and she was considered an attractive artist with a sweet voice and excellent diction. 'I'm sure she will steal everyone's heart in the song contest,' was the view of one sample-member.

THE RESULTS

The result was announced one week later, on Saturday 14 March, in that evening's edition of the *It's Cliff Richard Show*. The announcement was made by Deputy Head of Light Entertainment Bill Cotton, as Tom Sloan was in hospital at the time. In fact Sloan died just two months later, in May 1970.

The outcome this year was not without controversy, however, as Roger Reynolds explains: 'Our publishers said, "You'll earn quite well. You're not going to win it, but you're lying second or third" – and of course being second would be terrific, because you would go on and be the B-side of the record. Then on the Saturday morning [14 March], my future father-in-law woke me to tell me there was an article about our song in the *Daily Mirror*. We opened it up, and there it was, "*Eurovision* Song Fix". We couldn't believe it. What had happened was that during that week, our publishers had got all their staff to send in postcards for "You've Everything You Need" … Unfortunately that particular week a member of the staff got fired, so to take revenge he went to the *Daily Mirror* to sell them the story. The cat was out of the bag – it was absolutely devastating – so the BBC diplomatically put our song fifth. I saw Michael Hurll, the director, a little bit later, and he said to me that the publishers hadn't even been clever with it; they done all these postcards and put them all in the same post box. The postman had seen them, put a rubber band round them, and they'd all gone in to TV Centre, all for the same song. That would have been a bit suspicious anyway, so they weren't even subtle doing it. They might have got away with it, but as soon as the *Daily Mirror* published it, the BBC had to do something about it. So that was all rather distressing, as you can imagine.'

So, with apparently adjusted votes, the results were initially announced in reverse order; although, to add to the drama, when it came down to the last two songs, the winner was announced before the runner-up. Mary Hopkin then performed a reprise of the winning song, 'Knock, Knock, (Who's There?)'

Song	Title	Votes	Placing
2	'Early In The Morning Of Your Life'	15,090	Sixth
4	'You've Everything You Need'	39,360	Fifth
5	'Can I Believe'	42,160	Fourth
1	'Three Ships'	60,330	Third
3	'I'm Going To Fall In Love Again'	74,670	Second
6	'Knock, Knock, (Who's There)'	120,290	First

Analysis: The total voting figure of 351,900 was well up on the 125,209 recorded in 1969, even though the Final was broadcast in a similar time slot. It would appear that the votes were counted to the nearest ten, possibly adjusted as a result of the aforementioned irregularities. However, it was a pretty clear and comprehensive victory for the John Carter and Geoff Stephens composition. It was only the second time that the song performed last had won the contest; the other occasion prior to this had been in 1961.

CREDITS
Producer and director: Michael Hurll
Designer: Roger Ford
Sound supervisor: Hugh Barker
Orchestra conducted by: Norrie Paramor, Johnny Arthey and John Cameron

The results programme no longer exists in the BBC archives, although off-air audio recordings of the results announcement and the winning reprise exist. The 14 March edition of *It's Cliff Richard* was watched by 31.10 % (15.71 million) and scored an RI of 67.

Mary Hopkin's 18 January performances of all six songs were included on a series of BBC transcription disc LPs entitled *Top of the Pops*, which were sent out weekly to overseas radio stations. The first two songs were included together on disc 274, and the remainder singly on discs 275 to 278 inclusive. Disc 283 also featured the winning song. Another series of BBC transcription discs entitled *Pick of the Pops*, which were compilation versions of the *Top of the Pops* discs, also featured three entries on each of two discs.

All six songs were also recorded by Hopkin for record producer Mickie Most, ready for the release of the winner as a single. This 7" disc depicted an apple-shaped Union Flag on its cover and wasn't released until 23 March – two days after the 1970 *Eurovision Song Contest* took place in Amsterdam, which was unusual for the time. Despite this, 'Knock, Knock, (Who's There?)' reached number two in the charts. It was backed with the

SONGS FOR EUROPE VOLUME TWO

second-placed song, 'I'm Going To Fall In Love Again', which was in a slightly different arrangement from the version on the *Top of the Pops* BBC transcription disc 275. 'Can I Believe' appears on a Malaysian EP, though the remaining songs would appear not to have been released commercially.

The *NME*'s reviewer commented: 'I regarded "Knock, Knock (Who's There?)" as Britain's weakest entry since 1966, but it's simple, gay, catchy and light-hearted, with the air of banality of which pop hits are made. Not Mary's normal choice of disc material, I suspect, but with all the plugging it's had, and will still get, it's bound to be big.'

Music critic Peter Jones also reviewed the disc: 'We're going to hear a lot of this, he said knowingly. Messrs Carter and Stephens have hit a happy commercial feel here, with Mary doing her bell-like clarity bit as it jogs along. Probably a number one. And anyway the flip *Eurovision* runner-up is good value too.'

Apart from when she appeared in the final of the *Eurovision Song Contest*, Mary Hopkin rarely performed 'Knock, Knock (Who's There?)' again. The song did feature on *Top of the Pops* on the edition of 26 March, but this was possibly taken from either *It's Cliff Richard* or the *Eurovision Song Contest* performance – it is impossible to be certain, as this edition no longer exists in the archives. Hopkin did however perform the song 'You've Everything You Need' at the Expo 70 event in Osaka, Japan.

1970 EUROVISION SONG CONTEST

With four countries having come out as joint winners of the 1969 contest, there were several problems facing the 1970 event. The first was to find a host broadcaster. BBC paperwork confirms that there was only ever going to be a choice between two countries. As Spain had just hosted the 1969 event, and the BBC had staged the 1968 contest, it was down to either of the other two winning countries. A simple toss of the coin decided between France and the Netherlands, and the latter won (or lost, as one BBC official amusingly suggested in a memo). It was expected to cost Dutch broadcaster NOS (Nederlandse Omroep Stichting) £25,000 to stage the event.

The other problem, which wasn't totally resolved in time for the 1970 contest, was widespread dissatisfaction with the voting system that had allowed four countries to win. This led to Sweden announcing its withdrawal in April 1969, followed by Norway and Finland. Sweden had criticised the contest for its mediocre standard, but had informed the EBU that if it were to be redesigned they would reconsider their participation. Portugal also ultimately withdrew, though they still held a national contest.

Portugal (Withdrawn)	'Onde Vais Rio Que Eu Canto'	Sung by Sérgio Borges.	Composed by Nobrega e Sousa and Joaquim Pedro Gonçalves.

With just 12 countries remaining in the contest, the lowest number for over a decade, there were serious doubts as to its future. In light of the concerns expressed about the tied result in 1969, a rule was brought in to deal with any recurrence of that situation. The artists of the countries involved would have to perform again, and the juries in all the other remaining countries would determine the winner by a show of hands. If that too resulted in a tie, then the result would be a dead heat.

NOS came up with some innovations this year. The first was an extended opening film sequence, featuring the scenic delights of the host nation. By contrast, the 24-second introduction by presenter Willy Dobbe must go down as the shortest in the history of the contest. The second innovation was the inclusion of filmed 'postcards' between the songs. In this case, most of them showed the artists in settings in their respective countries. However, those for Luxembourg and Monaco were shot in Paris.

The ingenious set for the event, featuring changing mobile shapes, was designed by Roland De Groot. The artists were accompanied by an orchestra of 50 musicians. According to the *Daily Express*, the orchestra members were tipping the United Kingdom to win, followed by Spain and Germany.

Rehearsals had commenced on Wednesday 18 March at 10.00, with each country being given a 45-minute slot. On the first day, seven countries rehearsed: Netherlands, Switzerland, Italy, Yugoslavia, Belgium, France and Ireland. The United Kingdom was originally supposed to be one of the seven. However, as Mary Hopkin was contractually tied up with appearances at the London Palladium that day, the BBC requested that she be allowed to swap places with Ireland. On the second day, 19 March, rehearsals took place with Luxembourg, Spain, Monaco, Germany and the United Kingdom, with Hopkin's slot being from 14.45 to 15.30.

Friday 20 March saw all the countries have a second rehearsal of 20 minutes each, with the United Kingdom scheduled at 14.00. There was then a full rehearsal of the contest from 20.00.

There was a final dress rehearsal on the evening of Saturday 21 March from 18.00 to 20.00, which included a dummy voting sequence. The live transmission followed at 22.00 local time.

Although only 12 countries were participating, the programme was broadcast in a further 14 countries, including Iceland, Greece, Czechoslovakia, Tunisia, Israel, Bulgaria, Hungary, USSR, Romania, Brazil and Chile, winning a total audience of some 400 million.

1970 EUROVISION SONG CONTEST

So short was the gap between the final of *A Song for Europe* on 14 March and the main event on 21 March that it was too late for *Radio Times* to include details of the winning song in the edition covering the contest. This edition featured a colour photo of Mary Hopkin on the cover. Inside was a four page feature to promote the contest, including an interview with Hopkin, a score chart, and a retrospective look at previous British entrants.

There were trailers promoting the *Eurovision Song Contest* on Thursday 19 March, with a general trailer for *Radio Times* highlighting its coverage of *So You Think You Can Drive?* as well as the contest. Friday 20 March saw two further trailers, of 1'01" and 1'36" duration respectively, using footage of Hopkin performing 'Knock, Knock, (Who's There?)' from *It's Cliff Richard*. A similar trailer of 1'12" was shown on Saturday 21 March following that evening's edition of *It's Cliff Richard*.

EUROVISION SONG CONTEST 1970
Saturday 21 March at 22.00.00 (Duration 73'30")
From the RAI Congrescentrum, Amsterdam, The Netherlands
Presented by Willy Dobbe

David Gell provided the television commentary for BBC1, and Tony Brandon for Radio 1 and Radio 2 listeners. John Russell provided commentary for British Forces Radio.

Netherlands	'Waterman' (2'30")	Sung by the Hearts Of Soul (soloist Patricia).	Composed by Pieter Goemans.	Conducted by Dolf van der Linden.

SONGS FOR EUROPE VOLUME TWO

The Hearts of Soul comprised three sisters, Patricia, Stella and Bianca Maessen. However, as the rules of the contest still didn't allow for groups, Patricia took the lead vocal, and was credited accordingly, with her sisters providing backing vocals.

Switzerland	'Retour' (2'40")	Sung by Henri Dès.	Composed by Henri Dès.	Conducted by Bernard Gérard.
Italy	'Occhi Di Ragazza' (2'45")	Sung by Gianni Morandi.	Words by Sergio Bardotti and Gianfranco Baldazzi. Music by Lucio Dalla.	Conducted by Mario Capuano.
Yugoslavia	'Pridi, Dala, Ti Bom Cvet' (2'27")	Sung by Eva Sršen.	Words by Dušan Velkaverh. Music by Mojmir Sepe.	Conducted by Mojmir Sepe.
Belgium	'Viens L'Oublier' (3'00")	Sung by Jean Vallée.	Composed by Jean Vallée.	Conducted by Jack Say.

1970 EUROVISION SONG CONTEST

France	'Marie Blanche' (2'53")	Sung by Guy Bonnet.	Words by André-Pierre Dousset. Music by Guy Bonnet.	Conducted by Franck Pourcel.
United Kingdom	'Knock, Knock (Who's There?)' (2'35")	Sung by Mary Hopkin with Brian Bennett and John Evans (in vision).	Composed by John Carter and Geoff Stephens.	Conducted by Johnny Arthey.

Interviewed by Keith Altham of the *Record Mirror* before the contest, Mary Hopkin was asked if she liked her song. 'It was one of those I liked,' she replied guardedly. There was rumoured to be one song she didn't like? 'There was one I felt was too *Eurovision* manufactured'. With the 'la la' and 'knock knocks', couldn't that also be said of the song that won? 'Yes,' was her reply. Moving onto the subject of possible problems with the voting, Hopkin commented, 'I think they have ironed out most of the problems now. There are no questions of embarrassing ties or anything, so I think it's all right. The best song will win, as long as everyone votes fairly.'

Speaking to the press in Amsterdam, Hopkin had this to say: 'I think it would be better if it was not a contest. Some of the contestants seem to take it very seriously indeed, and that spoils it. I think a Eurovision song festival, where people could sing songs they like and not songs that must have a certain instant appeal, would be of much more value. I am going to have a good time here, whether I win or lose.'

Years later, Hopkin recalled the experience: 'I was so embarrassed about it. Standing on stage singing a song you hate is awful. Unless you are expressing what's inside, there is no point. For me it was the ultimate humiliation.'

Hopkin had a further top 20 hit in 1970 with 'Think About Your Children'. In 1971 she married record producer Tony Visconti and withdrew from the pop music scene to have a family, although it didn't prevent her from continuing to record and appearing occasionally on various television and radio shows. She made a return to the charts in 1976 with 'If You Love Me (I Won't Care)', which reached number 32. She and Visconti divorced in 1981.

Hopkin continued to work on projects that were very much of her own choosing, writing a number of her own songs and releasing several albums on her own label, as well as collaborating on albums with her daughter, Jessica Lee Morgan, and her son, Morgan Visconti.

Michael Hurll, the producer/director of her *A Song for Europe*, said, 'Mary Hopkin was a good singer, had a lovely voice, but was not a good performer; I think she lost it on that.'

Hurll had been part of the British delegation. 'We had gone out to Amsterdam, and Tom Sloan was confident we were going to win, and so were the press. We were staying in the Esso Hotel, and Tom instructed me to get the large ballroom booked up afterwards for a party, so I got it all booked and got the champagne in … and then of course she didn't win. I then had to go back to the management and say "I'm terribly sorry, we don't need all that anymore," and we had to pay up some guilders for cancelling it.

'Of course, Dana won. The Irish delegation didn't think she would win, didn't have any money, and hadn't organised a party. All they could get was a bedroom suite, so it was just a bedroom and a sitting room, which I think their delegation head had been using. The British press were invited, I was there, and so was Bill Cotton. We had joined them, and they were getting bottles in via room service, and after celebrating for about half an hour or so, there came a knock at the door, and there were about four rough Irish labourers, saying in strong Irish accents, "We'd like to say hello to Dana, we're working in Amsterdam". The Head of Delegation goes, "No, no, we don't want you here," and he slams the door shut. A short while later, another knock at the door, and it is these four Irish labourers again, who by now have had a bit more to drink, and are a bit more aggressive – "You're so bloody smart, we just want to congratulate Dana!" – and this time they punched him one! It then quickly developed into what I call a snowball fight, and it just kicked off all round the room. I thought, "I don't want to be involved in this," so I dived into the wardrobe and pulled the door shut … and of course there were clothes in there, and as I parted them, there was Bill Cotton in the other half of the wardrobe! This fight went round the room, out the door and down the stairs, and they smashed just about every pane of glass in the foyer.'

Alan Smith reviewed the contest in the *NME*: 'Right through the two days of rehearsals it became more and more apparent that "Knock Knock (Who's There)" and "All Kinds Of Everything" had to take the first or second places, even though the Irish number came in for some criticism for being "over sweet". Mary Hopkin's recording manager Mickie Most sat behind me during the event, and once "All Kinds Of Everything" had finished he said, "That's it. They've beaten us"; the man is a nit picking computer!

'Why did "Knock, Knock (Who's There?)" fail? Certainly, nobody I knew could fault Mary's performance. It came over beautifully; the orchestra belted away under the superb hand of Johnny Arthey; and in colour Little Miss Hopkin was a picture of beautiful professionalism with her blonde locks against a background of blue and a shimmering black dress.

'I name three factors. One, the incredibly high vote of nine votes for "All Kinds Of Everything" by the Belgian jury really swung the pattern away from Mary. Two, "All Kinds Of Everything" is indisputably a catchy and instantly commercial song. And three (and four), voting a slower number and an unknown artist to the top gave the annual jamboree something of a lift.'

'"All Kinds Of Everything" is a beautiful song,' said Hopkin in the same publication. 'I haven't been able to stop singing it for days. It was a fair competition, and the best song won. I really do wish Dana all the luck in the world.'

SONGS FOR EUROPE VOLUME TWO

Luxembourg	*'Je Suis Tombé Du Ciel'* (2'42")	Sung by David Alexandre Winter.	Words by Eddy Marnay. Music by Yves De Vriendt.	Conducted by Raymond Lefèvre.

Spain	'Gwendolyne' (2'50")	Sung by Julio Iglesias.	Composed by Julio Iglesias.	Conducted by Augusto Algueró.

Julio Iglesias' first big hit in the United Kingdom was 'Begin The Beguine', which went to number one in October 1981. At the time of the contest he was still relatively unknown.

Monaco	'Marlène' (2'38")	Sung by Dominique Dussault.	Words by Henri Dijan. Music by Eddie Barclay and Jimmy Walter.	Conducted by Jimmy Walter.

Germany	*'Wunder Gibt Es Immer Wieder'* (2'35")	Sung by Katja Ebstein.	Words by Günter Loose. Music by Christian Bruhn.	Conducted by Christian Bruhn.

The English language version, 'No More Love for Me', had lyrics written by the British husband and wife partnership of Barry Mason and Sylvan Whittingham.

1970 EUROVISION SONG CONTEST

| Ireland | 'All Kinds Of Everything' (3'00") | Sung by Dana. | Composed by Derry Lindsay and Jackie Smith. | Conducted by Dolf van der Linden. |

Dana (aka Rosemary Brown) was born in Islington, London in August 1951 and lived in Derry, Northern Ireland. 'All Kinds Of Everything' went to number one in the British charts. Dana appeared on *Top of the Pops* with the song on the editions broadcast on 2 April (possibly taken from the *Eurovision Song Contest*), 9 April (studio performance) and 16 and 23 April (these two being repeats of her 9 April appearance). In addition, as this was one of the best-selling songs of the year, she featured on the Christmas edition broadcast on 26 December. None of these programmes exists in the BBC archives. Other appearances included one on *The Golden Shot* broadcast on ITV on 12 April.

Dana had several more top ten hits, including 'It's Gonna Be A Cold, Cold Christmas' and 'Fairytale'. She became a regular on television and on stage in summer seasons, and was frequently cast as Snow White in pantomimes. Later she moved into politics. She stood in the Irish Presidential Elections, finishing third, and went on to become a member of the European Parliament.

THE VOTING

The same voting system was used as in 1969. The scoreboard showed the countries' names in Dutch, with '*Groot Brittannie*' for the United Kingdom.

The United Kingdom jury comprised Mr M H Preston, Mrs Altoft, Miss Bell, Reverend D Constable, Winston Jenkins, Sam Smith, Andrew Petitt, Shanna Houston, David Hammond and Alison Field. The United Kingdom spokesperson was Colin-Ward Lewis.

SONGS FOR EUROPE VOLUME TWO

	Netherlands	Switzerland	Italy	Yugoslavia	Belgium	France	United Kingdom	Luxembourg	Spain	Monaco	Germany	Ireland	TOTAL	POSITION
NETHERLANDS			3	3			1						07	7TH
SWITZERLAND	2					2	1				2	1	08	4TH=
ITALY				1					2		2		05	8TH=
YUGOSLAVIA							4						04	11TH
BELGIUM						3		1				1	05	8TH=
FRANCE			1	2						2		3	08	4TH=
UNITED KINGDOM	3	2	2	4		2		2		4	4	3	26	2ND
LUXEMBOURG													00	12TH
SPAIN			3					2		3			08	4TH=
MONACO		1			1	2			1				05	8TH=
GERMANY		1	1					3	4	1		2	12	3RD
IRELAND	5	6			9	1	4	2	3		2		32	1ST

1970 EUROVISION SONG CONTEST

Analysis: Ireland got off to a cracking start in the first round of voting and looked initially to be running away with the votes. When Yugoslavia drew the United Kingdom level, it looked as if it could now turn into something of a contest. But then came the Belgian jury, who delivered a knockout blow by awarding nine votes to Ireland. From that point on, the result never looked in doubt. Not since the 1958 contest had one country received as many as nine votes under the same scoring system. The United Kingdom was then reduced to playing catch up, and managed to reduce the final deficit to six points. No other country came close to challenging Ireland. Germany was the only other country to get a final total in double figures. Only two countries, Belgium and Spain, failed to award the United Kingdom any votes, while the United Kingdom itself was the only jury to give Yugoslavia any votes at all.

It must have come as something of a relief to the EBU Scrutineer that there was a clear outright winner this year; and with a different country, Ireland, winning for the first time, it gave the contest a much-needed boost. For the United Kingdom it marked the seventh time as runners-up.

The awards were presented by Lenny Kuhr, the Dutch singer who was one of the winners of the 1969 contest.

WINNING REPRISE

Ireland	'All Kinds Of Everything' (2'57")	Sung by Dana.	Composed by Derry Lindsay and Jackie Smith.	Conducted by Dolf van der Linden.

SONGS FOR EUROPE VOLUME TWO

CREDITS
Producer: Warner van Kampen
Director: Theo Ordeman
Designer: Roland De Groot
Musical Director: Dolf van der Linden
EBU Scrutineer: Clifford Brown

The programme was watched by 47.9 percent of the British population (24.19 million) and scored an RI of 61. Overall the response was less favourable than for the previous two to three years, according to a BBC Audience Research Report on the opinions of 200 viewers. This may have been due to the natural disappointment of Mary Hopkin being pipped at the post – although 'All Kinds Of Everything' did please most viewers – but another factor was a feeling that this year's contest had lacked any sense of occasion and atmosphere.

Nearly half of the sample reported considerable enjoyment of an entertaining and well-presented programme. A number were pleased that the preliminary chat and commentary had been kept to a minimum, making it more streamlined, and felt that the film introductions had been a good idea. The stage setting had been simple and effective, it was said, with the voting being fair. The majority agreed with the choice of the top two, although mainly because they could understand the English lyrics, and few would have reversed their positions. The Irish song was considered attractive and appealing, though some thought it was the best of a poor bunch, describing it as 'inoffensive', 'unoriginal' and 'colourless' and certainly not worthy of the nine votes given by Belgium.

With fewer countries participating each year, there was a feeling that the contest was becoming outmoded and there was a lack of excitement and glamour. The scoreboard and the reading of the votes were considered to have been not particularly clear. There were a few scattered complaints that both the Dutch presenter, Willy Dobbe, and the BBC commentator, David Gell, had been rather colourless, with the latter talking through announcements. Generally though there was warm praise for both, and it was said that David Gell's clear, unobtrusive comments had helped viewers follow what was happening

The BBC no longer holds its broadcast version of the contest in its archives, although an audio recording exists of the radio broadcast. It would also appear that no television archive in Europe has retained the opening sequence and the start of the Dutch song in colour, and the same applies to part of Dana's first performance of 'All Kinds Of Everything' (though her winning reprise exists in full in colour); and the interval act is also missing in colour. Black and white footage exists of all missing colour material.

After the contest, Tony Brandon continued live radio from Amsterdam with his *Saturday People* show, a mixture of chat and music, until midnight. The radio producer was John Hooper.

ITN has retained a 30" item that was featured in their news bulletin at 18.10 on 22 March, showing Mary Hopkin arriving back at Heathrow Airport and giving a short interview.

1971 UNITED KINGDOM

On 29 July 1970 the BBC held a photo call at TV Centre to announce the choice of entrant for the 1971 contest: Clodagh Rodgers. The announcement was also featured on the *BBC News* bulletins the same day, and the film footage (minus sound) has been retained in the archives.

As Rodgers was later to recall in an interview for *Radio Times*, the telephone had rung at nine o'clock one morning at her home in north London. Her husband and manager John Morris had taken the call. 'When I came downstairs, he just said "Guess who's been chosen to sing *A Song for Europe*?" He said it so casually that what I said to him in return isn't repeatable.'

Although the rules of the contest had now been changed to allow groups of up to six people to participate, the BBC opted not to take advantage of that change for 1971, and decided to keep to a female soloist, as the contest had been won by a female soloist every year from 1967, including all four winners in 1969.

'Girls have always had a tough time in the pop world,' Rodgers told *Radio Times*. 'I think it's because girls form the majority of the record buyers and you therefore have to identify very strongly with them before they'll accept you as a friend and buy your records. The *Eurovision Song Contest* is a way of really proving that a girl vocalist can get across a number on their behalf. Lulu, Sandie Shaw and Mary Hopkin have all benefited from it. It could well be the really big chance for me as well.'

As the contest was scheduled to take place in Dublin, the choice of artist was also perhaps a diplomatic move. Rodgers was born in March 1947 in Ballymena, County Antrim in Northern Ireland. She made her professional debut at the age of 13, opening for Michael Holliday. By 14 she had signed her first record deal. In 1965 she moved to EMI Columbia, initially performing with her name spelt Cloda Rogers. She appeared in a couple of films, *Just For Fun* and *It's All Over Town*. She was no stranger to song contests, either, having finished third in the *European Song Cup* in 1963, singing 'Powder Your Face In Sunshine' at the event in Greece.

In 1968, after her marriage to Morris, she signed a three year deal with RCA. A year later she had two top five hits, 'Come Back And Shake Me' and 'Goodnight Midnight'. Other chart songs followed, including 'Biljo' in 1969 and 'Everybody Go Home, The Party's Over' in 1970.

The six songs short-listed from the 212 submitted for the 1971 contest were announced in December 1970. They were then previewed at the rate of one a week on the *It's Cliff Richard* show, starting from 9 January. A memo was sent by the Executive Producer of Radio 2 stipulating that none of the songs could be broadcast on the radio prior to 1 March, as it could breach the contest rules. However, an exception was allowed for the Acker Bilk and Clodagh Rodgers-presented programme 'The Music Goes Round and Round', which went out between 19.02 and 20.00 on Radio 1 and Radio 2 on Tuesday evenings. This also previewed the six songs over six weeks, starting on 12 January.

The Final was recorded on Wednesday 17 February at BBC Television Theatre.

A SONG FOR EUROPE 1971
Saturday 20 February at 18.16.18 (Duration 43'55")
Presented by Cliff Richard

The programme opened with Cliff Richard singing the 1970 British entry 'Knock, Knock, (Who's There?)'. He then introduced Clodagh Rodgers, who was played on with 15" of 'Come Back And Shake Me', and after a brief humorous chat between the pair it was on to the contest. There was a specially-shot title sequence (19 feet of silent film) over which was played a lengthy fanfare (0.32") composed by Norrie Paramor. The orchestra under his direction comprised 28 musicians. Rodgers had vocal backing from the Breakaways, which included her sister Lavinia Rodgers plus Margo Newman, Jean Hawker and Vicki Brown. All the composers were present in the audience.

SONGS FOR EUROPE VOLUME TWO

Song One	'Look Left, Look Right' (2'19")	Sung by Clodagh Rodgers.	Composed by Alan Hawkshaw and Ray Cameron.	Arranged by Keith Mansfield.

This was the third year in succession that the songwriting team of Alan Hawkshaw and Ray Cameron had made the Final, following 'Are You Ready For Love', fifth in 1969, and 'Early In The Morning Of Your Life' in 1970.

'It was a bit nerve-wracking, but we believed we stood a chance,' said Hawkshaw. 'Seeing low numbers coming in was disappointing, of course.'

In the *NME*, Andy Gray reviewed the songs in the 1971 contest: 'From hearing the songs twice, most viewers would agree they are of a high standard, although there were some familiar passages in one or two of them. "Look Left, Look Right" had a little tinge of "Puppet On A String", a pop tune right enough, but it seemed a little intricate and not clean cut enough.'

The 9 January edition of *It's Cliff Richard* in which the song was previewed was watched by 25.9% of the population (13.08 million).

Song Two	'In My World Of Beautiful Things' (2'23")	Sung by Clodagh Rodgers.	Composed by Valerie Avon and Harold Spiro.	Arranged by Keith Mansfield.

Valerie Avon and Harold Spiro had their second entry in successive years in *A Song for Europe*, having achieved fourth place in 1970 with 'Can I Believe'.

'We pretty much knew we weren't going to win it. In those days, you were really taking a chance with a

1971 UNITED KINGDOM

ballad,' said Avon, 'because the British public wanted something instant, and not anything too clever. It had a few plays, though, but it wasn't instant enough.'

'Val Avon and Harold Spiro contributed a quiet, sweet, romantic kind of song with "In My World Of Beautiful Things"' was the *NME*'s verdict.

The 16 January edition of *It's Cliff Richard* in which the song was previewed was watched by 25.8% of the population (13.03 million).

| Song Three | 'Jack In The Box' (2'52") | Sung by Clodagh Rodgers. | Words by David Myers. Music by John Worsley. | Arranged by Johnny Arthey. |

Popular myth has it that the John Worsley who wrote the music for 'Jack In The Box' was actually Johnny Worth, who had composed 'Day At The Seaside' for Vince Hill in 1963.

'That is not me,' says Worth. 'This can oft be the bane of my life, and I hope I am not the bane of his! In all fairness, he is a very good songwriter, although I think I wrote a lot more songs, and probably a lot more hits. I often inadvertently get some of his money, which I endeavour to let the PRS (Performing Rights Society) know is not mine, and I hope he does the same for me!'

The actual writers, cockney David Myers, aged 30, and Worsley, aged 26, said to reporter David Wigg: 'We deliberately studied the style of "Puppet On A String" to write a *Eurovision* type song. Hence the idea of a toy with "Jack In The Box."'

Andy Gray wrote: 'The jaunty "Jack In The Box" song … used drum breaks to punctuate the lyric at the start. This number had a similar feel to "Puppet On A String" but was very well done by Clodagh.'

SONGS FOR EUROPE VOLUME TWO

The 23 January edition of *It's Cliff Richard* in which the song was previewed was watched by 24.90% (12.57 million).

| Song Four | 'Another Time, Another Place' (2'36") | Sung by Clodagh Rodgers. | Composed by Mike Leander and Eddie Seago. | Arranged by Keith Mansfield. |

One of the composers, Mike Leander, had previously written 'Little Rag Doll', which Cliff Richard had sung in the 1968 contest, finishing in fifth place.

Leander and Eddie Seago had composed 'Early In The Morning' and 'Come Tomorrow' for the group Vanity Fare, the former reaching number eight in the charts in 1969. The two composers had been schoolfriends, and Seago had previously had a career in advertising.

'One of the lines,' wrote the *NME*, 'reminded me of another hit tune (could it be "You Don't Have To Say You Love Me?") and has a Neapolitan sound at times, a romantic beat ballad, go-ey and interesting.'

The 30 January edition of *It's Cliff Richard* in which the song was previewed was watched by 27.20% of the population (13.74 million).

| Song Five | 'Wind Of Change' (2'18") | Sung by Clodagh Rodgers. | Words by Mike Hawker. Music by Brian Bennett. | Arranged by Johnny Arthey. |

1971 UNITED KINGDOM

Mike Hawker along with Ivor Raymonde had been behind several hits, including 'Walking Back To Happiness', which was a number one for Helen Shapiro, and 'I Only Want To Be With You' and 'Stay Awhile' for Dusty Springfield. With John Schroeder, Hawker also wrote two other songs for Shapiro, 'Don't Treat Me Like A Child' and 'You Don't Know', the latter of which was also a number one hit.

Brian Bennett was born in 1940 in Palmers Green, north London. When he left school at 16 he joined a skiffle group as a drummer, and after working in several groups, including a spell with Marty Wilde's Wildcats, he joined Cliff Richard's backing group, the Shadows, as their drummer. Along with Bruce Welch he co-wrote a number of hit songs for Richard and the Shadows, including 'Summer Holiday' and 'Time Drags By'. He was also a pianist, composer and arranger.

'A big voiced effort with a country-sound that was probably the most unusual of the six songs,' said reviewer Andy Gray.

The 6 February edition of *It's Cliff Richard* in which the song was previewed was watched by 24.20% of the population (12.22 million).

Song Six	'Someone To Love Me' (2'21")	Sung by Clodagh Rodgers.	Composed by Ernie Ponticelli and Gordon Rees.	Arranged by Johnny Arthey.

Gordon Rees had previously co-written, along with brothers Tony and Irving Hiller, the entry 'You're For Real' in the 1962 contest, which had finished in joint tenth position.

Amongst the songs composed by the team of Ernie Ponticelli and Rees was one called 'Decimalisation', recorded by Max Bygraves, as the country had just converted to the decimal system of currency. Ponticelli had worked with composer Norman Newell and together they wrote the top 20 song 'More Than Love' for Ken Dodd. Both Ponticelli and Rees had worked with Alan Moorhouse who had co-composed 'Boom Bang-A Bang'.

'Finally, "Someone To Love Me", with a rousing jog-trot, country sounding, with strings. Simple and very good,' was the verdict of the *NME*. 'Could be the winner.'

The 13 February edition of *It's Cliff Richard* in which the song was previewed was watched by 27.40% of the population (13.84 million).

THE ARRANGERS

Johnny Arthey had previously arranged 'My Continental Love' for Anne Shelton in the 1963 contest, and had conducted and arranged three of the songs in the 1970 competition – including the winner, 'Knock, Knock (Who's There?)', which he conducted at the *Eurovision Song Contest* in Amsterdam.

Keith Mansfield was born in 1943 and was well known for his television themes, including the *Grandstand* theme and 'Light And Tuneful', which was used for the BBC's coverage of the Wimbledon tennis championships. He arranged songs for the groups Marmalade and Love Affair amongst many others.

THE VOTING

There was one major problem when it came to the voting in 1971. Traditionally viewers had sent in their choice of song by postcard, but this year there was a national postal strike, which had been ongoing since 20 January. An emergency plan had to be put into operation, to use a system of juries throughout the country, with each jury comprising ten persons.

During the 17 February recording of the Final, two different endings were provided by Cliff Richard: one asking viewers to vote by post, in case the strike had ended by the time of transmission, and the other explaining about the jury system. Even if the strike was sorted out, it could still take several days before people would be even allowed to post, due to the backlog. The decision as to which ending to use was made on the morning of Saturday 20 February, just hours before the programme was transmitted. It had to be the jury system. (The postal strike didn't in fact end until 4 March.)

The juries were located in Belfast, Bristol, Birmingham, Cardiff, Glasgow, London, Manchester and Norwich. They watched the Final on 20 February and cast their votes, one per person, for their favourite song. The ballot boxes were sealed and brought to the BBC Television Centre.

The Final was watched by 30.80% (15.55 million). The postal strike also affected the Audience Research Report prepared for the programme, with just a small sample of 40 viewers able to respond. However, the Final had been well received by them, and most found the six songs moderately enjoyable, although few were enthusiastic. The complaints were that the songs were all very similar and manufactured for the occasion. (A frequent comment was that the final choice of 'Jack In The Box' sounded as if it was derived from 'Puppet On A String'.) Clodagh Rodgers was though considered to be an attractive singer.

All of the songs were also played by Terry Wogan in a show broadcast on Radio 1 and Radio 2, so listeners could still pick their favourite, even if they couldn't actually vote. An audio recording of this show exists.

THE RESULTS

The results were announced during the *It's Cliff Richard* show recorded on Friday 26 February and transmitted the following evening. The programme was promoted by a *Radio Times* cover for the 27 February edition, with a colour photograph of Clodagh Rodgers. Inside there was a half-page article, plus a black and white photo of the singer.

At the start of the programme the still-sealed ballot boxes were brought on stage. No-one knew the results at this time. They were then taken backstage to be opened and the votes counted. Then, later on in the show, BBC Head of Light Entertainment Bill Cotton announced how each jury had voted. Rodgers and Cliff Richard were also watching on stage as the scoreboard totalled up the votes.

SONGS FOR EUROPE VOLUME TWO

	Title	Belfast	Birmingham	Bristol	Cardiff	Glasgow	London	Manchester	Norwich	TOTAL	PLACING
1	'Look Left, Look Right'					1		4	1	06	5^(TH)=
2	'In My World Of Beautiful Things'		1		4	2	2	2	1	12	4^(TH)
3	'Jack In The Box'	1	1	4	1	6	4	3	2	22	1^(ST)
4	'Another Time, Another Place'		2	1		1	1		1	06	5^(TH)=
5	'Wind Of Change'	1	4	3	2		3		4	17	2^(ND)=
6	'Someone To Love Me'	8	2	2	3			1	1	17	2^(ND)=

Analysis: At first it looked as if it was going to be a runaway victory for 'Someone To Love Me' when it received a massive eight votes from Belfast and scored steadily over the next few rounds, while 'Jack In The Box' was well down the list. It was the Glasgow jury awarding six votes to 'Jack In The Box' that brought it up into contention, and high marks from London and Manchester edged it into a narrow lead. When Norwich spread their votes around, bringing 'Wind Of Change' into joint second place, it gave 'Jack In The Box' a close victory. Three juries – Bristol, Glasgow and London – correctly placed 'Jack In The Box' as the top song, with Bristol also managing to pick the joint second placed songs as their next favourites. 'Jack In The Box' was the only song to receive votes from every jury.

The composers were presented with their awards, and Rodgers reprised the winning song, 'Jack In the Box'(duration 2'55").

1971 UNITED KINGDOM

CREDITS
Producer: Michael Hurll
Designers: John Burrowes and Ian Rawnsley
Script: Eric Davidson
Musical Director: Norrie Paramor

The 27 February edition of *It's Cliff Richard* was watched by 31.50% of the population (15.91 million).

None of the *It's Cliff Richard* programmes is retained in the BBC archives, although the performance of 'Jack In The Box' from the 20 February edition survives, as it was used for the *Eurovision Song Contest* preview programmes (see below) and exists in the archives of those television stations that have retained copies. Audio recordings are known to exist of the 6 February edition of *It's Cliff Richard*, on which Rodgers performs 'Wind Of Change'; of the introductions and all of the songs from the final; and of the voting sequence from the 27 February edition.

The winning song was also featured in the Acker Bilk and Clodagh Rodgers-presented programme 'The Music Goes Round And Round' on Radio 1 and Radio 2 on Tuesday 2 March.

Rodgers said afterwards to Alan Smith of the *NME*: 'I thought "Jack In The Box" was the obvious choice, but that maybe people would have steered away from it. But for quite a while I thought "Someone To Love Me" was absolutely going to walk away with it, the way the votes were going. The funny thing about this contest is that you never know which song is going to get through, and which one you'll have to sing in the end. But you just have to do a good job. You have to do your best.'

Speaking to DJ Brian Matthew about the voting, Rodgers had this to say: 'The one thing that worried me with the postal strike was, would we pick the one the public wanted? That worried me more than anything else, because regardless of whether I liked the song or anybody at the studios liked it, whether the public like it is the most important thing, as we are representing the country. This time we had just 80 people deciding instead of thousands, but I really don't think it made a difference; it was between "Jack In The Box" and "Someone To Love Me". I'm not quite sure if "Someone To Love Me" might have beaten "Jack In The Box" in the long run [in a public vote], but "Jack In The Box" is like all the past winners rolled up into one, and something like this only comes out once a year, and I think it's got to be like that; no other kind of song could enter the *Eurovision*, so I think "Jack In The Box" would have won.'

The tie for second place in the contest resulted in a small dilemma for RCA records, as the rules stated that the runner-up had to go on the B-side of the subsequent single release. With two runners-up, the solution was to release a maxi-single with both songs on the B-side. This meant the record would be played at 33 1/3 rpm rather than the usual 45 rpm single format. There were further standard 45 rpm 7" singles that featured either "Someone To Love Me" or "Wind Of Change" on the B-side, and these were produced for jukeboxes to play.

Reviewing the winning song, the *NME* said: 'The United Kingdom may not have been very successful getting into Europe politically, but it's certainly broken down the barrier musically. This song has a tailor-made precision-built formula for the *Eurovision* contest … a slice of "Puppet On A String", a generous helping of "Congratulations", just a touch of "Boom Bang-A-Bang" and a la-la chorus. It's a tried and trusted pattern, and, as we shall doubtless be hearing it hundreds of times in the coming weeks, it's bound to be a hit in Britain – though whether or not the European juries will consider we're getting into a rut remains to be seen.'

The song reached number four in the charts and Rodgers appeared on *Top of the Pops* on the edition broadcast on 1 April. She also appeared again on *It's Cliff Richard* on 27 March, a week before the *Eurovision Song Contest*, to perform 'Jack In The Box'. Neither of these programmes exists in the BBC archives. 'Jack In The Box' also featured on the BBC *Top of the Pops* transcription disc LPs numbers 331 and 336 sent out to overseas radio stations.

Rodgers also recorded Spanish and Italian singles of 'Jack In The Box'. The former, as '*Caja De Sorpresa*' (lyric : Carmo), features 'Another Time, Another Place' on the B-side; the latter, as '*Pupazzo*' (lyric: Pino Perotti), has 'Wind Of Change' as the B-side.

1971 UNITED KINGDOM

To complicate things further, international releases of the English-language 'Jack In The Box' featured either of the runners-up on the B–side. For example the USA release has 'Wind of Change', while the German release has 'Someone To Love Me' (or as it is incorrectly titled on the sleeve and label, 'Some To Love Me'). A Portuguese EP features 'Jack In The Box', 'Someone To Love Me', 'Wind Of Change' and 'Another Time, Another Place'. 'Look Left, Look Right' was eventually released on the CD album *Clodagh Rodgers – The Masters* (1997). Although there appears to be no commercial recording available of 'In My World Of Beautiful Things', it does exist on a 7" acetate along with 'Look Left, Look Right'.

Engelbert Humperdinck also recorded 'Another Time, Another Place', which reached number 13 in the charts for him in September 1971, and performed it on *Top of the Pops* on the editions broadcast on 2 and 23 September. Neither edition exists in the BBC archives. However, his performance of the song from his own series in 1972 exists.

EUROVISION SONG CONTEST PREVIEWS
Presented by Cliff Richard

As part of the changes made by the EBU in 1971, the idea of preview programmes was introduced, the aim being to give the public a chance to familiarise themselves with all the national entries, and to try to give equal exposure to all the songs. The EBU rules required that participating broadcasters should prepare two or more preview programmes, i.e. the songs could not all be included in the same programme, and these could be broadcast only once. The preview videos (or films) of the songs were required to be ready for 12 March, for transmission across the Eurovision Network on 17 March. The BBC's two preview programmes were recorded on Thursday 18 March. The rules stated that they should be broadcast between 22 March and 30 March, though the BBC actually screened the first of them a day early, on 21 March. A specially-made trailer lasting 1'49" and narrated by David Reed, using footage of Dana singing 'All Kinds Of Everything' from the 1970 *Eurovision Song*

SONGS FOR EUROPE VOLUME TWO

Contest, was broadcast on BBC1 on the afternoon of 21 March to promote this first programme.

Part One: Sunday 21 March at 15.01.58 (Duration 30'37"). Audience 7.00% (3.53 million).
Part Two: Sunday 28 March at 14.59.25 (Duration 30'30"). Audience 5.90% (2.98 million).

All the songs were shown in the same order as in the contest itself, except for the United Kingdom entry, which was shown at the end of Part Two. This performance of 'Jack In The Box' was taken from the *It's Cliff Richard* programme of 20 February. The preview videos of the entries from Malta and Ireland were in black and white, but all the others were in colour.

The second preview programme was the subject of an Audience Research Report. 59% of those surveyed considered it a good idea to have the preview, 23% thought it not a particularly good idea, and 18% responded with a definite 'No'. The balance was in favour, it being said, 'When you hear songs only once they don't make much impression.' There was however a widespread feeling that the previews might lessen the impact of the Final, by taking away the element of surprise. Only 29% liked the songs very much, with 60% moderately liking them and 11% not liking them at all. The most favourable reactions were for the entries of the United Kingdom and Norway. There were also appreciative references to the varied and imaginative settings, and it was said that Cliff Richard had introduced the programme in a pleasant and relaxed manner.

CREDIT
Television Presentation: Michael Hurll

The BBC has not retained copies of the preview programmes in its archives.

1971 EUROVISION SONG CONTEST

Only 12 countries having participated in the 1970 event, the EBU decided that this would be the absolute minimum required in future; if the number fell below that, then they should look at reorganising or replacing the entire event. They also planned to extend the contest outside the geographical boundaries of Europe to encompass the European Broadcasting Area as a whole, and to ask Greece, Tunisia, Algeria, Morocco and Malta if they would be interested in participating.

A few more rule changes were introduced. Up until the 1971 contest, only one or two principal vocalists had been allowed, with a maximum of three supporting artists. Now for the first time groups would be allowed, with a maximum of six performers in total on stage.

In addition there was a change to the voting system. The new system was designed to produce a clear-cut winner, by resolving a tie should it occur, and also to avoid any country scoring no points all. ARD (Germany) had proposed a system of ten points for the song a jury placed first, five points for second, four points for third, three points for fourth, two points for fifth and one point for sixth. However, it was Bill Cotton of the BBC who devised the new system actually adopted. In this, juries marked songs out of five votes (though for a brief period ten votes was considered).

With the changes agreed, in August 1970 the Scandinavian countries of Norway, Sweden and Finland agreed to return to the contest, though Denmark was at that stage still undecided and ultimately declined. In addition, Portugal returned and Malta made their debut, bringing the total number up to a healthy 17 nations by the time the draw for the running order was made in Dublin on 8 October. The draw had Malta at number one, all the way through to Norway at number 17. However on 23 October Austria indicated that they would also like to participate. After consulting the host Irish broadcaster RTÉ (Raidió Teilifís Éireann) and pointing out that having 18 nations would be quite useful, as the number was divisible by three for the voting sequence, a Programme Committee meeting in

Zagreb confirmed that Austria could compete in the contest. A suggestion was made that all 18 numbers should be put into a hat and whichever one was pulled out would be the position in which Austria would perform. In the end, however, Austria were told that as a consequence of their late admittance they would have to perform at position number one. The addition of Austria meant that the contest now had the highest number of participants since 1966.

For RTÉ, staging the event was a massive undertaking with a huge investment required, as at that time they did not have a colour television service. The cost to Irish taxpayers was estimated at £35,000. The BBC helped out with technical support and cameras, and the 1971 contest would mark the very first programme broadcast in colour on the Irish network. Some 29 countries took the broadcast, including for the first time the USA.

Work started in the Gaiety Theatre venue on Sunday 21 March, with the erection of scaffolding plus the scoreboard on stage, as well as the lighting rig. Removal of some of the theatre seats also commenced. The main construction of the stage set was begun on Tuesday 23 March. The orchestra, comprising 48 musicians, started their rehearsals on Saturday 27 March, while on Monday 29 March there were rehearsals with the scoreboard and the standby scoreboard.

Camera rehearsals got under way on Tuesday 30 March, with presenter Bernadette Ni Ghallchoir being rehearsed in the morning from 10.00. (Lorna Madigan was the standby presenter.) At 11.15 there were rehearsals for the award presentation and for the opening film and all inserts. In the afternoon, from 14.00, the first five countries in the draw each had a 45 minute slot to rehearse.

On Wednesday 31 March, from 10.00, it was the rehearsals of Spain through to Sweden, with the United Kingdom having the 14.00 to 14.45 slot. There was a jury briefing and a dry run of the voting sequence from 19.00 to 21.00.

On Thursday 1 April, rehearsals took place for Ireland through to Norway, as well as the interval piece. There was a further jury run-through from 16.30. The commentators' briefing took place from 19.30.

Friday 2 April saw all the acts rehearsed, with 20 minutes allocated to each country. The United Kingdom rehearsed from 14.20 to 14.40. After another rehearsal from 18.00 to 18.30 with the jury and the scoreboard, there was a first full dress rehearsal, including dummy voting, from 20.00 until 22.00.

On the day of the contest, there were rehearsals during the morning with the jury, which included the procedure to be used in case of a tie. In the afternoon there was a technical rehearsal between 14.00 and 15.00, followed at 17.00 by a second full dress rehearsal, again with dummy voting, through until 19.00. Everyone then had a meal break prior to the live transmission at the unusual time of 21.45 local time.

BBC News bulletins on 31 March broadcast footage of Clodagh Rodgers and her husband flying out to Dublin the previous day. The film footage (minus sound) has been retained in the archives.

Bookmakers had United Kingdom 3/1 favourite, Luxembourg 5/1, Spain 7/1, Germany 8/1 and Monaco, Norway and Malta 10/1.

The contest was promoted with a *Radio Times* colour cover, with a photograph of Rodgers surrounded by members of her family. Inside there was a one page feature with an interview with the singer. The Saturday television programme page also featured a black and white photograph of Rodgers with the two composers of 'Jack In The Box', while the radio programme page had a further black and white photo of Rodgers, this time with conductor Johnny Arthey.

A 32" trailer was broadcast on BBC1 on the evening 3 April, just before the evening news at 17.50. This had Rodgers singing 'Jack In The Box' with a voiceover by actor Gordon Clyde.

EUROVISION SONG CONTEST 1971
Saturday 3 April at 21.45.00 (Duration 105'45")
From the Gaeity Theatre, Dublin, Ireland
Presented by Bernadette Ni Ghallchoir

The BBC television commentator was Dave Lee Travis (real name David Patrick Griffin). He was born in May

SONGS FOR EUROPE VOLUME TWO

1945 in Buxton, Derbyshire, and began his broadcasting career working for offshore pirate radio in 1965. In 1968 he moved to BBC Radio 1, and in 1969 he took over presenting the Sunday morning show.

Commentating for BBC Radio 1 and Radio 2 was Terry Wogan. Michael Terence Wogan was born in Limerick in Ireland. After a brief spell in the banking profession, he joined RTÉ as a newsreader and announcer before moving onto being a disc jockey and host of light entertainment television shows. He joined Radio 1 when it started in 1967, initially presenting late night programmes, and he regularly commuted between London and Dublin until he got a regular afternoon slot on Radio 1. He had presented all six songs for Clodagh Rodgers on his radio show. The radio coverage commenced at 21.43, and it was planned that in the event of any technical failure Peter Latham would take over the commentary.

John Russell provided commentary for British Forces Radio.

Owing to the smallness of the venue, presenter Bernadette Ni Ghallchoir did her introductions, and the voting sequence, seated in one of the balcony seats in the theatre. She had previously worked for RTÉ but had moved to Switzerland, and was brought back for the programme due to her linguistic skills.

Austria	'Musik' (2'40")	Sung by Marianne Mendt.	Composed by Richard Schönherz and Manuel Rigoni.	Conducted by Robert Opratko.

Malta	'Marija L'Maltija' (3'00")	Sung by Joe Grech.	Words by Charles Mifsud. Music by Joe Grech.	Conducted by Anthony Chircop.

1971 EUROVISION SONG CONTEST

Monaco	'Un Banc, Un Arbre, Une Rue' (2'54")	Sung by Séverine.	Words by Yves Dessca. Music by Jean-Pierre Bourtayre.	Conducted by Jean-Claude Petit.

A later *Record Mirror* review of this entry, which won the contest for Monaco, said: 'The tested formula for a *Eurovision* winner is essentially that of any top of the pops song; get a punchy chorus with a catchy line and repeat it over and over again. Putting as little as possible into the intervening verses. The winner, Monaco's "*Un Banc, Un Arbre, Une Rue*", which any linguist will tell you means "A bench, a tree, a street" followed that principle right down the line. But that aside, and taken as a top tenner that will stick in everybody's mind on one listening, "*Un Banc, Un Arbre, Une Rue*" happens to be a damn good song, and Séverine is a damn fine singer.'

Séverine, real name Josiane Grizeau, was born in Paris in October 1948. She recorded an English version of her winning song with lyrics by John Clunie as 'Chance In Time', but it was the original French-language version that made the British charts, peaking at number nine. She appeared on the edition of *Top of the Pops* broadcast on 6 May, which no longer exists on video in the BBC archives, although a low-quality audio recording is known to exist. She also performed the song on the London Weekend Television series *Whittaker's World of Music*, on the edition broadcast on Saturday 15 May.

Switzerland	'Les Illusions De Nos Vingt Ans' (2'38")	Sung by Peter, Sue and Marc.	Words by Maurice Tézé. Music by Peter Reber.	Conducted by Hardy Schneiders.

SONGS FOR EUROPE VOLUME TWO

| Germany | 'Diese Welt' (2'59") | Sung by Katja Ebstein. | Words by Fred Jay. Music by Dieter Zimmerman. | Conducted by Dieter Zimmerman. |

Katja Ebstein had finished third in 1970 for her country with 'Wunder Gibt Es Immer Wieder'.

| Spain | 'En Un Mundo Nuevo' (3'01") | Sung by Karina. | Words by Tony Luz. Music by Rafael Trabucchelli. | Conducted by Waldo de Los Rios. |

| France | 'Un Jardin Sur La Terre' (2'51") | Sung by Serge Lama. | Words by Henri Dijan and Jacques Demarny. Music by Alice Dona. | Conducted by Franck Pourcel. |

| Luxembourg | 'Pomme, Pomme, Pomme' (2'45") | Sung by Monique Melsen. | Words by Pierre Cour. Music by Hubert Giraud. | Conducted by Jean Claudric. |

'The Love Beat' was the title of the English version, with lyrics by Jack Fishman.

1971 EUROVISION SONG CONTEST

United Kingdom	'Jack In The Box' (2'51")	Sung by Clodagh Rodgers with Lavinia Rodgers, Margo Newman, Jean Hawker and Vicki Brown.	Words by David Myers. Music by John Worsley.	Conducted by Johnny Arthey.

The film postcards this year featured scenic stock footage, accompanied by appropriate music related to the country in question. For the United Kingdom the traditional melody 'Greensleeves' (0'29") was used. Richie Burbridge performed the music for all the postcards.

Speaking to Alan Smith in the *NME*, Clodagh Rodgers had this to say: 'It's silly to try and change this kind of event, because it exists of what it is. People have to realise that within three minutes you've got to race on and catch people's attention there and then. You could write the most beautiful and clever song, and it would be lost because of the language problem. You've got to go on and bash away and really sell it.'

Andy Gray, reviewing the contest in the same publication, agreed about the language problem: 'Until all the competitors can sing in one language, the *Eurovision Song Contest* will never be fair. That's my contention anyway. The new two persons per country juries did one good thing, by seeing that every country got a good lot of votes and not none at all, as has happened in previous years, but it also brought into focus more than ever the language factor. English is a good tongue, of course, because it is the second language of most juries, but the cards were against us winning, because "Jack In The Box" was too like "Puppet On A String". Clodagh Rodgers didn't seem to zip it out with enough vivacity, and her stunning hot pants rig-out was killed by the appearance of Luxembourg's Monique Melsen just before her, in virtually the same costume! Pity. The fact that the United Kingdom's song wasn't the best we could produce is one that I can grumble about.'

Rodgers had actually rehearsed in a different outfit, in order to keep the surprise back of her wearing sparkly hot pants as long as possible.

'It's the luck of the game,' said Rodgers afterwards. 'When you enter these things you have got to be prepared to lose, but you hope you are going to win. I felt as though I did my best, and that's all you can really do. Maybe [the single] will do well all over the world. Can you imagine, I'm going to be played on and off stage with this for the rest of my life?'

Speaking years later Rodgers said: 'The media exposure was incredible, in the lead up to it, for about six months before; and by the time of the contest, they were putting us in the top three. About three minutes before I went on stage, I couldn't remember a word, but as soon as the band struck up, I remembered them. There was a wonderful atmosphere, and the singers backstage were all rooting for each other. We had a ball.

'We used to go into it with such clout; it was Sandie, Cliff and Lulu. I don't regret it at all. I think though that you have to be careful what you do afterwards, and I changed drastically and recorded a ballad, and it really wasn't the right thing to do. I should have kept to the up-tempo style.'

Belgium	*'Goeie Morgen, Morgen'* (2'35")	Sung by Lily Castel and Jacques Raymond.	Words by Phil van Cauwenbergh. Music by Paul Quintens.	Conducted by Francis Bay.

This song was originally due to be sung by Nicole Josy and Hugo Sigal, but unfortunately Josy came down with jaundice shortly before the contest, and Jacques Raymond and Lily Castel were brought in at short notice. Raymond had previously sung for Belgium in 1963 with '*Waarom*'.

1971 EUROVISION SONG CONTEST

Italy	'L'Amore È Un Attimo' (2'57")	Sung by Massimo Ranieri.	Words by Giancarlo Bigazzi and Gaetano Savio. Music by Enrico Polito.	Conducted by Enrico Polito.

The English version was called 'Goodbye My Love' with lyrics by the husband and wife team of Tony Hatch and Jackie Trent.

Sweden	'Vita Vidder' (2'54")	Sung by the Family Four.	Composed by Håkan Elmquist.	Conducted by Claes Rosendahl.

Ireland	'One Day Love' (2'52")	Sung by Angela Farrell.	Composed by Donald Martin and Ita Flynn.	Conducted by Noel Kelehan.

Netherlands	'De Tijd' (2'16")	Sung by Saskia and Serge.	Words by Gerrit den Braber. Music by Joop Stokkermans.	Conducted by Dolf van der Linden.

Portugal	'Menina Do Alto Da Serra' (3'06")	Sung by Tonicha.	Words by José Carlos Ary dos Santos. Music by Nuno Nazareth Fernandes.	Conducted by Jorge Costa Pinto.

SONGS FOR EUROPE VOLUME TWO

| Yugoslavia | 'Tvoj Dječak Je Tužan' (2'34") | Sung by Krunoslav Slabinac. | Words by Zvonimir Golob. Music by Ivan Krajač. | Conducted by Miljenko Prohaska. |

| Finland | 'Tie Uuteen Päivään' (2'44) | Sung by Markku Aro and Koivisto Sisters. | Composed by Rauno Lehtinen. | Conducted by Ossi Runne. |

| Norway | 'Lykken Er' (2'52") | Sung by Hanne Krogh. | Composed by Arne Bendiksen. | Conducted by Arne Bendiksen. |

THE VOTING

Each country had two jurors – one below the age of 25, the other above – who both had to give between one and five points to each song, except for their own country's. The juries were present at the venue in Dublin and watched the transmission on television, during which they had to record their votes, so they could not be altered later. For the voting sequence, they were brought on stage to deliver their points, voting in groups of three countries at a time.

The United Kingdom jurors were company director Jeremy Paterson Fox and 21-year-old Gay Lowe, a receptionist from Liverpool. Reports that attempts had been made to fix the results were refuted by Lowe, and she told the press, 'It all started with light-hearted remarks when two Spaniards came up to me and in a joking manner asked how much it cost to buy votes on the black market. I said I didn't know and I wasn't interested. A

1971 EUROVISION SONG CONTEST

BBC man was with me at the time. He realised it was not a serious attempt at bribery, just a joke, and we left it at that. I was amazed when people started getting in touch with me and asking how the fix attempt was made.'

	Austria	Malta	Monaco	Switzerland	Germany	Spain	France	Luxembourg	UK	Belgium	Italy	Sweden	Ireland	Netherlands	Portugal	Yugoslavia	Finland	Norway	TOTAL	POSITION
AUSTRIA		3	5	2	7	2	3	2	3	3	6	4	6	3	5	4	3	5	66	16TH
MALTA	4		2	2	3	5	3	2	3	4	4	2	4	5	2	2	3	2	52	18TH
MONACO	4	5		10	10	2	8	4	8	10	4	10	9	9	8	10	7	10	128	1ST
SWITZERLAND	5	5	4		6	2	6	2	6	3	7	4	5	5	6	4	4	4	78	12TH
GERMANY	6	5	7	6		8	8	2	6	7	6	6	5	5	7	7	5	4	100	3RD
SPAIN	4	8	10	5	7		10	4	7	4	5	6	9	6	7	7	9	8	116	2ND
FRANCE	3	2	8	8	5	5		2	5	3	4	4	6	9	5	5	3	5	82	10TH
LUXEMBOURG	2	7	6	3	2	4	5		6	3	3	2	5	3	6	4	5	4	70	13TH
UNITED KINGDOM	4	8	8	6	5	2	8	4		8	3	5	7	5	7	6	6	6	98	4TH

SONGS FOR EUROPE VOLUME TWO

BELGIUM	3	2	5	4	2	2	5	2	6	▓	3	5	4	6	6	3	6	4	68	14TH=
ITALY	4	6	9	8	6	6	9	2	6	2	▓	7	6	2	3	8	2	5	91	5TH
SWEDEN	7	4	4	9	4	2	5	2	5	6	6	▓	3	9	3	6	4	6	85	6TH=
IRELAND	7	6	6	3	4	5	7	2	6	3	6	2	▓	5	4	5	4	4	79	11TH
NETHERLANDS	6	2	6	5	4	5	7	2	5	2	2	6	5	▓	9	5	6	8	85	6TH=
PORTUGAL	4	3	6	2	5	10	8	5	6	4	4	2	3	5	▓	6	5	5	83	9TH
YUGOSLAVIA	6	2	4	2	7	6	6	2	3	2	5	2	5	4	4	▓	3	5	68	14TH=
FINLAND	4	4	4	4	4	3	4	2	10	10	2	4	6	3	8	6	▓	6	84	8TH
NORWAY	3	3	6	4	2	2	5	2	7	6	2	2	7	2	5	4	3	▓	65	17TH

Analysis: The new scoring system did indeed produce clear-cut positions at the top. What was most striking was the low points awarded by the Luxembourg jury; with the sole exception of the three points given by the over-25 juror to Portugal, no song rated more than one or two points from each of them. The United Kingdom fared better than most countries here, receiving Luxembourg's second-top mark of just four points in total from the two jurors. Spain was the least generous country to the United Kingdom, giving just two points in total; the lowest possible. The highest scores received for the United Kingdom were several eights, from Malta, Monaco,

France and Belgium. Full marks from the United Kingdom went to Finland, followed by an eight to eventual winners Monaco. British over-25 juror Jeremy Paterson Fox was in marked contrast to the Luxembourg juror seated next to him, and awarded no song as low as one point; two points was his minimum.

Séverine received the awards and plaudits on stage for winning the contest. In addition there were flowers and scrolls for the second and third placed entrants, and Karina and Katja Ebstein took their places on stage. Clodagh Rodgers just missed out by finishing in fourth place.

For all of those involved there was a reception held by RTÉ afterwards in the state apartments of Dublin Castle.

WINNING REPRISE

| Monaco | *'Un Banc, Un Arbre, Une Rue'* (2'50") | Sung by Séverine. | Words by Yves Dessca. Music by Jean-Pierre Bourtayre. | Conducted by Jean-Claude Petit. |

CREDITS
Producer: Tom McGrath
Musical Director: Colman Pearce
Designer: Alpho O'Reilly
EBU Scrutineer: Clifford Brown

The contest was watched by 40.20% of the British population (20.31 million) from the start of the programme at 21.45, rising to 42.80% (21.61 million) from 22.30.

It wasn't so much the songs as the element of international competition that attracted viewers, according to the Audience Research Report compiled for the programme. Less than half of those sampled (46%) agreed with the choice of winner. Some felt the United Kingdom should have won, although several others wished that we could have entered something away from the typical *Eurovision* song, and others had plumped for Italy or Spain

Almost all were in favour of the new voting system. Some felt it was drawn out and lacked the excitement of the telephone juries, and that two jurors was hardly representative, but a greater number found it quicker and more efficient to have an on-the-spot jury.

43% had liked the commentary by Dave Lee Travis. The main complaint was that he had far too much to say, without explaining what a given song was about. A few also grumbled that the stage setting was unattractive and there had been not enough close-ups, but admitted that technically it had been well organised and there were no problems in seeing or hearing. Several had enjoyed the introductory film and the films of each country used in the postcards, as well as the interval item from Shannon Castle.

BBC News featured Clodagh Rodgers' return from Dublin in their bulletin of 4 April, along with a short interview in which she stated, 'Britain must change its tune'. This item has been retained in the BBC archives.

The BBC no longer holds its broadcast version of the contest in its archives, although an off-air domestic video exists. Copies of the transmitted programme exist in various European television archives.

1972 UNITED KINGDOM

The New Seekers would be the first group ever to represent the United Kingdom in the *Eurovision Song Contest*, following the rule change that had come into force prior to the 1971 event.

The New Seekers had evolved from the Australian group the Seekers. They were formed in 1969 by Keith Potger, one of the original members of the Seekers, who would perform with the new group. The initial line-up included Chris Barrington, Laurie Heath, Marty Kristian, Eve Graham and Sally Graham (the latter two being unrelated). After just one single, the line-up changed to the more familiar one that would appear in the contest, comprising Peter Doyle, Paul Layton, Marty Kristian, Lyn Paul and Eve Graham. With this line-up the group achieved success with their first single release, 'What Have They Done To My Song Ma', although it did better in the USA than in the UK.

Their next big successes came with 'Never Ending Song Of Love', a number two hit in the charts in June 1971, and the first to be produced by David MacKay. Their next song, however, was to make the biggest impact of all. 'I'd Like To Teach The World To Sing' reached number one in December 1971. It had originally achieved fame in a Coca-Cola advert, as 'I'd Like To Buy The World A Coke', but such was its popularity that it was reworked to drop the brand name.

'It was the famed Bill Cotton who approached our management and said that the New Seekers seemed like a good group to represent the UK in the contest,' says bass player Paul Layton, 'and we were absolutely chuffed to be asked, especially when we found out we were going to be performing the final six songs on the *It's Cliff Richard* series. One thing led to another, and we ended up contributing to the whole 13 week series; so it wasn't just the six shows. We were able to participate in all aspects of the shows, including comedy sketches and songs with Cliff.

'We didn't have any input on the final song selection for the contest; that was down to the MPA.'

The six songs were previewed one song per week on the *It's Cliff Richard* show from Saturday 1 January to Saturday

SONGS FOR EUROPE VOLUME TWO

5 February. The Final, featuring all the songs together, was transmitted on Saturday 12 February, having been recorded just the night before. The songs were also previewed on Radio 2 on Pete Murray's *Open House*. In line with standard practice, a memo was sent from the Executive Producer of Radio 2 specifying that none of the songs in the contest could be broadcast on the radio before 21 February, apart from on the aforementioned Pete Murray programme.

Television at the time was being hit by industrial action, though not by the broadcasting unions. A national miners' strike had by 9 February 1972 led to a state of emergency being declared, and in order to conserve supplies of electricity, television had to stop broadcasting by 22.30 each day. An edition of *Top of the Pops* due to be broadcast on 10 February was blacked out due to power cuts. The cuts were also starting to hit private households, and many people may well have missed viewing the *A Song for Europe* programme. For those affected, there would be a chance to hear the songs recapped on the Pete Murray show on radio on 14 February.

A SONG FOR EUROPE 1972
Saturday 12 February, 1972 at 18.17.57 (Duration 44'53")
Presented by Cliff Richard

An orchestra of 32 musicians was used for the show. This was under the direction of Norrie Paramor for those parts involving Cliff Richard, and conducted and arranged by David MacKay for the section with the New Seekers. The programme opened with Cliff Richard performing 'Goodbye Sam, Hello Samantha', backed by Bones and the orchestra. Then, after a short comedy sketch about Napoleon and Josephine featuring the New Seekers, Richard made the introductions, starting with the *A Song for Europe* titles, specially shot on film, and accompanied by 10" of the 'Eurovision Short Fanfare' composed by Paramor. Richard provided a brief piece of background information about the composers before each song, then the cameras would cut to the respective composers seated in the audience.

1972 UNITED KINGDOM

| Song One | 'Out On The Edge Of Beyond' (2'20") | Sung by the New Seekers. | Composed by John Bendall and Mike Sammes. |

Composer Mike Sammes was born in Reigate in 1928. He learned the cello while still at school and played piano for a local dance band called the Meltones. He and fellow Meltones band member Bill Shepherd joined the George Mitchell Singers, and then formed the splinter group the Coronets. Sammes himself had sung as part of the group in two of the Heats for the *Festival of British Popular Songs* 1956 on a total of four songs, the best result being achieved with 'The Heart Of A Child', which came third in Heat Six. He later formed the vocal group the Mike Sammes Singers, and they provided backing vocals for Matt Monro in the 1964 *A Song for Europe*. Sammes was a prolific backing vocalist, and amongst the many hits on which he can be heard are Tom Jones' 'The Green Green Grass Of Home' and Helen Shapiro's 'Walkin' Back To Happiness'. Other top stars he worked with included Cliff Richard, Tony Bennett and Judy Garland, though to his regret he never worked with Frank Sinatra. Sammes also provided various vocal sounds and effects on comedy records, including those of Pinky and Perky. Though featuring on many hits recorded by other artists, the Mike Sammes Singers had only one under their own name. This was 'Somewhere My Love', which peaked at number 22 in 1966 and re-entered the charts the following year, this time reaching number 14.

Sammes wrote many songs and commercials with various lyricists, but never achieved a hit record in this capacity. 'Out On The Edge Of Beyond' was his only song as a composer to feature in *A Song for Europe*. 'The week that they were featuring my song, there was a power strike and only about three people saw the broadcast,' said Sammes years later. Mike Sammes died in May 2001.

The 1 January edition of *It's Cliff Richard* in which the song was previewed was watched by 20.30% of the population (10.25 million).

SONGS FOR EUROPE VOLUME TWO

Song Two	'Sing Out' (2'05")	Sung by the New Seekers.	Composed by Ronnie Dunlop.

Ronnie Dunlop was a civil servant and had released two singles as a performer on the Pye record label, 'It Would Only Take A Lifetime To Explain' and 'Dream Of The Future', both in 1970. He had also written hit songs for the likes of Malcolm Roberts and Daliah Lavi.

'This one was quite commercial too,' Paul Layton remembers.

The 8 January edition of *It's Cliff Richard* in which the song was previewed was watched by 25.00% (12.63 million).

Song Three	'Why Can't We All Get Together' (2'40")	Sung by the New Seekers.	Composed by Ray Davies.

Ray Davies was born in Swansea in 1929. He enrolled in the Sea Cadets at the start of the Second World War, and quickly joined their brass band as a trumpet player. He studied musical composition at the Royal College of Music and joined the Teddy Foster Band, accompanying singers including Vince Hill. He left the band in 1953 and was then much in demand as a session musician, playing trumpet for Bob Hope and Bing Crosby amongst others. He composed a number of instrumental tracks, mainly for the brass section of the orchestra, and featured on tracks for the Rolling Stones, the Beatles, Petula Clark, Shirley Bassey and Tom Jones. He had a long stint in the orchestra on *Top of the Pops* under the direction of Johnny Pearson, and regularly recorded with Johnny Gregory and his orchestra. Davies founded his own small brass led band, the Button Down Brass, releasing several albums, initially in an easy listening style but progressing through the years to soul and funk.

This was the only song in the contest to have been written by Davies, and he also recorded it as the title track

1972 UNITED KINGDOM

on one of his own albums. Since the mid-'70s he has concentrated more on composing, including jingles and library music. He has also served on committees for both the PRS and BASCA.

'That was the waltz song,' notes Paul Layton of this contribution to the contest, still remembering the melody years later.

The 15 January edition of *It's Cliff Richard* in which the song was previewed was watched by 24.20% (12.22 million).

| Song Four | 'One By One' (3'00") | Sung by the New Seekers. (Lead vocal Eve Graham.) | Composed by Mike Leander and Eddie Seago. |

Mike Leander and Eddie Seago were the only composers in the 1972 event who had had entries in previous contests. Leander had written 'Little Rag Doll' in the 1968 contest, finishing fifth, while as a duo they had written 'Another Time, Another Place', which had come fifth for Clodagh Rodgers the previous year and gone on to become a hit for Engelbert Humperdinck.

It was the last time that either composer had an entry in the Final of *A Song for Europe*.

Leander, also known as Michael Farr, went on to work with Gary Glitter, producing a string of hits, including 'I'm The Leader Of The Gang' and 'I Love You Love Me Love'. Apart from writing, he played virtually all the instruments on the tracks, except brass. He received an Ivor Novello Award and a Certificate of Honour for services to British Popular Music. In later years he divided his time between London and Majorca, loving all things Spanish, and no doubt this inspired him to write the West End musical *Matador*, based on the bullfighter El Cordobes. He produced a concept album of the show, providing Tom Jones with a hit single, 'The Boy From Nowhere'. Leander died in April 1996.

SONGS FOR EUROPE VOLUME TWO

Seago, as a close colleague of Leander, set up the publishing side to Leander's management company, was involved with the careers of Gary Glitter, the Glitter Band and Barry Blue aand helped Adrian Baker set up the band Liquid Gold.

'David MacKay, our producer, would very much decide who sung which vocals,' recalls Paul Layton. 'We were very much directed in those; he would have picked who he felt was the strongest to sing, and done the vocal arrangement to incorporate those voices.'

The 22 January edition of *It's Cliff Richard* in which the song was previewed was watched by 26.50% of the population (13.38 million).

| Song Five | 'Songs Of Praise' (2'30") | Sung by the New Seekers. (Lead vocal Peter Doyle.) | Composed by Roy Wood. |

Born in November 1946, Roy Adrian Wood formed his first band, the Falcons, in the early 1960s in Birmingham. From this he progressed onto the Move, a group that included Carl Wayne. It was their single 'Flowers In The Rain' that had the distinction of launching Radio 1 in 1967. Keen to experiment with different genres of music, such as combining rock and roll with classical, Wood next founded the Electric Light Orchestra with a couple of the band members of the Move, while still on tour with them.

'I was a fan of Roy Wood,' says Paul Layton. 'I liked his style of music anyway, and I particularly enjoyed this one.'

It was the only song of Wood's to make the final stages of *A Song for Europe*. A few months later, after differences with the Electric Light Orchestra, he left and formed a new group called Wizzard, with whom he achieved the hits 'See My Baby Jive' and the particularly memorable 'I Wish It Could Be Christmas Every Day', which has re-entered the charts several times over the decades, having reached number four in 1973 on its first release. Wood also released his own version of 'Songs Of Praise' on single.

The 29 January edition of *It's Cliff Richard* in which the song was previewed was watched by 25.7% (12.98 million).

Song Six	'Beg, Steal Or Borrow' (2'45")	Sung by the New Seekers. (Lead vocals Lyn Paul and Peter Doyle.)	Composed by Tony Cole, Graeme Hall and Steve Wolfe.

'We did like "Beg, Steal Or Borrow",' says Paul Layton. 'We saw it as being strong and very much a favourite; by the time we had worked through them, done the vocal arrangements, and the way they were shaping up, it was probably going to win.'

This was the first attempt that the three young songwriters had made at writing a song together. Tony Cole was a former schoolteacher who had written songs for Tom Jones and Petula Clark.

The 5 February edition of *It's Cliff Richard* in which the song was previewed was watched by 27.60 % (13.94 million).

After the initial performances, all six songs were shown again from a recording made of the main session. Cliff Richard then gave the details of the postal voting address and closing date. The programme closed with the orchestra playing 25" of 'Congratulations'.

The Final of *A Song for Europe* was watched by 25.00% (12.62 million). An Audience Research Report conducted for the programme found that most of the 387 sampled viewers had found the songs unimpressive.

SONGS FOR EUROPE VOLUME TWO

It was said that 'none stood out' and that they were 'not as good as [in] other years', varying 'from mediocre to poor'. 'All sounded alike,' said one respondent, 'and I don't think any one of them would stand a chance of winning [the international contest].' The New Seekers were considered to have sung very well, but one viewer commented, 'I don't think the songs are worthy of them,' and the opinion was expressed that 'the style of the New Seekers emphasised the monotony of the entries.' The fact that the songs were shown twice seemed to bother quite a few, and only 16% of the sample declared their intention to vote. Some thought the songs had taken up too much time, and that they preferred *It's Cliff Richard* without *A Song for Europe*. 'Beg, Steal Or Borrow' was especially fancied by the viewers, though only one or two songs were seen as likely winners. A minority view was that they were all so good that it was impossible to make a decision. According to these respondents, the songs were of a higher standard than in previous years, and 'Thank goodness they are not of the "Puppet On A String" variety'.

THE CONDUCTOR

David MacKay was born in Sydney, Australia. He started his career in music aged just 15 in a theatre production of *Bye, Bye Birdie*. He later joined EMI in Australia as a recording engineer, and then as head of A&R, and produced several hits for many pop acts, including 'The Pushbike Song' by the Mixtures, a number two hit in the UK charts in 1970. He transferred to Abbey Road studios in London and produced the New Seekers' singles, starting with 'Never Ending Song of Love', and their albums.

THE RESULTS

The results were announced by Bill Cotton one week later, on the *It's Cliff Richard* edition of Saturday 19 February.

1972 UNITED KINGDOM

Song	Title	Votes	Placing
1	'Out On The Edge Of Beyond'	14,645	Third
2	'Sing Out'	7,412	Fifth
3	'Why Can't We All Get Together'	11,337	Fourth
4	'One By One'	27,314	Second
5	'Songs Of Praise'	3,842	Sixth
6	'Beg, Steal Or Borrow'	62,584	First

Analysis: No postal vote having taken place in 1971, we have to go back two years to draw a comparison. With just over 127,000 votes submitted in total, this was well down on the nearly 352,000 recorded in 1970. As mentioned above, power cuts were starting to hit homes, so many potential viewers may have missed seeing all or part of the show; also inflation was running high in Britain, and the cost of postage had risen by about 33%.

For the third time, the song performed last won the contest. 'Beg, Steal Or Borrow' took nearly half the total vote, at 49.23%; more than double that of the second place entry 'One By One', which received 21.48%.

The winning composers received their awards and were played off with a burst of 'Congratulations'.

The reprise of 'Beg, Steal Or Borrow' was actually taken from the broadcast of 12 February.

CREDITS
Designer: David Chandler
Producer: Michael Hurll
Musical Director: David MacKay

SONGS FOR EUROPE VOLUME TWO

The 19 February edition of *It's Cliff Richard* that included the results was watched by 22.00% of the population (11.11 million).

'Beg, Steal Or Borrow' was released on a 7" picture-sleeve single, backed with the second-place song, 'One By One'. The record peaked at number two in the charts. The group performed the winning song on *Top of the Pops* in the 24 February edition. This recording was then repeated in the 2 March and 30 March editions, and the song was also played from disc on the 16 March edition. None of these *Top of the Pops* programmes is known to exist in the BBC archives.

The New Seekers made a number of concert appearances throughout February and March, including in Hemel Hempstead, Manchester, Stockton and Bournemouth, and also undertook a series of dates in Belgium, Switzerland and France prior to the international contest.

The group was featured in an item on *Blue Peter* on 13 March, which exists in the BBC archives. Some viewers had apparently reckoned that presenter Peter Purves looked similar to lead singer Peter Doyle. The item included photos of the group, and an extract of the soundtrack of 'Beg, Steal Or Borrow'. There was also a mention of the first *Eurovision Song Contest* preview programme, which would be broadcast later that same evening.

The New Seekers appeared again on *It's Cliff Richard* on the edition broadcast on 18 March, just a week before the *Eurovision Song Contest*, performing 'Beg, Steal Or Borrow'.

A number of European releases of the 7" single featured 'Sing Out' on the B-side instead of the runner-up. The group also recorded a German-language version of the winning song as '*Oh, Ich Will Betteln, Ich Will Stehlen*' (lyric: Elisabeth Bertram). 'We learned that all phonetically,' says Paul Layton. A USA promo single features both mono and stereo versions of 'Beg, Steal Or Borrow'.

All six songs from *A Song for Europe* 1972 appeared across two albums by the New Seekers. On *We'd Like To*

1972 UNITED KINGDOM

Teach The World To Sing appear 'One By One', 'Songs Of Praise' and 'Beg, Steal Or Borrow', and on *Look What They've Done To My Song, Ma* are 'Sing Out', 'Why Can't We All Get Together' and 'Out On The Edge Of Beyond'.

Although none of the *It's Cliff Richard* shows is known to exist, those international broadcasters that have retained copies of the 1972 previews have the New Seekers performing 'Beg, Steal Or Borrow' from the Final. Off-air audio exists of the introductions and songs from the Final on 12 February, and of the results on 19 February.

EUROVISION SONG CONTEST PREVIEWS
Presented by Cliff Richard

Richard took time out from rehearsing *It's Cliff Richard* on Thursday 9 March between 11.00 and 12.45 to record the linking material for the preview programmes.

Part One: Monday 13 March at 19.30.00 (Duration 29'17"). Audience 15.90% (8.03 million).
Part Two: Monday 20 March at 19.31.13 (Duration 29'35"). Audience 10.10% (5.10 million).

The songs were shown in the same order as they would appear in the *Eurovision Song Contest*, except for the United Kingdom entry, which unusually was shown at the end of Part One rather than the end of Part Two. The United Kingdom preview of 'Beg, Steal Or Borrow' was taken from *It's Cliff Richard* transmitted on 12 February.

CREDIT
Television Presentation: Michael Hurll.

The BBC has not retained the preview programmes in its archives, though copies exist on audio.

1972 EUROVISION SONG CONTEST

Originally the Monaco broadcaster RMC (Radio Monte-Carlo), winner of the 1971 *Eurovision Song Contest*, wanted to host the 1972 event, and proposed staging it outdoors in June 1972. Construction was also under way on a suitable concert hall, which RMC was trying to get accelerated to finish in time. The BBC was against the event taking place in June, as it would impact on contractual arrangements for the *It's Cliff Richard* show (which of course was being used for selection of the United Kingdom entry), and they forwarded their objections at the end of May 1971.

In June 1971 it was known that TVE (Spain) and ARD (Germany), the previous year's second- and third-placed prize winners, would turn down the opportunity to stage the 1972 contest, and that the EBU office was 'calling loudly' for volunteers. The BBC hinted that ORTF (France) could offer, as they had escaped when they tossed a coin with NOS (Netherlands) for the staging of the 1970 contest. However the BBC eventually decided to take on the task if Monaco had to bow out. RMC finally declared on 6 July that it would be unable to organise the 1972 contest.

By 16 September 1971, the BBC was starting to firm up its plans. It proposed 25 March as the date for the event, and suggested either Edinburgh or Blackpool as the venue. The starting time would be 21.30. The BBC stated that it was not prepared to start any later than that, and any country that couldn't take the show live might have to tape it.

As regards the budget, the BBC indicated that it was prepared to work to the 1971 figure of £25,000 that was the direct cost to RTÉ, although it actually expected to spend £30,000 on the staging. The BBC agreed to pay half of the £25,000, with the rest coming from the EBU. This meant that its own costs would be £17,500. (When everything was finally taken into account – production staff, scenery, costumes, Eurovision lines, the orchestra, hospitality, film and videotape, artists fees and outside broadcast – the actual total came to £81,000.)

The following day there came a counter-offer made to the EBU by Frank Copplestone of ITV: 'This is to confirm that ITV offers to act as host and provide the British entry for the 1972 *Eurovision Song Contest* to be held on 25 March, or any other date to be agreed, and will bear all costs usually attributed to the host organisation.' The memo was copied to the BBC in order that they could respond.

The EBU decided to go ahead with the BBC's offer, and the contest would be staged in the Usher Hall in Edinburgh. This venue was built in 1914 and named after Andrew Usher, who had donated £100,000 to the city in order to build a concert hall. Sadly Usher died before the building started construction.

For the contest, the audience in the hall was around 1,500, and the worldwide audience was put at 400 million, with the programme being broadcast to 28 countries. The draw for the running order was made in London on 1 December 1971.

The BBC appointed Terry Hughes to produce the contest. 'I imagine the reason I did it was that I was available at the time,' says Hughes. 'There was probably a break from doing *The Two Ronnies*, which was the main show I was involved with at the time. I had also done a lot of music shows previously, like *Val Doonican* and *Billy Cotton*, and it would have been Bill Cotton Jnr who would have called me in and asked me to do it. At the BBC in those days I was a producer and a director, but you couldn't take both credits on a programme, so I was credited as the director and Bill was executive producer. That was an honorary credit that went back to the days when Tom Sloan was involved with the contest, both emotionally and personally, which meant the buck stopped with him; so in terms of international recognition with the other heads, he was the top guy, the president if you like.

'I'm sure the venue had already been decided on before I became involved, though I think it was my idea to have the jury in Edinburgh Castle, which I thought would be suitably different. They were always going to be in a different venue, as we simply didn't have the room in the Usher Hall. I was instrumental in choosing Moira Shearer as the presenter; we had a short list and I pushed for her. I remember going to see her, and she was kind of reluctant at first, as she had never done anything like it before, but she was a lovely lady and brought an elegance and class to it, and she could speak enough French. The musical director, Malcolm Lockyer, was a lovely man. I can't remember though who appointed him. I think he came as part of the package when I took the job on. But he was charming and delightful to work with.

'We used the outside broadcast crew, and as I recall we brought most of them up from London.'

When reminded about the £30,000 budget, Hughes adds: 'I don't remember there being any budgetary restrictions. It was going to cost what it cost in order to do it well. It was kind of daunting to do it when you realised how many people would be watching it, and how seriously some countries took it. It was like the World Cup!'

Rehearsals commenced on Tuesday 21 March, with presenter Moira Shearer from 14.30 onwards. Shearer was born in January 1926 in Dunfermline, and was best known as a ballet dancer and actress. She had been with the Sadler's Wells Ballet School, and in 1948 came to international attention in the film *The Red Shoes*. She retired from ballet in 1953 and continued her acting career; other films included *The Tales of Hoffmann* and *Peeping Tom*. She was married in 1950 to journalist and broadcaster Ludovic Kennedy, with whom she had four children. Shearer died in January 2006 aged 80.

Not long after the contest took place there came a shocking terrorist incident at the 1972 Olympic Games, so what had security been like at the *Eurovision Song Contest*? 'To be honest, I don't remember there being any,' says Hughes. 'It wasn't a consideration at that time; and if it had been, it would have probably been more about the IRA than anything else. I don't remember it being a major point of discussion or having big meetings about it, and people just seemed to come and go. These were earlier times, they were wonderful, nobody worried about such issues, and we had no vision of what was to come.'

On Wednesday 22 March two days of rehearsals started with the artists and the BBC Radio Orchestra, which comprised 44 musicians. These rehearsals were without costumes, and commenced at 10.30 each morning, with each act having a 50 minute slot allocated to them. The first eight countries rehearsed throughout the first day, and the remaining ten on the second, in the same order as they would appear in the contest itself, except that France swapped places with Belgium, so Belgium rehearsed on the Wednesday in second position, and France rehearsed the following day in position number 16. The New Seekers, representing the United Kingdom, were scheduled to rehearse from 15.25 to 16.15 on the Wednesday. The Swiss brought the first day's rehearsals to a conclusion at 19.25.

'I would have had my ideas as to how each song should look,' says Hughes, 'and I remember having consultations with the other countries. I had prepared a camera script. Each contestant had their rehearsal, and their television guys would be looking to see what I had done, and they might ask for a close-up here or there or whatever, but there was certainly a lot of time allowed for all of that.'

On the evening of Thursday 23 March there was an hour's dinner break and a commentators' briefing scheduled before the last two countries rehearsed, and the final entry from the Netherlands finished at 22.15.

Friday 24 March saw another full day of rehearsals, with each country having a 20 minute slot in full costume, this time in the correct running order. The United Kingdom had the 12.20 to 12.40 slot, and the Netherlands wrapped things up, finishing at 18.40. Following a 20 minute period set aside for any notes to the artists, and a break for dinner, there was then a camera rehearsal of the entire show in full costume along with dummy voting from 20.00 to 22.00.

In Edinburgh Castle meanwhile, the jury members assembled at 10.00 on Friday 24 March. They were given a briefing on the voting procedure and from 11.00 to 13.00 had a dummy run of the voting. In the afternoon, starting at 14.30, there was a further dummy run using a VT playback of the songs, and the session finished at 17.30. After an extended break for dinner etc, at 20.00 the jury members were back in place to take part in the complete run-through of the show.

Saturday 25 March, the day of the Final, saw technical rehearsals take place in the Usher Hall with Shearer and the scoreboard from 10.30 to 12.30, while the artists had the morning off before being required at 14.00 for a technical and dress rehearsal, with the orchestra taking their places from 14.30. The jurors were also back in the Great Hall of Edinburgh Castle to play their part in the rehearsals. By 17.00 the rehearsals were completed and everyone could take a break in readiness for the live transmission at 21.30.

Radio Times had a colour cover photo of the New Seekers to promote the contest, with an article inside. On Friday 24 March on BBC1, just before that evening's edition of *The Liver Birds* was shown, there was a 1'13" trailer featuring the New Seekers with 'Beg, Steal Or Borrow' and footage taken from *It's Cliff Richard*, voiced over by Dick Graham. There were two further trailers on Saturday 25 March. The first, just before *Doctor Who*, was a general Saturday night programmes trailer and included 15" of 'Beg, Steal Or Borrow'. The second, this time specific to the contest, followed *The Dick Emery Show* and included 30" of 'Beg, Steal Or Borrow'.

Bookmakers had made the United Kingdom 7/2 favourites to win the contest.

EUROVISION SONG CONTEST 1972
Saturday 25 March at 21.30.00 (Duration 104'31")
From the Usher Hall, Edinburgh, United Kingdom
Presented by Moira Shearer

Commentating for BBC1 viewers for the first and only time was the distinguished broadcaster Tom Fleming. He was born in Edinburgh in 1927 and started his career as an actor, making his stage debut in 1945 in a company led by Edith Evans. In 1953 he joined the BBC to commentate on the Coronation, and from then on he became associated with covering big state occasions and similar events, including royal weddings, state funerals and enthronements of Popes and Archbishops, as well as the annual Edinburgh Military Tattoo. He died in April 2010 aged 82.

On radio, Pete Murray commentated for listeners, and had a short interview with the New Seekers during the interval item. After the contest he continued his radio show until midnight, including interviews with artists and composers who had been involved in the contest.

Terry James provided commentary for British Forces Radio.

Moira Shearer was played onto the stage by a fanfare composed by Musical Director Malcolm Lockyer. He had previously used the same fanfare in the opening title music of the film *Dr Who and the Daleks* for which he had provided the score. Lockyer had previously appeared in the *Festival of British Popular Songs* in 1956 and

1972 EUROVISION SONG CONTEST

1957. In the latter he had performed the instrumental version of the winning song 'All'. In 1966 he had served as the Musical Director on *A Song for Europe*. The 1972 contest marked his final association with the event. Lockyer died in June 1976.

Germany	*'Nur Die Liebe Lässt Uns Leben'* (2'49")	Sung by Mary Roos (with Susanne Jage, Rolf Jage, Rosi Rohr, Angelika Metzger and John Wiseman).	Words by Joachim Relin. Music by Joachim Heider.	Conducted by Paul Kuhn.
France	*'Comé-Comédie'* (2'41")	Sung by Betty Mars (with Joss Baselli).	Composed by Frédéric Botton.	Conducted by Franck Pourcel.
Ireland	*'Ceol An Ghrá'* (2'36")	Sung by Sandie Jones.	Words by Liam MacUistin. Music by Joe Burkett.	Conducted by Colman Pearce.

This was the first, and to date only, entry sung in the Irish language.

SONGS FOR EUROPE VOLUME TWO

Spain	'Amanece' (2'56")	Sung by Jaime Morey (with Marti-Carmen Ros, Montserrat Ros, Jose Tudela and Angel Pascual).	Words by Ramón Arcusa. Music by Augusto Algueró.	Conducted by Augusto Algueró.
United Kingdom	'Beg, Steal Or Borrow' (2'44")	Sung by the New Seekers (Eve Graham, Lyn Paul, Peter Doyle, Paul Layton, and Marty Kristian).	Composed by Tony Cole, Graeme Hall and Steve Wolfe.	Conducted by David MacKay.

'We were photographed on a baggage trolley at King's Cross Station for the front of the *Radio Times*,' recalls Paul Layton, 'and in keeping with that we had to travel up by train, and I think we had a film crew on the train with us. There was a banner spread across the terminal at Edinburgh Airport saying "Edinburgh Welcomes The New Seekers" ... and we were the only act to arrive by train!

'The experience in Edinburgh was incredible; it was the first experience of being adulated in a ridiculous way. We were in the hotel and the fans broke down the revolving door. The police came up to our rooms and asked us not to go near the window, as they would book us for inciting a riot, so of course Peter Doyle would wave his pants out of the window! The girls were going berserk in the street below and keeping vigil all night.

1972 EUROVISION SONG CONTEST

'We saw bits of the other acts rehearsing during the week, although all I can remember now is the winner, Vicky Leandros. She had a good ballad, a catchy song, but we claim we were robbed a bit with politics, with low votes from Spain and Malta.

'It was very nerve-wracking before going on stage. The occasion was very formal. I was faced with a problem of logistics. I was often on television, playing my bass guitar, with a drummer who was some distance away in the orchestra, and no matter how well they hooked up the monitors in those days, it was always going to be a nervous situation, to try to make sure I could hear him as he was playing, without there being any time lag. We tried to give a relaxed rendition of the song and get it across. It hung largely on Peter and Lyn as lead vocalists to do it, and I think they did great. It was a bit disappointing to be second, but it had been very much the New Seekers' week in Edinburgh, and it launched us onto a UK tour that started in Scotland. Having spent 13 weeks in people's living rooms on the *It's Cliff Richard* series, we hadn't realised the popularity of the group. We started concerts off without security on board, but had to quickly organise that as we were getting mobbed on stage.'

Lyn Paul had told the press, 'I'm feeling nervous. I hate contests of any kind,' while Marty Kristian had said, 'I'm treating it like a normal concert. We can only give our best.'

Mike Nevard, writing in the *Sun*, said this about the United Kingdom entry: 'Corny, rickety-tick. Old fashioned, peasant-rousing. Rating 20/50.' The same journalist rated Austria at the top, followed by Netherlands, Switzerland and Sweden.

The New Seekers immediately followed up their success with another top ten single, 'Circles', in July 1972. Other hits followed, including 'You Won't Find Another Fool Like Me' and 'I Get A Little Sentimental Over You', and numerous albums also charted. The group had several changes of line up over the years. Of the 1972 line-up, Paul would feature again in *A Song for Europe* in 1977, and Layton and Kristian planned to return in the 1980 competition. Layton is the longest-serving member of the group and still performs with them. Eve Graham married fellow group member Kevin (aka Danny) Finn, and still records albums. Peter Doyle died in October 2001.

SONGS FOR EUROPE VOLUME TWO

Norway	'Småting' (2'57")	Sung by Grethe Kausland and Benny Borg.	Composed by Kåre Grøttum and Ivar Børsum.	Conducted by Carsten Klouman.

Portugal	'A Festa Da Vida' (2'06")	Sung by Carlos Mendes (with Laura Lee, Gill Gray and Sylvia King).	Words by José Niza. Music by José Calvário.	Conducted by Richard Hill.

In 1968 Carlos Mendes had represented Portugal, finishing in eleventh place with 'Verão'. Conductor Richard Hill was born in Renfrew in Scotland in 1942 and had studied at the Royal College of Music in London. As well as being a conductor he was a composer, working in television, film and theatre. The song was given an English lyric by actor Bill Owen under the title 'Shadows'.

Switzerland	'C'est La Chanson De Mon Amour' (3'00")	Sung by Véronique Müller.	Words by Catherine Desage. Music by Véronique Müller.	Conducted by Jean-Pierre Festi.

Malta	'L-Imhabba' (2'51")	Sung by Helen and Joseph.	Words by Albert Cassola. Music by Charles Camilleri.	Conducted by Charles Camilleri.

1972 EUROVISION SONG CONTEST

Finland	*Muistathan* (2'53")	Sung by Päivi Paunu and Kim Floor.	Words by Juha Flinck. Music by Juha Flinck and Nacke Johansson.	Conducted by Ossi Runne.

Austria	*Falter Im Wind* (2'45")	Sung by the Milestones (Beatrix Neundlinger, Günther Grosslercher, Norbert Niedermeyer and Christian Kolonovits).	Words by Heinz Unger. Music by Richard Schönherz and Manuel Rigoni.	Conducted by Erich Kleinschuster.

The Austrian entry required a piano to be shifted on stage, so to allow time for this it was scripted that the cameras would show shots of the juries in Edinburgh Castle at this point.

The English version was titled 'Dance Butterfly' with lyrics by Richard Gillinson.

SONGS FOR EUROPE VOLUME TWO

Italy	'I Giorni Dell Acrobaleno' (2'52")	Sung by Nicola di Bari.	Words by Dalmazio Masini. Music by Piero Pintucci and Nicola di Bari.	Conducted by Gianfranco Reverberi.

Yugoslavia	'Muziki I Ti' (2'57")	Sung by Téréza.	Words by Ivan Krajač. Music by Nikica Kalogjera.	Conducted by Nikica Kalogjera.

Téréza Kesovija had represented Monaco in the 1966 contest with '*Bien Plus Fort*', which finished seventeenth.

Sweden	'*Härliga Sommerdag*' (2'36")	Sung by the Family Four (Berndt Ost, Agneta Munther, Marie Bergman and Pierre Isacsson).	Composed by Håkan Elmquist.	Conducted by Mats Olsson.

For the second year in succession the Family Four were representing Sweden, having come sixth in Dublin with '*Vita Vidder*'.

1972 EUROVISION SONG CONTEST

Monaco	*'Comme On S'aime'* (2'50")	Sung by Peter McLane and Anne-Marie Goddart.	Words by Jean Drejac. Music by Raymond Bernard.	Conducted by Raymond Bernard.

Before the Monegasque entry, the camera showed the 1971 winner, Séverine, in the audience. This shot would later become infamous as she was seen glancing down at her watch in apparent boredom. It was however planned in the camera script that there would be a cut to her at this point, so it was not an opportunistic move.

Belgium	*'À La Folie Ou Pas Du Tout'* (2'19")	Sung by Serge and Christine Ghisoland (with Claude Lombard, Annie Gerard and Michelle Paquay)	Words by Daniël Nelis. Music by Daniël Nelis and Bob Milan.	Conducted by Henri Segers.

Luxembourg	*'Après Toi'* (2'50")	Sung by Vicky Leandros (with Susanne Jage, Rolf Jage, Rosi Rohr, Angelika Metzger and John Wiseman).	Words by Klaus Munro and Yves Dessca. Music by Mario Panas and Klaus Munro.	Conducted by Klaus Munro.

SONGS FOR EUROPE VOLUME TWO

Vicky Leandros was born Vassiliki Papathanasiou in August 1949 on the island of Corfu. She was the daughter of musician Leandros Papathanasiou, otherwise known by his pseudonym Mario Panas. Performing simply as Vicky, she released her first single in 1965, and two years later was invited to sing for Luxembourg in the *Eurovision Song Contest* with 'L'amour Est Bleu'. She finished in fourth place, but the song went on to become a big international hit as 'Love Is Blue', notably in an instrumental version by Paul Mauriat. In the 1970s she changed her stage name to Vicky Leandros, taking her father's first name, and her 1970 television show *Ich Bin* was shown in many European countries.

'Après Toi' was given an English lyric by Norman Newell and released as 'Come What May'. Leandros was seen performing the song on *Top of the Pops* on the editions broadcast on 13 and 27 April and 11 May, with the latter two appearances being repeats of the first. None of these editions of *Top of the Pops* exists in the BBC archives. Leandros also appeared on the ITV series *The Golden Shot* broadcast on 23 April. The single eventually reached number two in the charts in May 1972. In total Leandros recorded seven different language versions for the worldwide market, and the song sold six million copies.

Two other singles by Leandros made the top 50 in the charts in 1973, 'The Love In Your Eyes' and 'When Bouzoukis Played'. Leandros made numerous television appearances in the UK, including on *The Morecambe and Wise Show*, and hosted the series *Music My Way*. She continued to be popular on the continent, particularly in Germany and Greece. In 2006 she made an attempt to represent Germany in the *Eurovision Song Contest*, but her song 'Don't Break My Heart' failed to win the national selection.

| Netherlands | 'Als Het Om De Liefde Gaat' (2'57") | Sung by Sandra and Andres (with Judith Sinninge, Titia den Bosch, Yvonne Paay, and Wanda Stellaert). | Words by Hans van Hemert. Music by Dries Holten. | Conducted by Harry van Hoof. |

1972 EUROVISION SONG CONTEST

INTERVAL ACT

The interval act wasn't specially shot for the contest. It was stock footage taken from coverage of the 1968 Edinburgh Military Tattoo, with the bands of eight Scottish regiments marching to the tune of 'Inverness Gathering'. The sequence lasted 3'58". 'We were originally going to film it ourselves,' says producer Terry Hughes, 'but we came across that footage, and it saved us a lot of time and money to use that.'

THE VOTING

The system of voting introduced in the 1971 contest was used again, although one major change was that the juries were kept away in a separate part of the city until the dress rehearsals. The United Kingdom jurors were Robert Walker and Doreen Samuels.

The juries were based in the Grand Hall of Edinburgh Castle, and while television viewers at home could see them in colour, the pictures were projected in black and white on an Eidophor screen for the benefit of the audience in the Usher Hall. Hughes remembers, 'The Eidophor screen would have been the height of technology at the time!'

'I looked after the juries,' says Michael Hurll. 'There were two of them from each country, and several of them turned out to be friends of their respective country's management, girlfriends of the directors of programmes or whatever, and – how shall I put it? – having jollities together. I could just about say who would vote for whom, based on who had been with whom. So that voting system simply didn't work. Too many people had a hidden agenda, and sometimes not so hidden, and it didn't last much longer.'

SONGS FOR EUROPE VOLUME TWO

	Germany	France	Ireland	Spain	UK	Norway	Portugal	Switzerland	Malta	Finland	Austria	Italy	Yugoslavia	Sweden	Monaco	Belgium	Luxembourg	Netherlands	TOTAL	POSITION
Germany		8	6	9	5	6	6	5	4	5	5	7	5	8	8	7	7	6	107	3RD
France	5		5	2	9	7	2	3	5	4	2	3	5	2	6	7	8	6	81	11TH
Ireland	4	3		4	4	6	4	3	6	3	4	3	3	5	5	4	6	5	72	15TH
Spain	7	5	5		3	8	6	3	4	4	5	3	2	7	8	3	5	5	83	10TH
United Kingdom	8	9	6	2		10	4	8	2	7	7	7	9	6	9	4	8	8	114	2ND
Norway	4	3	6	5	4		5	2	5	7	3	2	5	4	4	4	6	4	73	14TH
Portugal	3	4	7	7	4	2		6	5	2	4	9	4	7	4	7	10	5	90	7TH
Switzerland	4	5	6	5	4	7	2		4	7	8	5	5	4	6	4	7	5	88	8TH
Malta	3	2	4	2	6	2	2	2		5	2	2	2	3	3	2	2	4	48	18TH
Finland	4	3	3	6	5	6	4	3	3		3	3	4	4	5	8	6	8	78	12TH
Austria	6	6	6	6	3	5	5	7	5	4		6	8	10	5	4	5	9	100	5TH
Italy	4	5	3	2	3	6	7	9	6	6	6		4	8	6	6	6	5	92	6TH

1972 EUROVISION SONG CONTEST

																			Total	Place
Yugoslavia	7	4	5	8	5	4	5	2	4	3	3	2		4	9	8	8	6	87	9TH
Sweden	5	3	5	3	3	5	4	2	4	5	4	3	7		5	7	5	5	75	13TH
Monaco	4	3	4	3	5	6	2	2	5	5	3	3	4	3		4	4	5	65	16TH
Belgium	2	3	4	2	5	2	3	3	5	4	2	3	2	2	4		6	3	56	17TH
Luxembourg	9	8	9	2	10	8	7	6	4	6	8	9	10	8	7	8		9	128	1ST
Netherlands	6	6	8	8	9	8	5	6	3	9	6	3	9	6	5	2	7		106	4TH

Analysis: Luxembourg went straight into the lead from the opening round, and kept it throughout the voting. Only in the second block of voting, with Spain, UK and Norway allotting their points, did Luxembourg look challenged. Spain awarded just two points to Luxembourg and to the United Kingdom, and this allowed the Netherlands to come within a point of Luxembourg. But following that round, Luxembourg extended its lead with each subsequent one, and going into the last round it had an almost unassailable 14 point advantage. The Netherlands fell from second to fourth place in the end, while the United Kingdom finished in second place for the eighth time, once again behind Luxembourg. Every win so far by the Grand Duchy had been at the expense of the United Kingdom as runners-up.

The United Kingdom had been one of two juries to award the maximum of ten points to Luxembourg, helping them take their third Grand Prix and making them the second most successful nation in the contest after France. Their score of 128 points was identical to the winning total the previous year. The United Kingdom achieved one maximum score thanks to the Norwegian jury.

SONGS FOR EUROPE VOLUME TWO

Germany finished in third place for the third year in succession, and Portugal achieved their best result so far with a seventh place. Malta once again managed to finish in last place on their second appearance, with an even lower score than their debut.

WINNING REPRISE

| Luxembourg | 'Après Toi' (2'50") | Sung by Vicky Leandros. | Words by Klaus Munro and, Yves Dessca. Music by Mario Panas and Klaus Munro. | Conducted by Klaus Munro. |

There had been consideration given to repeating the idea used in the 1971 contest of having the second- and third-placed artists on stage at the presentation of the awards, to receive flowers. However, apparently the artists in the 1971 contest had not been too happy to appear on stage in this capacity and the idea was dropped from future editions.

CREDITS
Executive Producer: Bill Cotton
Assistant to Executive Producer: Queenie Lipyeat
Producer: Terry Hughes
Assistant to Producer: Jenny Mercer
Designer: Brian Tregidden

1972 EUROVISION SONG CONTEST

Costume Supervisor: Kirstie Colam
Make-Up Supervisors: Rosemary Burrett and Tulah Tuke
Sound Supervisor: Chris Holcombe
Vision Mixer: Tony Rowe
Production Assistants: Tony Newman and Alex Young

Edinburgh Castle Team:
Associate Producer: Iain MacFadyen
Assistant to Producer: Anne Carroll
Sound Supervisor: Ian Dunn
Vision Mixer: David Gloag
Production Assistant: Hal Duncan

Music Director: Malcolm Lockyer
EBU Scrutineer: Clifford Brown

The contest was watched by 38.20% (19.29 million) at the start of the programme at 21.30, rising to 40.20% (20.30 million) by 22.00 and reaching 42.20% (21.31 million) by 22.30.

The views of 548 viewers were canvassed for the Audience Research Report. The range of opinions expressed was much the same as in previous years. The contest was said to be 'pretty much as expected; nothing new or startling' and 'decidedly wearisome with 18 songs, all bar one in a foreign language.' According to one respondent, 'It's Monday now and I can't remember any of them, except our one, and that's because I've heard it so many times before'.

The new voting system was still popular, with just a few preferring the old one. 'It might not have been quite so business-like, but definitely more exciting,' was one viewpoint. About half approved of '*Apres Toi*' as the winner, and of the others the Netherlands' entry would have been the first choice of many. Some said the United Kingdom would have won had it not been for some distinctly political voting.

Moira Shearer was considered to have been charming and gracious. A few had thought her a little bit stiff and lacking in warmth, but most had found her quite delightful, poised and confident. Tom Fleming had set the scene well, it was felt, and technically the presentation had left little to be desired, although once again a sizeable number had commented that the orchestra had drowned out the singers at times.

The BBC has retained a copy of the broadcast version in its archives. A copy also exists of the BBC radio broadcast.[1]

Just as in 1968, there had been a big joke played on a member of the production team during the staging of the contest. Whereas the story of the supposed Albanian delegation turning up in 1968 has been often repeated, the 1972 prank is less well known.

'It became incumbent on whoever was doing the contest to come up with a practical joke,' explains Terry Hughes, 'and we had a very elaborate one on this occasion. I had a very close friend and fellow producer, a wonderful guy called Colin Charman, who sadly was to die at a young age from a brain haemorrhage. He had just finished producing *The Dick Emery Show* for the season, and approached Bill Cotton to ask if he could come up to Scotland for the contest. He didn't want any credit or anything, he just wanted to come up and do any job, as he thought it would be a fun place to be. So Bill told him that we could use him up at the Castle with the jury, and that he could supervise that. Colin was very excited to be involved and came up for the week. Bill Cotton and I were at rehearsals and Bill suggested that we should really try and come up with something to hit Colin with …

---

[1] From this point, copies also exist of all subsequent BBC radio broadcasts of the *Eurovision Song Contest*.

1972 EUROVISION SONG CONTEST

'In parallel to this, there was a plan to have a big party as always following the production. But whoever was in charge of the local authority informed us that there were restrictions on the licensing hours. The cut-off time for serving alcohol was something like 22.00, and the show didn't end until 23.00, and we wanted to have this party afterwards. Now this part is true. The local authority had threatened to raid the party, telling us that we couldn't do it, and Alisdair Milne, who was Controller of BBC Scotland at that time, was having an ongoing correspondence with them. He explained about the foreign visitors coming to Edinburgh, and the business it was generating, and the fact that it was tradition to hold a post-contest function, and that it would be in the confines of the big hotel we were using, but the local authority were being unyielding.

'So what we did, in order to catch Colin out, was we got some correspondence supposedly from Alisdair Milne to Bill Cotton, which went something like this:

'Dear Bill,

'As you know, we are having an ongoing contretemps with the Lord Provost of Edinburgh, who is insisting that we may not have any alcoholic beverages at the event following transmission of the *Eurovision Song Contest*. He is of course also aware of the importance of the visiting foreign delegations and of the image of Edinburgh, and that it is expected that such a function forms part of the tradition associated with hosting the contest. He is therefore making noises about arresting someone as a token gesture, but it would be extremely embarrassing if this person was to be one of our staff members from BBC Scotland. So I am asking you if you could nominate one of your London members of staff as the person to be arrested.

'Yours
'Alisdair Milne

SONGS FOR EUROPE VOLUME TWO

'So we got that letter typed up, and Bill also made up a reply to it, which read something like:

'Dear Alisdair,

'Thank you for letter. This is a very irritating situation. I cannot tell you how angry I am about this, but I understand the delicate position you are in. I will however nominate one of my staff to take the fall for this on the BBC's behalf.

'Yours
'Bill Cotton

'Anyway, Colin Charman flies up from London, and Bill goes to meet him at the airport. In the taxi from the airport to the hotel, Bill explains that he is glad Colin is there, but he has a difficult assignment to give him. He shows Colin the supposed correspondence from Alisdair Milne, and says that they need someone to be the nominated person to be arrested on behalf of the BBC. Bill explains that while he is delighted that Colin is up in Edinburgh to help out, he isn't absolutely essential to the event, and therefore he would have to be the nominated person to take the fall!
'Naturally Colin wanted to know what it would involve. So Bill explained that at most the police would come in and arrest him at the party, and would take him away to a police station and probably keep him in overnight. The BBC lawyers would be on hand to make sure the incident didn't go on record!
'Colin was worried about what his wife would think of him being taken away and put in prison for the night, but Bill said he would have a word with his wife to reassure her that everything would be okay. So Colin, who was an ex-soldier, could see that it made sense that he should be the fall guy, as everyone else was too important

and involved with the contest, so he agreed to go along with it.

'That Thursday night I'd finished the rehearsals and Colin was anxious to talk to me. Of course I knew what it was going to be about. He came up to my hotel room and said, "Terry, I know I've said yes to this, but I'm feeling really bad about it," and I was telling him that it would be okay, and that it would be for only one night, and that they "probably" wouldn't handcuff him. So he was reassured, but as he left the room I added, "I just hope you haven't got any previous criminal record, because that could come up," and he assured me he hadn't and he left.

'However, about one o'clock in the morning I get a phone call in my room, and it's Colin. "Terry I can't sleep," he says, and when I ask him why, he replies, "Well you know you asked if I had any criminal record … Well I was fined once … for not having a television licence … and if that comes out it is going to be so embarrassing as a BBC television producer!" It was so hard for me to contain my laughter! I was telling him that we would talk to the BBC lawyers in the morning; and then of course he was worried about telling the BBC lawyers, and that he might get fired from his position in the BBC!

'Well, I know the poor guy didn't get a wink of sleep that night, so I had to call Bill Cotton early in the morning in his hotel room. I could hardly get the story out for laughing so much, and Bill was in hysterics as well. We talked about it over breakfast, and I said, "We have to tell him and let him off the hook." But Bill said, "Let's wait at least until we have this afternoon's dress rehearsal done."

'So after the run-through in the afternoon, Bill gets hold of Colin and says to him, "Colin how would you feel if I told you this whole thing was a scam?" Colin replied, "I'd like to think it was, but I've seen the correspondence from Alisdair Milne, so I know it isn't." Then Bill assured him it was a scam and that the letters had been made up, and Colin couldn't believe it, as it had all been so elaborate.

'Colin was the perfect person to play the trick on, and he took it very well.'

As an addendum, the post-contest party did go ahead in Edinburgh, without the approval of the local authority, so the threat of it being raided still hung over the BBC. 'I think they knew we were going to do it anyway, and thankfully turned a blind eye to it,' adds Hughes. 'I really enjoyed the whole experience. It was so wonderful being up in Scotland. It was the only time that I had spent a great deal of time there, and I really liked it. I was surrounded by musicians, a great team, people from other countries who have stayed good friends and contacts, and it was great to be part of such an event.'

1973 UNITED KINGDOM

To represent the country in 1973, BBC Head of Light Entertainment Bill Cotton turned once more to Cliff Richard, who had come a close second in the 1968 *Eurovision Song Contest* with 'Congratulations', had hosted the selection of the past three United Kingdom entries on his show *It's Cliff Richard* and had presented the 1971 and 1972 preview programmes. This made Richard only the second artist to have the honour of performing twice for the country, the other being Ronnie Carroll in 1962 and 1963. One crucial difference was that Richard had been specifically chosen, whereas Carroll had had to actively compete to gain his place.

Since his 1968 appearance, Richard had continued to enjoy chart success, with songs like 'Good Times (Better Times)' and 'Goodbye Sam, Hello Samantha'. He also had a number 22 hit in 1968 with an English cover version of the Italian entry to the 1968 contest, 'Marianne'.

At the end of November 1972, negotiations took place for Richard to appear on Cilla Black's show *Cilla* to perform the final six entries. Nearly 300 songs were submitted to the MPA, which were whittled down to a short list of 15 by a committee, before Richard was allowed to add a further three songs of his choice, leaving just 18 to go forward to the BBC.

In alphabetical order the final 18 songs were: 'All Get Together', 'Ashes To Ashes', 'Come Back Billie Jo', 'The Days Of Love', 'Do I Hear Music', 'The Good Book', 'Help It Along', 'I Can See', 'Jeannie', 'Jigsaw World', 'A Little Understanding', 'May The Sun Never Set', 'Never Found A Girl To Love', 'Power To All Our Friends', 'Songs', 'This World Is Ours Today', 'Tomorrow Rising' and 'Where In The World'. Each song was listened to twice by a panel comprising Cotton, two BBC producers, two MPA officials and two representatives of Richard, before the final six emerged. Richard recorded the final six songs in the recording studios on 27 and 28 December 1972 in preparation for the release of the single and subsequent EP.

SONGS FOR EUROPE VOLUME TWO

The performance of the first song for *Cilla* was scheduled for recording on 12 January 1973, for transmission in the following day's show. The remaining five songs were all recorded on 17 January, and inserted one a week into the editions of *Cilla* transmitted from 18 January through to 17 February.

On 18 January Richard recorded all six songs again, for the *A Song for Europe* programme to be broadcast on 24 February. He was also contracted to perform the winning song over 2 and 3 March for that week's *Cilla* show, and to rehearse in Luxembourg from Tuesday 3 April to Saturday 7 April, for which the BBC would pay his fares and £20 per day expenses in Luxembourg.

Richard would be backed by John Farrar, Alan Tarney, Terry Britten and Trevor Spencer, sometimes called the New Shadows in paperwork. The musical director for *A Song for Europe* would be David MacKay, who had done the same job in 1972. He would have an orchestra of 29 musicians at his disposal. Ronnie Hazlehurst would conduct all the other music in the programme, including Cilla Black's opening number, 'Something Tells Me'. The programme was recorded in the BBC Television Theatre in Shepherds Bush.

Radio Times had featured Richard and Black on the cover for the edition of 13 January to promote the first programme in the series. It also carried a one-and-a-half-page feature on the contest in the 24 February edition, with biographies and photographs of all the composers taking part, plus a short interview with Richard.

BBC1 broadcast a 1.00" trailer on 24 February, just after *The Wonderful World Of Disney*, which featured clips of the New Seekers performing 'Beg, Steal Or Borrow' and Vicky Leandros performing '*Apres Toi*' and featured a voiceover by Dick Graham.

A SONG FOR EUROPE 1973
Saturday 24 February 1973 at 20.16.01 (Duration 50'08")
Presented by Cilla Black

1973 UNITED KINGDOM

Cilla Black opened the programme by explaining that it was a special show to select the United Kingdom entry for the *Eurovision Song Contest*. She introduced Cliff Richard, who was played on with a Norrie Paramour arrangement of 'Congratulations' (duration 10"). After a brief chat with Richard, there was a specially-shot 16mm film that featured the names of 17 countries in a descending circular pattern. The observant viewer would have noticed that these graphics included Malta, although that country would end up not being in the Final of the 1973 contest, but made no mention of Israel, which would be participating.

Black introduced each song, with details of the composers, and the camera cut to shots of the respective composers sitting in the Television Theatre audience. All the composers were present for the recording.

Song One	'Come Back Billie Jo' (2'30")	Sung by Cliff Richard.	Composed by Mitch Murray and Tony Macaulay.

Mitch Murray had previously composed two runners-up for the contest: 'I've Got The Moon On My Side' in 1964 and, alongside Peter Callander, 'Tell The Boys' in 1967.

'I founded SODS (Society of Distinguished Songwriters) in 1971,' says Murray. 'The whole idea of SODS was to do nothing at all, no charity, no good to anybody else. As a result they all love it, just turn up, have nothing to do except eat nicely, laugh and enjoy each other's company. But as a spin-off, sometimes collaborations come out of it, because you might want to spend some time with a particular person. Tony Macaulay probably said to me "Do you fancy writing for the *Eurovision*?", and I would have said "Yes," and we wrote it at Tony's flat near Edgware Road. We are both all-rounders, so that would be throwing stuff around, but Tony is a bit of a powerhouse when it comes to writing, and whenever he's cooking as it were, you just leave him to it, because there's no point in getting your tuppence in when the other guy is really hot. So that sort of collaboration could have been mainly me, but it was mainly him. I just went along with it, and made some sort of adjustments, but I remember it being very much Tony.'

'Come Back Billie Jo' was the only song that Murray and Tony Macaulay ever wrote together. Macaulay was voted Songwriter of the Year by the Songwriters' Guild of Great Britain in 1971, and his hits had included 'Love Grows' recorded by Edison Lighthouse, and 'That Same Old Feeling' recorded by Pickettywitch.

'We were both members of SODS,' recalls Macaulay. 'It's still going, and I was very into it at the time. It encouraged a lot of us to write together, or to write with people we might not have written with before, and Mitch was some years ahead in terms of success and his career, and I wanted to write with him. He was a very basic musician, and wrote some very good songs. I tended to write with people who came up with as much of the melody as I did, or as much of the lyrics as I did. It was fine, he's a very talented guy, but that was the only song we ever wrote together. I seem to remember I did most of the melody. I work from a guitar and the piano. Some songs would start on one instrument and end up on the other.

'I thought the winner had a good hook and chorus, and was better than ours. To be honest I was never into that *Eurovision* style; that central European, almost Germanic feel, that one-in-a-bar, two-four time, was alien to me. About the only thing I ever wrote in that style was the theme tune to *New Faces*. It was not a feel I enjoyed much. When I write from the wallet, rather than my heart, it never really works.'

Murray would try with a couple of songs each year, in the hope of getting one through. 'It was just a good way of writing commercial songs, having something to aim for. If you are given an artist to write for, it gives you a shape to write for. I thought we were in with a really good chance with "Come Back Billie Jo". I don't remember "Power To All Our Friends" worrying me at the time, but it was not up to me, and I was second again. I remember Tony Orlando and Dawn doing a cover version, but it never made the money that it should have.'

Having come second on every attempt, this was the last time that Murray would have composition in the Final. 'I can't remember if I tried again. It wouldn't have been crucial. If I didn't try again, then it was because that was the way it had worked.' He went on with songwriting partner Callander to form the Bus Stop record label, which launched Paper Lace, and they wrote the group's hits 'Billy, Don't Be A Hero' and 'The Night Chicago Died'. Murray has since built up his reputation for comedy, including voice characterisations, is a prolific after-dinner speaker, and has written various books on speechwriting.

The 13 January edition of *Cilla* in which the song was previewed was watched by 36.40% of the population (18.38 million). The Audience Research Report compiled for that programme, from a sample of 321 viewers, recorded the opinion that Richard had sung the first song well, and that he was 'the best possible choice' for the contest, although some thought 'Cliff would never win with that song.'

| Song Two | 'Ashes To Ashes' (3'00") | Sung by Cliff Richard. | Composed by Tony Cole. |

Australian Tony Cole had been one of the team of songwriters that composed the winning entry in the 1972 contest, 'Beg, Steal Or Borrow'. As a singer he had a couple of minor hits in Australia, including 'Beat It' and 'The Hook'. In 1972 he spent four weeks in the USA charts with his single 'Man And Woman'. He composed the score and songs for the 1973 Cliff Richard film *Take Me High*. Its title song, recorded by Richard, reached number 27 in the charts. He also composed for Johnny Halliday. Cole died in 2001.

The 20 January edition of *Cilla* in which the song was previewed was watched by 31.80% (16.06 million).

Richard had to do two retakes of this song on the recording for the Final. On the first performance he fluffed his lines, and on the second take there was a false start.

| Song Three | 'Tomorrow Rising' (2'10") | Sung by Cliff Richard. | Words by Mike Hawker. Music by Brian Bennett. |

Mike Hawker and Brian Bennett had previously composed 'Wind Of Change' for Clodagh Rodgers in the 1971 competition, which was one of the songs that finished in second place.

Hawker had further chart success with the song 'I Only Want To Be With You', written with Ivor Raymonde. It was originally a hit for Dusty Springfield; the Bay City Rollers reached number four in the UK charts with it in 1976; and the Tourists also reached number four with their version in 1979.

The 27 January edition of *Cilla* in which the song was previewed was watched by 32.30% (16.31 million).

| Song Four | 'The Days Of Love' (3'28") | Sung by Cliff Richard. | Words by Dougie Wright. Music by Alan Hawkshaw. |

Alan Hawkshaw had previously composed entries along with Ray Cameron for the 1969, 1970 and 1971 contests. This was the first time that he had collaborated on a song with Dougie Wright.

'Dougie Wright and I had known each other for years and we met often on our various recording sessions as session men,' says Hawkshaw. 'We probably wrote that song on somebody else's time while they were listening to playbacks. Doug Flett and Guy Fletcher's song "Power To All Our Friends" was more than a cut above the average and deserved to win.'

'I was interested in music at school,' recalls Dougie Wright, 'and took piano for a couple of years, but I took up percussion quite late at 18. I did a lot of practice, had lessons on a drum kit, and eventually after a little while got into semi-pro dance band work around the Leeds area. That brought me into contact with Alan Hawkshaw, as the first band we ever started with was the same band … but at different times.'

Wright started his professional career in 1958 as drummer with the John Barry Seven. He remained with the band for four years, worked in film, theatre, radio and television broadcasts, and appeared on the *Royal Variety Show* in 1960 backing Adam Faith. He then became a freelance session drummer and was much in demand, featuring on tracks performed by Kathy Kirby, Matt Monro, Cilla Black, Sandie Shaw and Vince Hill.

1973 UNITED KINGDOM

He was also the regular drummer on the ITV pop programme *Ready Steady Go!*

Of his break into songwriting, Wright says: 'I started jotting stuff down, and saying to a few people, "I think I'm going to have a go at lyrics". I asked my good friend Vic Flick [of the John Barry Seven] to see if he would be interested in collaborating with me, which he did, and we jotted down quite a lot of stuff, and it took off from there. We had a few very near misses, a close call with the big time, and from a writing point of view it was touch and go whether we would make it or not. But we were two very busy musicians in London at that time doing sessions, as well as other things between times. Eventually I started to write with other people, including Herbie Flowers, Mike Redway and Johnny Arthey, jotting stuff down, but never had any great success. I remember entering a song for the contest with Johnny Arthey; it never got beyond first base, but I can't recall any more details about it.

'With "Days Of Love", that came about when I was on a session (I can't even remember who for) at De Lane Lea studios in Wembley. Alan [Hawkshaw] was on organ, and I was on drums, and he said to me, "I've got a little tune here. Would you like to jot some lyrics down to it?" I said, "Sure," and had a look at it, and he played around with it a bit on keyboards. So in between takes in the studio, while people were listening back in the control room, we were writing a song. We knocked it up in an hour, and so and I left it with Alan, and he said, "I'm going to take it down to KPM, and get a publishing deal on it," which he did, with Peter Maurice Music. Anyway, a short while later, Alan told me we had got into the last so many hundred of the whittling down system for the choice for *A Song for Europe,* and I thought "Great," and then eventually, later on, we got into the last six. I was most surprised and delighted when it got to that point.

'Now I thought, "This is going to be interesting," as session musicians are not really acknowledged as being songwriters. If you cracked the *Eurovision,* then you could make a lot of money. I had the gut feeling, but don't have any proof, that we were kind of relegated a little bit. The song was given a nice arrangement by David MacKay, if a bit theatrical, and it was interesting from a string point of view. A couple of things didn't knock me sideways, but generally speaking it was a good arrangement. I didn't think we were going to win; we had heard things through the grapevine, that this other song, "Power To All Our Friends", was going to go through, so we had an inkling.'

Wright had played the drums on the demo discs of two other songs entered into the contest, 'Power To All Our Friends' and 'Help It Along'. He entered a few more songs, on his own, in subsequent years, but without success. Apart from drumming, songwriting and singing, Wright also went into teaching percussion, and giving his own talk shows on the many songs on which he has performed.

The 3 February edition of *Cilla* in which the song was previewed was watched by 32.70% (16.51 million). A BBC Audience Research Report for the programme, based on the views of a sample of 303, recorded the opinion that the weekly presentation of the songs for the contest 'had been disappointing, though Cliff did his best to make them appealing'.

'Days Of Love' required a second retake during recording of the Final, owing to a false start on the first retake.

| Song Five | 'Power To All Our Friends' (3'00") | Sung by Cliff Richard. | Composed by Guy Fletcher and Doug Flett. |

The songwriting team of Guy Fletcher and Doug Flett had written 'Wonderful World', which Cliff Richard had sung in the 1968 competition. They had returned in 1970 with 'Three Ships' for Mary Hopkin. Both songs had finished in third place in their respective years. The pair hadn't tried in either 1971 or 1972, but came back to write again for Richard.

'It was a killer song,' says Fletcher. 'There wasn't any doubt in my mind. We put it in, and in those days there were about 30 teams of songwriters who were really totally professional, and we are all friends, and still good friends. We went along to the Final of *A Song for Europe*, and we were nervous, because you never know what's going to happen. It was a fantastic, friendly rivalry, and a very important event in the music calendar, as all the great writers went in for it. If you had a winner it was huge, and it could make a lot of money; and we won it by a landslide.'

The 10 February edition of *Cilla* in which the song was previewed was watched by 30.50% (15.40 million).

1973 UNITED KINGDOM

Song Six	'Help It Along' (3'05")	Sung by Cliff Richard.	Composed by Christopher Neil.

Christopher Neil started his career as a singer with the Manchester group the Chuckles. In 1970 he played the lead in the London production of *Hair* and in 1972 he released a solo album entitled *Where I Belong*. At the time of the contest he was playing one of the apostles in the rock musical *Jesus Christ Superstar*, in which he also understudied for Paul Nicholas in the lead role.

This was his only song to make the Final of *A Song for Europe*. It was as a record producer that Neil was to make his name, working with artists including Sheena Easton, Dollar and in particular Mike and the Mechanics. He has worked with several artists associated with the contest, including Morten Harket of Aha, Johnny Logan and Edyta Gorniak, and he produced the Celine Dion track 'Think Twice'. In the 2009 *Eurovision Song Contest* he was one of the songwriters behind the Icelandic entry, 'Is It True?', which finished in second place.

The 17 February edition of *Cilla* in which the song was previewed was watched by 28.30% of the population (14.29 million).

There had to be a second retake of Cilla Black's introduction to Neil during the recording of the Final.

As in 1972, the songs were shown for a second time, broadcast from the video taken of the earlier performances. This time Black and Richard took turns with the introductions but there was no reference to the composers or shots of them in the audience. However there were some retakes required here as well. A second retake was necessary on Black's introduction to 'Ashes To Ashes', and one retake required on each of her introductions to 'The Days Of Love' and 'Help It Along'.

At the conclusion of the second run-through, Black then provided details of the address for postal votes, the deadline for which was the first postal delivery on Thursday 1 March. She also had to do a retake of this announcement, as she had fluffed it the first time. Finally Richard had to do a retake on his 'I'll be back on Saturday night …' speech, before Black closed the show with 'I Don't Know How To Love Him'.

The Final of *A Song for Europe* was watched by 28.60% (14.44 million). The BBC again prepared an Audience Research Report on the programme. Reaction was pretty mixed from the 402 viewers questioned. The main feeling seemed to be that the songs were 'very ordinary', with a few even going as far as to say that they were 'extremely poor'. Though the sample members had hoped they were wrong, they felt there didn't appear to be a likely winner amongst them, and that they all sounded 'very similar', 'unoriginal' and 'lacked punch'. Additional sources of dissatisfaction were the playing of each song twice, particularly in their entirety, and the relatively little amount of screen time given to Cilla Black. It was commented that perhaps the programme should have been sub-titled *The Cliff Richard Show*, and some suggested that *A Song for Europe* should actually be done as a separate show. However there were some viewers who had watched and listened purely for the *A Song for Europe* aspect. Several were irritated by Black, and her coy manner and accent, while others regarded Richard as 'nondescript' and felt that some of the songs had 'not suited his voice' or not made 'the best of the material.' Many more, however, were enthusiastic about both artists, commenting that Black had been entertaining in the little she had to do, and that Richard had a pleasing personality and had put the songs over in a professionally polished manner. The songs themselves struck about a third of the sample as all very good, and melodious and catchy. Those who appreciated them most said that it was difficult to single one out, and that they had been fairly presented. The backing group was also separately commended.

All six songs were played again on Pete Murray's *Open House* from 11.00 on Radio 2 on Monday 26 February.

THE RESULTS

The results were announced one week later, on the Saturday 3 March edition of the *Cilla* show, which had been recorded the previous day. The results were announced by Bill Cotton, along with Cilla Black, in the order they

1973 UNITED KINGDOM

were presented. The votes for each song were illustrated on a barometer graphic, which went as high as 40,000. When it came to 'Power To All Our Friends', it went off the scale. Cotton made the presentations of the awards to composers Guy Fletcher and Doug Flett. Cliff Richard then reprised the winning song, 'Power To All Our Friends'.

	Title	Votes	Placing
1	'Come Back Billie Jo'	34,209	Second
2	'Ashes To Ashes'	17,115	Sixth
3	'Tomorrow Rising'	21,858	Fourth
4	'The Days Of Love'	18,304	Fifth
5	'Power To All Our Friends'	125,505	First
6	'Help It Along'	25,369	Third

Analysis: A huge postal vote, with almost twice as many votes cast as the previous year, produced a comfortable winner in 'Power To All Our Friends'. It scored more than all the other songs put together, with 51.78% of the total, and was well ahead of the runner up, 'Come Back Billie Jo', at just 14.11%. The closest battle was actually for last place, with just under 1,200 votes separating the bottom two.

CREDITS
Producer: Michael Hurll
Designers: David Chandler and Valerie Warrender
Costume Designer: Linda Martin
Make-Up: Ann Rayment
Sound Supervisor: Len Shorey

SONGS FOR EUROPE VOLUME TWO

Lighting: Bill Millar
Musical Director: David MacKay

The 3 March edition of *Cilla* that included the results was watched by 27.00% of the population (13.64 million). A panel of 357 replied to questionnaires for the Audience Research Report on the programme. Of those, about 40% were enthusiastic about the music, and agreed on the result, feeling that the chosen song was a potential winner of the international event. Some though expressed disappointment because it wasn't the song they would have chosen, while others thought it was the best of a bad bunch, and a few went as far as to say it was 'ghastly', 'a disgrace to our country' and 'not worthy of representation'. Some felt Richard had been defeated by poor material, though Richard was also described as 'marvellous as always' and a 'true professional who put *A Song for Europe* over beautifully'.

Of the *Cilla* show in general, some said that if it returned they would like it to be more like Black's other shows, and not combined with *A Song for Europe*.

The BBC has retained in its archives all the *Cilla* shows with Cliff Richard performing the entries each week, as well as the Final, and the edition featuring the results.

The winning song, 'Power To All Our Friends', was released on 7" single, backed with the second-placed song, 'Come Back Billie Jo'. It peaked at number four in the charts, and Richard appeared twice on *Top of the Pops*, on the editions broadcast on 8 and 15 March, the latter performance being a repeat of the former. Neither edition exists in the BBC archives.

Reviewing the single in *Record Mirror*, Peter Jones said: 'The Fletcher-Flett song … goes into the *Eurovision Song Contest* and will probably be in the first three … what with it suiting Cliff's style so well. It's a mixture of the pop, the near gospel and the big beat, and the basic chorus is just fine. No point going further in a critical survey of it. Except to say it's probably the one I would have picked had I been on the panel.'

Richard appeared on the BBC1 show *They Sold a Million*, broadcast on 25 March, which was introduced by

1973 UNITED KINGDOM

Terry Wogan. He sang a number of his hits, then in the latter section of the show there was a *Eurovision* medley, with songs performed by Vince Hill, Julie Rogers and the Young Generation. The songs included were '*Volare*', 'Sing Little Birdie', 'Looking High, High, High', 'Jack In The Box', 'La, La, La', 'Knock, Knock (Who's There?)', 'Congratulations' (sung by Richard), 'Puppet On A String', 'Love Is Blue', 'Come What May', 'Boom Bang-A-Bang' and 'Beg Steal Or Borrow'. The medley erroneously contained the Matt Monro song 'My Kind Of Girl', which had actually been the runner-up in the *ITV Song Contest* of 1961. Richard concluded the programme with a full version of 'Power To All Our Friends'. This programme exists in the BBC archives.

'Power To All Our Friends' later featured on the *It's Cliff Richard* edition broadcast on 14 September 1974. 'Help It Along' was performed by Richard on the edition broadcast on 31 August 1974 and also on *It's Cliff And Friends* broadcast on 3 January 1976. All these programmes have been retained in the BBC archives.

Richard recorded several different language versions of 'Power To All Our Friends' between 21 and 23 March. In French it became '*Il Faut Chanter La Vie*' (lyric: Michel Jordan), in German '*Gut, dass es Freunde gibt*' (lyric: Michael Kunze) and in Spanish '*Todo El Poder A Los Amigos*' (lyric: A Belgrano). 'We didn't have any input on the different language versions,' says Guy Fletcher. 'The local publisher would decide who would write the different versions. I wouldn't let that happen now, but in those days we didn't really know what was going on with publishers; we just went along with it.'

On the programme *Made In Britain: It's A Record*, broadcast on 26 August, with Clive Jacobs reporting on the record industry, there was a short extract showing the German version of 'Power To All Our Friends' being mixed in the recording studio at Abbey Road. This programme has been retained in the BBC archives.

Some European releases of 'Power To All Our Friends' featured 'Days Of Love' on the B-side, rather than the runner-up. A Danish single was released with two of the losing entries, 'Ashes To Ashes' on the A-side and 'Days Of Love' on the B-side.

A maxi single entitled *Eurovision Special* was issued in a picture sleeve in the UK, with the third- to sixth-placed songs from the contest. It reached number 29 in the UK charts in May 1973. Although to all intents it was an EP, officially it was called a maxi single and therefore eligible for the charts.

EUROVISION SONG CONTEST PREVIEWS
Presented by Terry Wogan
Recorded: Saturday 23 March

The previews had to be ready by 17 March, for transmission on international circuits by German broadcaster ARD on 21 March, to be broadcast nationally between 26 March and 3 April. Once again the BBC broadcast Part One before the first of the permitted dates.

Part One: Saturday 24 March at 17.05.23 (Duration 29'13"). Audience 8.80% (4.44 million).
Part Two: Saturday 31 March at 17.05.11 (Duration 29'25"). Audience 8.10% (4.09 million).

The songs were shown in the same order as they would appear in the *Eurovision Song Contest*, except for the United Kingdom entry, which was shown at the end of Part Two. The preview of 'Power To All Our Friends' was taken from the *Cilla* show of 24 February. Part One concluded with '*Apres Toi*' from the 1972 *Eurovision Song Contest*. The preview of the Italian entry was in black and white.

CREDIT
Television Presentation: Michael Hurll

The BBC has not retained copies of the preview programmes in its archives, though copies exist on audio.

1973 EUROVISION SONG CONTEST

Within just four days of winning the 1972 contest, the Luxembourg broadcaster CLT (Compagnie Luxembourgeoise de Télédiffusion) had not only confirmed they were prepared to stage the 1973 event, but had proposed the Nouveau Théâtre in Luxembourg as the venue, and possible dates of either 28 April or 5 May 1973, avoiding the Easter weekend date of Saturday 21 April. With the exception of the very first contest held on 24 May 1956, this was the latest calendar dates yet proposed for the contest. However, by 22 April 1972 CLT were able to come back with a revised date of 7 April 1973 – which was quickly accepted.

There were several changes in the rules for the *Eurovision Song Contest* of 1973. The main one the audience would have noticed was that there was no longer any restriction on the use of national language, so performers were free to choose any language or languages they wished to sing in. The use of backing tapes was also permitted for the first time, although this was to prove controversial. All national selections had to be completed by 4 March 1973.

The line-up of countries had remained stable for the past two years, but there were changes for 1973. Austria withdrew, and Israel made their debut at the contest. In October 1972 Greece enquired about entering the contest, but at this stage they were too late for the 1973 event. In January 1973 Cyprus declared an interest in being a participant in the contest in the future, but were informed that until they had the appropriate sound and vision circuits in place and were able to broadcast (or even stage) the contest live, they would have to wait. This would have left a line-up of 18 countries again, but Malta, who originally applied to participate and were placed at number six in the running order when the draw was made on 8 January, pulled out very late in the day, citing that the songs submitted to the Maltese national selection programme were not up to *Eurovision* standard. This left 17 countries in the contest, and would have an effect on the voting sequence.

32 countries were expected to broadcast the programme in addition to those participating; these included

Austria, Bulgaria, Czechoslovakia, East Germany, Greece, Hungary, Malta, Poland, Romania, the Soviet Union and for the first time Turkey. Japan took the broadcast on radio. The total audience was again in the region of 400 million.

When Cliff Richard flew out to Luxembourg, this was reported by *BBC News* on their broadcasts of Wednesday 4 April. That was also the date on which rehearsals got under way, with each country allocated a 45-minute slot from 10.00 onwards. In a departure from past practice, the order in which the countries rehearsed was determined by how close they were to host nation Luxembourg. Luxembourg thus went first, followed by Belgium, the Netherlands, France, the United Kingdom (from 16.20 to 17.05), Germany and Switzerland.

Thursday 5 April saw the rehearsals continue. Monaco were up first at 10.00, followed by Italy, Ireland, Spain and Yugoslavia and Portugal, ending at 18.15. (Had Malta competed, they would have been the last country of the day to rehearse, from 18.20 until 19.05.)

Friday 6 April saw the remaining four countries, Sweden, Norway, Finland and Israel, rehearse between 09.30 and 13.05.

With Israel participating for the first time, and in light of the tragic events at the 1972 Olympic Games when 11 Israeli athletes had been killed as a result of terrorism, Luxembourg mounted its biggest-ever security operation. The authorities sealed off the Nouveau Théâtre concert venue, and when not required there, the Israeli delegation were isolated in the top floor of the local Holiday Inn Hotel, surrounded by armed guards, some of whom had come from Israel itself. Bill Cotton from the BBC was particularly concerned about security with the inclusion of Israel in the contest, and had sought assurances from the organisers that it would be increased from that used in previous editions.

Security however didn't seem to be so strict when it came to the jurors, who had been housed in a hotel some 25 miles away from the city and had been forbidden to mix with singers or promoters. There were allegations that several jurors, including a Portuguese one, had been entertained by Dutch record pluggers at a late-night party. Producer Paul Ulveling commented: 'I have ordered the heads of the delegations to speak very strongly to the jurors who were guilty of breaking the rules.'

The jurors were briefed on Friday 6 April from 10.00, before having their first rehearsal later that day from 16.00 in a television studio in Luxembourg. At the Nouveau Théâtre, the interval act was rehearsed from 15.00, while the presenter was rehearsed from 16.00. There had been concerns expressed previously that the jury members shouldn't see too many of the artists' rehearsals, as these entailed a lot of stopping and starting for lighting, sound quality etc, which could be irritating. However, the jurors actively participated in the complete dress rehearsal that took place from 19.30 until 22.00 that evening.

Saturday 7 April saw technical rehearsals take place in the theatre from 10.00, whilst the jurors also had a rehearsal at the same time until 12.00. A further full dress rehearsal of the entire show took place from 15.00 until 17.00. The jurors had another short rehearsal from 17.00 until 17.30 before everyone had a break for dinner; the live transmission took place at 21.30 local time (which was the same as in the UK).

This was the third *Eurovision Song Context* to have been organised by CLT, though they received some technical help from German broadcaster ARD. The venue normally seated around 800 people, but around 100 seats had to be removed to make way for technical equipment. This meant that the national delegation received only 15 tickets each. Bill Cotton on behalf of the BBC had requested 18 tickets, and was dismayed to be told he couldn't receive more than the standard allocation. It was suggested that if one of the smaller delegations such as Malta didn't use its full allocation then he might get the extra tickets he was seeking; and it is highly likely that, with Malta's late withdrawal, this did indeed happen. Less fortunate were the organisers of the international Cliff Richard Fan Club, who had also requested tickets to see their idol, only to be informed that this wouldn't be possible.

There was a 46-piece orchestra located on stage along with the performers.

The bookmakers had the United Kingdom as favourite to win, followed by, in order, Spain, Monaco, Luxembourg, Germany and Ireland.

Radio Times promoted the contest with a two-page feature on the 1972 winner Vicky Leandros. On Friday

SONGS FOR EUROPE VOLUME TWO

6 April, just before that evening's edition of *The Good Old Days*, BBC1 broadcast a 1'06" trailer featuring Terry Wogan and a voiceover by Dick Graham. There were two further trailers broadcast on the evening of 7 April. The first, just before *Doctor Who*, was a general trailer for Saturday evening programmes and included 15" of 'Power To All Our Friends'. The second came after *Doctor Who* and was specifically to promote the contest. Narrated by John Brahan, it lasted 50" and included the '*Te Deum*' anthem.

EUROVISION SONG CONTEST 1973
Saturday 7 April at 21.30.00 (Duration 99'45")
From the Nouveau Théâtre, Luxembourg
Presented by Helga Guitton

Commentating for BBC television was Terry Wogan, while Pete Murray fulfilled that role for Radio 2. Making his debut as commentator for British Forces Radio was Richard Astbury.

Astbury had put himself through drama school, having obtained a grant, and spent three years at the Birmingham School of Speech and Drama, followed by two or three seasons at the Alexandra Theatre Repertory Company in Birmingham. Having got married, and also having a young son to support, he decided to get a more responsible job in a creditable organisation, and joined the BBC. He was a props man on the studio floor, and worked on the soap opera *The Newcomers* for three years. He then applied for a job as a BBC announcer, but was turned down through lack of experience in that capacity; the senior announcer, Victor Hallam, suggested he apply instead to the British Forces Broadcasting Service (BFBS). Astbury took this advice and passed the voice test, but the BFBS board initially turned him down as well, this time through lack of life experience. Astbury joined the Birmingham Hospital Broadcasting Association and worked part-time in the evenings for around six months, before he got a further call from BFBS inviting him to join the organisation in May 1969.

1973 EUROVISION SONG CONTEST

Initially posted to Cyprus, Astbury spent 18 months as a radio announcer. He was heard by BFBS colleagues in Cologne, Germany, and John Russell, who had commentated on the *Eurovision Song Contest* for British Forces Radio from 1969 to 1971, decided that he should join the staff there. In 1972 Astbury was given the prestigious mid-morning show, which he would continue to present until 1976.

'John [Russell] called me in one day in 1972 and suggested I do a European pop show,' recalls Astbury. 'I didn't want to do it at all, as I knew nothing about European pop, and I didn't like the idea very much, so I said no. But he diplomatically persuaded me, by twisting my arm, that this would be a very good gateway for BFBS to become better known in Germany, and therefore to other European radio stations, and it would be a good flag-waver for the organisation. So I started a radio show called *Pop Around Europe*, which went out every Sunday afternoon.

'I had to work very hard. I had to get to know all the record companies, and they had to get to know me, and some I had to coax to get me non-released material from Spain, Portugal, Italy, Denmark, Sweden and Greece etc. I got all these records that weren't necessarily released in Germany, and I played them on *Pop Around Europe*.' The programme would eventually run from 1972 to 1978.

'It was because of John that I got to do the *Eurovision Song Contest*,' Astbury continues, 'and Terry James [who had provided the commentary in 1972] acted as my producer in Luxembourg.

'The one thing that was always very difficult was that, although we were doing it on radio, it was really for television. What the television show always used to do in those days was to paint a portrait of the city it was coming from, and you would see the local tourist attractions, a famous building, the industry etc, and they would play music for a minute and a half while this was happening. It was very difficult to cover this on radio; you would wonder what to say. So we tried to prepare our commentary so that it would match the television picture, describing the landmark or whatever, and very often it worked extremely well, though sometimes more by luck than judgement.

'Doing the commentary, it was absolutely vital that you stopped talking as soon as a song started, and sometimes that would be quite difficult, so it was important to be at as many rehearsals as possible. We would

SONGS FOR EUROPE VOLUME TWO

also go to the very early rehearsals of the songs, so that we would get some idea of them, whether they were any good … or not.'

Finland	'Tom, Tom, Tom' (2'49")	Sung by Marion Rung.	Words by Bob Barratt. Music by Rauno Lehtinen.	Conducted by Ossi Runne.

Marion Rung had represented Finland in 1962 with '*Tipi-Tii*', when coincidentally she had likewise been first to perform and the contest had also been staged in Luxembourg. 'Tom, Tom, Tom' was performed in English.

Belgium	'Baby, Baby' (2'29")	Sung by Nicole Josy and Hugo Sigal.	Words by Erik Marijsse. Music by Ignace Baert.	Conducted by Francis Bay.

Nicole Josy and Hugo Sigal had been due to sing for Belgium in the 1971 contest, before Josy contracted jaundice and they had to be replaced. The song 'Baby, Baby' was predominantly sung in Dutch.

Portugal	'*Tourada*' (2'56")	Sung by Fernando Tordo.	Words José Carlos Ary dos Santos. Music by Fernando Tordo.	Conducted by Jorge Costa Pinto.

1973 EUROVISION SONG CONTEST

Germany	*Junger Tag* (2'50")	Sung by Gitte.	Words by Stephan Lego. Music by Günther-Eric Thöner.	Conducted by Günther-Eric Thöner.

Norway	'It's Just A Game' (2'22")	Sung by The Bendik Singers	Words by Bob Williams. Music by Arne Bendiksen.	Conducted by Carsten Klouman.

The song was given an English title, but its lyrics feature a multitude of languages.

Monaco	*Un Train Qui Part* (3'00")	Sung by Marie.	Words by Boris Bergman. Music by Bernard Liamis.	Conducted by Jean-Claude Vannier.

Spain	*Eres Tú* (2'56")	Sung by Mocedades.	Composed by Juan Carlos Calderón.	Conducted by Juan Carlos Calderón.

This entry became a big international hit, reaching number nine in the Billboard Hot 100 in the USA sung in Spanish, although an English version with lyrics by Mike Hawker entitled 'Touch The Wind' was available on the B-side. It has been covered by many artists including Johnny Mathis, who sang it with an English verse and Spanish chorus.

SONGS FOR EUROPE VOLUME TWO

Switzerland	'Je Vais Me Marier Marie' (2'50")	Sung by Patrick Juvet.	Words by Pierre Delanoë. Music by Patrick Juvet.	Conducted by Hervé Roy.

In 1978 Patrick Juvet had two UK chart songs, 'Got A Feeling' and 'I Love America', with the latter peaking at number 12.

Yugoslavia	'Gori Vatra' (2'54")	Sung by Zdravko Čolić.	Composed by Kemal Monteno.	Conducted by Esad Arnautalić.

Italy	'Chi Sarà Con Te' (2'50")	Sung by Massimo Ranieri.	Words by Giancarlo Bigazzi. Music by Enrico Polito and Gaetano Savio.	Conducted by Enrico Politi.

Massimo Ranieri had represented Italy in the 1971 contest, finishing fifth with 'L'amore È Un Attimo'.

Luxembourg	'Tu Te Reconnaîtras' (2'30")	Sung by Anne-Marie David.	Words by Vline Buggy. Music by Claude Morgan.	Conducted by Pierre Cao.

1973 EUROVISION SONG CONTEST

Anne-Marie David was born in May 1952 in Arles, France. When she was 18 she moved to Paris and got involved with musical theatre. She went on to play the role of Mary Magdalene in *Jesus Christ Superstar*. In 1979 she returned to the *Eurovision Song Contest*, this time representing her native France. In 1987 she retired from the music business, although she made a comeback in 2003 and subsequently appeared in the contest's celebratory fiftieth anniversary show.

This winning song was released in English as 'Wonderful Dream', with lyrics by Shaun Lawton, and reached number 13 in the UK charts. David appeared on the editions of *Top of the Pops* broadcast on 27 April, 11 and 18 May, with the latter two performances being repeats of the first. None of these editions exists in the BBC archives, though audios exist of her performance as seen on the 11 and 18 May programmes. She also appeared on the edition of London Weekend Television's *The Rolf Harris Show* broadcast on 16 June.

'I had a feeling about Anne-Marie David,' states BFBS commentator Richard Astbury. 'It was such a wonderful ballad, and she was such a beautiful young girl, that I thought it was going to win.'

Sweden	'You Are Summer' (2'57")	Sung by the Nova.	Words by Lars Forssell. Music by Monica Dominique and Carl-Axel Dominique.	Conducted by Monica Dominique.

The duo was also known as Malta, but to avoid any confusion with the country of the same name, which had been due to participate, they renamed themselves the Nova. Monica Dominique was the first female conductor in the history of the contest; she was shortly followed by the second female conductor, the Israeli Nurit Hirsh, later in the same event.

| Netherlands | *De Oude Muzikant* (2'57") | Sung by Ben Cramer. | Composed by Pierre Kartner. | Conducted by Harry van Hoof. |

| Ireland | 'Do I Dream?' (2'35") | Sung by Maxi. | Composed by Jack Brierley and George F Crosbie. | Conducted by Colman Pearce. |

| United Kingdom | 'Power To All Our Friends' (2'59") | Sung by Cliff Richard (with Alan Tarney, Trevor Spencer, Terry Britten and John Farrar). | Composed by Guy Fletcher and Doug Flett. | Conducted by David MacKay. |

'Power To All Our Friends' had the distinction of being the first song ever in the contest to use backing tracks in addition to the live orchestra. But this could have been a disaster, as it transpired there had been some confusion in the rules between the English and the French text. The rules were clarified for future contests to specify that any backing tracks used should be only instrumental, and not vocal.

Discussing the rehearsals with reporter Robert Elphick on *BBC News*, Cliff Richard, who was the oldest competitor in the contest at the age of 32, said: 'They've rehearsed us so that the countries nearest Luxembourg rehearse first. So far all I've seen is the artist in front of me, which was France. A very lovely lady singer, but I didn't think much of the song. The Dutch song I heard a couple of weeks ago. That's quite good, really, an Engelbert Humperdinck-type waltz, but again, I'd rather have our song.'

Richard told the press: 'We could be number one or somewhere in the top five. It is a better song than "Congratulations", which I sang for *Eurovision* in 1968.'

In the book *Which One's Cliff?*, Richard recalled: 'With "Power To All Our Friends" I knew we had a great song and that, whether we won or lost, it would be a smash hit. I remember telling my band that the only way to treat the contest was as the biggest plug anyone could give their latest record. 400 million people were watching, a sort of world *Top of the Pops*. Sure enough, we lost, but sold one and a half million copies.'

After the contest, Richard said: 'So many people told me that I should have won that I didn't understand why I didn't. I simply wanted to represent my country. I feel very proud to have done so. It's not sour grapes, but I just didn't like the winning song.'

Composers Guy Fletcher and Doug Flett went to Luxembourg for the contest. 'It was appalling,' recalls Fletcher. 'The BBC didn't really look after us properly. David MacKay was our musical director, a wonderful arranger and conductor and a good friend. I remember him phoning me up and saying that the BBC had asked him to go to Luxembourg to conduct the orchestra for Cliff Richard. I thought that was great, that was exactly what should happen, and they took him over there … and paid him £35. We had no control at all; the BBC didn't recognise that we were even there. Doug and I had to get our own taxi to take us to the venue, where we were representing the country as composers and having to do everything ourselves. I didn't like the evening at all. I didn't like Cliff's performance, it was ludicrous; and I've done a lot of work with Cliff over the years. He

SONGS FOR EUROPE VOLUME TWO

was very nervous, as it had an *a cappella* opening and it was an unusual song. I did think though that we would do well and win it. As far as success goes it was the winner, as it was a huge seller, and we got an Ivor Novello Award as well, so I had no problems with losing, I wasn't upset by it.'

France	'*Sans Toi*' (2'50")	Sung by Martine Clémenceau.	Words by Anne Grégory. Music by Paul Koulak.	Conducted by Jean Claudric.

Israel	'*Ey Sham*' (2'50")	Sung by Ilanit.	Words by Ehud Manor. Music by Nurit Hirsh.	Conducted by Nurit Hirsh.

Tony Waddington and Wayne Bickerton wrote the English version as 'All Make Believe'.

THE VOTING

The same voting system was used as in the recent past. The juries were present in a television studio in Luxembourg and voted in groups of three countries at a time, with the last two countries, France and Israel, voting as a block of two. The scoreboard was in French. The United Kingdom jurors were Pat Williams and Catherine Woodfield.

1973 EUROVISION SONG CONTEST

	Finland	Belgium	Portugal	Germany	Norway	Monaco	Spain	Switzerland	Yugoslavia	Italy	Luxembourg	Sweden	Netherlands	Ireland	UK	France	Israel	TOTAL	POSITION
FINLAND		9	5	6	6	5	6	6	7	2	6	7	5	5	9	4	5	93	6TH
BELGIUM	4		3	4	3	6	6	4	4	2	4	2	3	4	5	2	2	58	17TH
PORTUGAL	4	6		5	5	4	8	8	6	3	4	2	5	4	5	6	5	80	10TH=
GERMANY	2	5	6		4	5	9	7	4	3	7	6	5	6	5	7	4	85	8TH=
NORWAY	8	5	5	6		7	6	7	6	5	7	3	3	3	3	6	9	89	7TH
MONACO	6	3	2	4	3		6	5	9	8	6	4	5	6	9	5	4	85	8TH=
SPAIN	3	8	9	9	4	9		8	9	10	8	7	10	10	4	9	8	125	2ND
SWITZERLAND	4	3	3	4	7	5	7		6	4	6	3	8	7	7	2	3	79	12TH
YUGOSLAVIA	5	3	3	4	2	5	8	6		2	4	2	4	5	4	4	4	65	15TH=
ITALY	2	5	3	5	5	5	5	7	5		5	5	4	4	5	5	4	74	13TH
LUXEMBOURG	6	6	8	7	8	7	6	10	9	9		8	9	8	10	10	8	129	1ST
SWEDEN	8	4	4	5	8	5	7	9	6	5	6		6	5	7	4	5	94	5TH

SONGS FOR EUROPE VOLUME TWO

NETHERLANDS	4	4	2	5	5	4	5	5	5	4	7	3	▓	5	3	6	2	69	14TH
IRELAND	3	7	2	4	6	6	7	5	5	5	6	5	6	▓	5	4	4	80	10TH=
UNITED KINGDOM	9	6	6	7	7	8	4	8	8	5	10	9	10	9	▓	8	9	123	3RD
FRANCE	4	3	2	4	4	5	5	4	7	2	3	5	5	5	5	▓	2	65	15TH=
ISRAEL	6	6	5	7	5	7	4	6	7	7	8	6	6	7	5	5	▓	97	4TH

Analysis: This was the closest contest under this voting system, with just six points separating the top three countries, in marked contrast to the previous two years. In effect it meant that once more the decision of just one person could affect the outcome. As the voting progressed, the lead kept changing between Luxembourg and the United Kingdom, if only because the United Kingdom was drawn so late in the running order and therefore at first had an artificial lead, especially after the round where Luxembourg couldn't vote for themselves. With just two countries in the last block, the voting ended on more of a whimper than a bang. The United Kingdom received its fewest marks once again from Spain, just four points. Luxembourg and the Netherlands were the most generous, giving 'Power To All Our Friends' the maximum of ten points each. With the United Kingdom awarding Luxembourg the maximum ten points, and awarding Spain just four points, it was enough to hand the title once more to Luxembourg.

Luxembourg thus became the first country to win the contest outright twice in succession, eclipsing the achievement of Spain, who'd had to share their second consecutive win in 1969. It also gave the Grand Duchy its fourth victory in the contest, making it the most successful country to date, surpassing France with its three outright victories and one shared victory.

1973 EUROVISION SONG CONTEST

WINNING REPRISE

Luxembourg	'Tu Te Reconnaîtras' (2'30")	Sung by Anne-Marie David.	Words by Vline Buggy. Music by Claude Morgan.	Conducted by Pierre Cao.

A second, shorter reprise of 51" was played over the closing credits.

CREDITS
Producer: Paul Ulveling
Director: René Steichen
Designer: Jo Dzierzenga
Music Director: Pierre Cao
EBU Scrutineer: Clifford Brown

The contest was watched by 45.30% of the British population (22.87 million) from the start of the programme at 21.30, rising to 50.30% (25.40 million) from 22.15.

There was a mixed response from the 488 viewers that made up the panel for the BBC's Audience Research Report, with some disappointed with the songs, the singers and the result. Some were even disappointed with Cliff Richard; they felt that he had sung less well than at home, and had disliked his jumping about and waving of arms. 'The British song was by far the best, but the wrong singer was chosen,' was the opinion of one viewer.

Despite this, just over half of the sample had enjoyed the contest, and while they were disappointed with the United Kingdom's failure to win, they added that the songs and singers seemed better than before and that

SONGS FOR EUROPE VOLUME TWO

Richard was by far the most professional. Only 28% agreed with the choice of the winning song, and the chief criticism was that it had sounded like the previous year's winner. Their votes would have gone to Spain, the United Kingdom or Ireland, and they had disliked the relatively new method of voting, feeling that the previous system of the judges telephoning in their decisions had seemed fairer. A minority though did agree with the result and had thought the voting to be fair, faster and better than telephoning round different countries. They considered that the contest had produced 'a good winner, pleasant song and singer.'

There was also a mixed response to the commentary by Terry Wogan. He had irritated many by talking too much, particularly at the same time as the official announcers, and had appeared muddled at times. Some thought he had failed to give as many details about entries as in previous years, and in the last round when it was obvious the United Kingdom could not win, he had annoyed many viewers by trying to maintain an air of suspense. Nevertheless a sizeable minority thought he had gone a long way to brightening up an otherwise dull show, and endeavoured to sound enthusiastic and had a pleasant and relaxed manner.

The BBC budget for the programme was £8,750. The BBC has retained a copy of the broadcast version in its archives.

1974 UNITED KINGDOM

Few can have been surprised when it was announced that Olivia Newton-John would be the singer to represent the United Kingdom in the 1974 contest. She had made frequent appearances on the *It's Cliff Richard* show, and was the natural choice to succeed him in *A Song for Europe*. Around 400 songs were submitted to the MPA, from which six would go forward to the Final.

   Amongst the songs that didn't make it around this period was 'Sugar Baby Love' by Wayne Bickerton and Tony Waddington. 'It had a potted history, that song,' explains Wayne Bickerton. 'We wrote it for Showaddywaddy, but they turned it down, so we went into the studios, did some vocals, finished it off, and put it in for the contest, but it didn't get through the various committees.' The composers then went back to the session musicians who had recorded the original demo in October 1973, and from them formed a band called the Rubettes, for whom 'Sugar Baby Love' went on to become a number one hit in May 1974.

   Newton-John was born in the United Kingdom on 26 September 1948 but grew up in Melbourne, Australia when the family emigrated there in 1954. At the age of 14 she formed a short-lived all-girl band with some schoolfriends, performing in a coffee shop owned by her brother-in-law. It wasn't long before she was performing on local radio and television, as Lovely Livvy. She entered and won a television talent show called *Sing, Sing, Sing*, and the prize was a trip to Britain.

   In 1966 she recorded her first single, 'Till You Say You'll Be Mine'. She soon teamed up with an Australian friend, Pat Carroll, and they formed a duo, touring nightclubs in Europe. When Carroll's visa expired, Newton-John remained in Britain to pursue a solo career. She recorded her first album, *If Not For You*, in 1971, and the title track became her first international hit, reaching number seven in the UK charts. Her follow up single, 'Banks Of The Ohio', went one better at number six later in the year. Further top 20 hits followed with 'What Is Life' and 'Take

Me Home Country Roads'. She was voted Best British Female Vocalist two years in succession by *Record Mirror*.

The programme chosen to showcase *A Song for Europe* this year was *Clunk-Click*, a Saturday evening chat and variety show hosted by Jimmy Savile. Savile was best known as a presenter on *Top of the Pops* and a radio disc jockey. *Clunk-Click* was named after a contemporary series of public information films in which he promoted the use of car seat belts with the slogan 'Clunk-click every trip.' Savile died in October 2011 aged 84, after which he became notorious as details emerged of a string of sex offences he had committed over many years.

The original plan was for two songs to be previewed in each of three weekly *Clunk-Click* programmes, starting from the 2 February edition. However, industrial action affected the transmission of the first programme, so the plan quickly changed to having three songs previewed in each of just two editions, shown on 9 and 16 February respectively. The 9 February edition was watched by 15.70% of the population (7.93 million) and scored a RI of 54, while the 16 February edition was watched by 13.30% (6.72 million) and scored an RI of 48.

The 9 February edition of *Clunk-Click* was also the subject of an Audience Research Report, and included comments from the sample of 241 viewers on the first three songs. These were generally well received. A number of viewers complained bitterly about the lack of originality and 'the same old style of song every year,' and said that although they had been well sung by Newton-John, they were 'just not winners.' Quite a few however felt that they were above the average of recent years. There were a few scattered objections that Newton-John had little personality and gave a rather wooden performance, although there was also considerable praise for the singer, it being said that her 'pleasant singing style and attractive appearance made her an excellent choice to represent the United Kingdom.'

The songs were also previewed on the Terry Wogan show on Radio 2 on 11 and 18 February, around 08.05.

The Final was recorded on Thursday 21 February, two days before transmission. Nick Ingman was the musical director and conductor of the orchestra.

With much of that week's *Radio Times* devoted to coverage of the General Election taking place on 28 February, promotion of the Final was limited to six small black and white photos of Newton-John on the

1974 UNITED KINGDOM

programme pages for 23 February. The caption read: 'Olivia Newton-John puts forward all six candidates for your votes in the poll for this year's British entry in the *Eurovision Song Contest*. Her non-party, unpolitical broadcast goes *Clunk-Click* tonight.'

A SONG FOR EUROPE 1974
Saturday 23 February at 17.54.36 (Duration 43'41")
Presented by Jimmy Savile

Before the first song there was the Eurovision Short Fanfare that had been composed by Norrie Paramor and had been used on several previous *A Song for Europe* broadcasts. This was played over a specially-made film, which included the names of all the participating countries and a photograph of Olivia Newton-John.

| Song One | 'Have Love, Will Travel' (2'42") | Sung by Olivia Newton-John. | Composed by Roger Greenaway and Geoff Stephens. | Arranged by Nick Ingman |

Both composers had had entries in previous *A Song for Europe* contests. Roger Greenaway had co-written the 1968 runner-up 'High 'n' Dry' along with Roger Cook, while Geoff Stephens had co-written with John Carter the 1970 winner 'Knock, Knock (Who's There?)'.

    Greenaway wasn't present for the recording of the Final, as he was in the USA. He was represented instead by his wife.

SONGS FOR EUROPE VOLUME TWO

Song Two	'Lovin' You Ain't Easy' (2'48")	Sung by Olivia Newton-John.	Composed by Bob Saker, Stuart Leathwood and Gary Sulsh.	Arranged by Brian Bennett

Stuart Leathwood was born in Merseyside in 1942. He was in the school choir at the age of six, and had an extraordinary vocal range. At the age of 21 he decided to pack up work at a local firm to become a full-time musician. He became a guitarist with the group the Midnighters, and then formed the group the Kubas, who toured with the Beatles. They changed their name to the Koobas, recorded several singles and albums without great success and broke up in 1969. Another group followed called Harlan County, which included in its line up Peter Skellern and Gary Sulsh. Leathwood was lead vocalist, while Sulsh was on lead guitar. Leathwood also teamed up with Gary Holton to form March Hare. He was, in addition, a writer of fiction and a talented cartoonist.

Leathwood and Sulsh had previously written the single 'Good Old Fashioned Music' for the New Seekers, which was released in 1971.

Bob Saker was a singer, and had been one of the many session singers in Soul Train, a group that did cover versions of current hits for the David Hamilton show on Radio 2. Since the mid-'70s there will always have been an advert running somewhere with his voice, as he is also a talented and prolific voiceover artist.

Song Three	'Long Live Love' (2'45")	Sung by Olivia Newton-John.	Composed by Valerie Avon and Harold Spiro.	Arranged by Nick Ingman

1974 UNITED KINGDOM

Valerie Avon and Harold Spiro had written two previous songs for the contest. In 1970 they had contributed 'Can I Believe', finishing in fourth place, and a year later 'In My World Of Beautiful Things', also finishing in fourth place.

Did the duo like writing for a given artist, or would they have preferred to choose their own? Avon discusses: 'The year of Olivia Newton-John, I had a group called Reflections, which consisted of three girls and two boys who had come out of the Second Generation. I used to vocal-coach the Second Generation, so we split this group off, and they did the demo for me. The demo was fantastic, even if I say so myself. They really sounded terrific, and I know had they been singing it in the international event, they would have given ABBA a run for their money. I'm not saying they would have won, as I rate ABBA very highly, but I don't think Olivia was right for the song. She was too namby-pamby for the song; she didn't have the energy it required.'

Despite this, how had Avon rated the song's chances in *A Song for Europe*? 'I knew we stood a chance, as it was the first time we had done a song that was in the idiom, very instant. When we were taken in and positioned as to where to sit. Harold and I were down near the front and the others further back. I didn't realise it, but my husband worked it out that we had won. It didn't occur to me until it was announced that we had got through … I was very excited, but from then on it was downhill. As composers we were very much secondary after that. We had to wait nine months until we actually got our plaques.'

| Song Four | 'Someday' (2'55") | Sung by Olivia Newton-John. | Composed by Gary Benson and David Mindel. | Arranged by Nick Ingman |

'When I was a kid, like everybody I was in a band and wanted to write songs … and was pretty bad at it!' says

SONGS FOR EUROPE VOLUME TWO

David Mindel. 'Then I was in a duo with a friend of mine and we started writing songs together and got signed to EMI. We had an agent called Noel Gay Artists, and when it was obvious we weren't going very far, they offered me a job there. They had a writer called Gary Benson, and eventually he and I started writing things together. This song was pretty much the first thing we wrote together. We both had strong choruses, and we didn't know what to do, so eventually we put them together and that became "Someday".'

Gary Benson was born Harry Hyams in London, and was a singer as well as a songwriter.

Song Five	'Angel Eyes' (2'47")	Sung by Olivia Newton-John.	Composed by Tony Macauley and Keith Potger.	Arranged by Nick Ingman

'Keith Potger ran my publishing company,' said Tony Macauley. 'I can't remember the order of events, but I was writing for the New Seekers, I co-produced an album for them, I did their songs "You Won't Find Another Fool Like Me" and "I Get A Little Sentimental Over You". Keith was in the office. We only ever did two things together; we did Duane Eddy's "Play Me Like You Play Your Guitar" [1975] and "Angel Eyes".'

Of Olivia Newton-John, Macauley had this to say: 'I couldn't stick her voice, absolutely loathed it. I thought she was a dreadful person, a dreadful singer, and she came across that she didn't want to do the whole thing … After all these years I can say these things. I didn't enjoy that experience at all. I thought the song though was better than the others I did. It was in three-quarter time and not in that Germanic beat.'

Potger was born in Ceylon (now Sri Lanka) in 1941. He was one of the founding members of the Australian group the Seekers, and was a guitarist and vocalist. He also wrote for the group, sometimes under a pseudonym. The Seekers split in 1968 and, realising there was a gap in the market for the same type of music, Potger formed

1974 UNITED KINGDOM

the New Seekers, initially performing with the group and subsequently taking a management role. This was his only contribution to the British selections. He has appeared several times on various Seekers reunion tours, and even a New Seekers reunion performance. In 2003 he had a singer's worst nightmare and lost his voice, but with the aid of a speech therapist he regained it and is still singing and working.

Song Six	'Hands Across The Sea' (2'50")	Sung by Olivia Newton-John.	Composed by Ben Findon and Geoff Wilkins.	Arranged by Brian Bennett

'Hands Across The Sea' was planned as the first release for a new family group called the Dooleys. Once it was accepted for *A Song for Europe*, its release was delayed, although ultimately it failed to chart for them.

Ben Findon (Benjamin David Findon) had previously composed and produced records with Peter Shelley.

This was the only entry in the contest by Geoff Wilkins. He and Findon also wrote 'Wild Beautiful Woman' for Billy Ocean and 'Stone Walls' for Mac Kissoon.

After the final song, Jimmy Savile had a brief chat with Olivia Newton-John before all six songs were shown again, courtesy of the videotape. At the end of the programme, details were given of where to send the postcard votes and of the deadline for their receipt, which was the first post on Thursday 28 February. The programme was watched by 15.40% (7.78 million) and scored an RI of 56.

The Final was again the subject of an Audience Research Report. This found that all six songs had disappointed regular viewers, who felt *A Song for Europe* should be a separate programme. However, the contest had also attracted some viewers who wouldn't normally have watched *Clunk-Click*. 39% had enjoyed the songs very much,

51% had moderately enjoyed them, while 10% hadn't enjoyed them at all. Some thought they had been a definite improvement on previous years' entries, and that there was a fair chance of the United Kingdom winning the *Eurovision Song Contest*. More general was a rather depressed feeling, that while on the whole the songs had been unobjectionable, they were almost all mediocre and unimaginative. It would be a miracle if any of them won the contest, many felt; and, once more, hearing the same songs twice had been considered pretty boring.

The panel was more positive about Newton-John, commenting that she had performed the songs beautifully and had got the best out of every one.

THE CONDUCTOR

Nick Ingman studied at the Berklee College of Music in the USA for three years. 'When I came back in the early 1970s,' he says, 'I knocked on a lot of doors, and Norrie Paramor's was one of them. He took me on for a six week probationary period, and fortunately I passed the test and stayed there for about five years until Norrie retired.'

His work with Paramor had brought Ingman into contact with Cliff Richard, as he explains: 'Norrie had a close association with Peter Gormley, who was Cliff's manager at the time, and also managed Olivia Newton-John, and that was the direct connection when *A Song for Europe* came up. There were two arrangers, myself and Brian Bennett, and we each got songs to arrange. It was literally a case of whichever song got voted through, then the musical director associated with it would be the one who got the contest. I arranged "Long Live Love", it won, so I got the gig. We had no say in the selection of the songs; it was a *fait accompli*: "Here are your songs, and get on with it." We recorded them pretty much all together at Abbey Road, as I remember.'

So what did Ingman get from the composers to turn into the finished versions? 'Demos then were much cruder than they are now. I can't remember much about the others, but with "Long Live Love", although I can't remember how I first heard it, it could have been as crude as a piano and a top line. The brief was from John Farrar, and he was unofficially producing the tracks for the whole contest. He had some fairly definite ideas,

1974 UNITED KINGDOM

and with "Long Live Love" there was an intro figure that he came up with, so he was quite involved at that level. Musically, that was whom I was taking the information from. I remember at the recording session when we were doing all six and we came across this one, and it had a four-to-the-floor beat to it in the chorus, we all laughed and said "That's the one."

All six songs were played on the Terry Wogan show on Radio 2 on Monday 25 February, from around 08.05.

THE RESULTS

The results were announced on the *Clunk-Click* programme one week later, on 2 March. Although the bulk of the programme had been pre-recorded on 28 February, the results section was dropped in at the last minute, and was announced by Bill Cotton.

Song	Title	Votes	Result
1	'Have Love Will Travel'	15,266	Fourth
2	'Loving You Ain't Easy'	5,905	Fifth
3	'Long Live Love'	27,387	First
4	'Someday'	5,520	Sixth
5	'Angel Eyes'	18,108	Second
6	'Hands Across The Sea'	15,365	Third

With their song 'Someday' coming last, this was a disappointing first effort in the contest for Gary Benson and David Mindel. 'It was rather strange really,' says Mindel. 'Most of the people who had songs in it had come back time and time again, and were well-known writers. My closest friends who had a song in that year were Gary Sulsh, Bob Saker and Stuart Leathwood. I remember we were there, and the results were being read out, and when it came to their song ["Loving You Ain't Easy"], they got about five thousand odd votes, and I thought "Poor devils, how embarrassing". Then they read out ours and we had even fewer! I remember laughing; I thought it was so funny that I had felt sorry for them … and then I spoke to my mother later and she was asking "Why were you laughing, you came last!" I thought, "By the time you take off all the members of my family who voted, especially my brother-in-law, the public vote must have been about two!"

'I think it was Tony Macauley who pointed out that [Olivia Newton-John] had said in the paper that day she had a favourite. When she was singing "Someday", Tony said, "We all know which one is her favourite now …" So I know she liked it, even if it came last.'

Analysis: The total number of votes was well down on the previous year – over 150,000 fewer. This could be explained by a number of factors. When Cliff Richard had sung on the *Cilla* show, it had gone out in a slot after 20.00 on the Saturday evening, whereas *Clunk-Click* was transmitted around two hours earlier. With just two weeks of previews in 1974, as opposed to the six weeks in 1973, there was also less time for the public to become aware that *A Song for Europe* was taking place. The difference could also have been due partly to the relative popularity of the artists, or of the songs themselves. But perhaps another factor was that the public had another vote on their minds: the General Election of 1974 was to take place a few days later, on 28 February, and campaigning was at its height on the last weekend before polling day.

The vote in *A Song for Europe* gave 31.28% to 'Long Live Love', a pretty comfortable margin over the second-place song 'Angel Eyes', which got 20.68%. It was pretty close though for that second-place spot, which would secure a financially-rewarding place on the B-side of the subsequent single. 'Angel Eyes' took that by just a few thousand votes. Third and fourth were separated by just 99 votes, the closest margin between any two songs with postal voting.

There was a performance of Newton-John singing 'Long Live Love' (2'45") before cutting back to the pre-recorded section of *Clunk-Click* for Savile to wrap up the programme.

1974 UNITED KINGDOM

CREDITS
Executive Producer: Michael Hurll
Producer: Roger Ordish
Director: Bruce Milliard
Designer: Geoffrey Patterson
Costume Designer: Joyce Mortlock
Make-Up Designer: Monica Ludkin
Sound Supervisor: Laurie Taylor
Lighting: Duncan Brown
Production Team: Patricia Houlihan, Gill Stribling Wright, Ken Smith
Musical Director: Nick Ingman

The 2 March edition of *Clunk-Click* that included the result was watched by 16.90% of the population (8.53 million) and scored an RI of 54. The BBC archives hold recordings of *Clunk-Click* from 9 and 16 February with the previews of the songs. The *Clunk-Click* edition of 2 March exists, but without most of the *A Song for Europe* section; it has just the intro and outro by Savile. The performance of 'Long Live Love' from 23 February also exists in the archives of those broadcasters who have retained the international preview programmes. Audio also exists of the 23 February edition containing all the songs in the Final of *A Song for Europe*.

The winning song, 'Long Live Love', was released as a single, with 'Angel Eyes' on the B-side. It peaked at number 11 in the charts. Newton-John appeared on *Top of the Pops* with the song, on the editions broadcast on 7 and 28 March, neither of which exists in the archives. All six songs were included on Newton-John's album *Long Live Love*. A single was released in Barbados featuring the fourth- and fifth-placed songs, 'Have Love Will Travel' and 'Loving You Ain't Easy'.

SONGS FOR EUROPE VOLUME TWO

Not everyone was happy with the result. In the Letters page of the *Radio Times* of 6 April, Miss Julie White wrote: 'Isn't it about time that the BBC changed the system that every year fails to find a decent song to enter in the *Eurovision Song Contest*? Every year we are given a selection of six songs, and every year the same people vote for the same boom-boom rhythms. Why not have a panel of judges who know what to look for in a winning song? Why not even let the singer choose? What a waste of extremely good ballads we see every year. I find it not only disturbing but annoying. "Puppet On A String" was lucky being the first in the line. I am afraid I cannot say much for the chances of this year's entry.'

EUROVISION SONG CONTEST PREVIEWS
Presented by David Vine

Vine was born in 1935 in Newton Abbott, Devon. As a reporter he joined Westward TV in 1961, and BBC2 in 1966. As BBC2 wasn't yet available in the South West area, he found that he was able to work for both broadcasters at the same time. It was only an article in the *Daily Mail*, drawing attention to this moonlighting, that led to him having to quit his job at Westward TV. He was mainly known for presenting sports programmes such as *Grandstand* and *Match of the Day* as well as international events like *Miss World* and *Jeux Sans Frontières*. 1974 was the only year he was involved in the song contest, not only presenting the preview programmes, but also providing the BBC television commentary on the *Eurovision Song Contest* itself. He continued presenting programmes like *Question of Sport*, *Ski Sunday* and the *World Snooker Championships* until he retired in 2000. He died in January 2009 aged 74.

As in previous years, the EBU rules required that the previews had to be shown in two or more programmes (i.e. they could not all be broadcast in the one programme). The previews had to be ready by 16 March for transmission over the Eurovision Network on 20 March, and were then supposed to be broadcast between 25 March and 2 April, though once again the BBC screened Part One a day early.

1974 UNITED KINGDOM

The BBC had always split the previews over two programmes, with half the songs in each show. Sometimes due to the uneven number of entrants one programme would feature one more song than the other. However 1974 was the big exception. Just six songs were shown in Part One, with the remaining 12, including the United Kingdom entry, in Part Two.

Part One: Recorded on Saturday 23 March
Broadcast: Sunday 24 March at 16.51.14 (Duration: 20'20"). Audience 5.50% (2.78 million), RI 50.
Finland, Spain, Norway, Greece, Israel and Yugoslavia.

Part Two: Recorded on Saturday 30 March
Broadcast: Sunday 31 March at 16.45.00 (Duration: 39'57"). Audience 4.80% (2.42 million), RI 55.
Sweden, Luxembourg, Monaco, Belgium, Netherlands, Ireland, France, Germany, Switzerland, Portugal, Italy and United Kingdom.

For the first and only time, the preview programmes were recorded on two separate dates. There was a trailer for Part Two broadcast just after *Clunk-Click* on 30 March; this included approximately 10" each from the entries of Monaco, France, Italy and the United Kingdom, and was voiced over by John Braban. The preview of 'Long Live Love' was taken from *Clunk-Click* transmitted on 23 February. The previews of Greece and Italy were in black and white.

CREDIT
Television Presentation: Michael Hurll

The BBC has not retained copies of the preview programmes in its archives, though copies exist on audio.

1974 EUROVISION SONG CONTEST

Both Luxembourg, the winners in 1973, and Spain, the runners-up, turned down the opportunity to stage the 1974 contest. Initially the EBU asked the BBC, the third-placed country, not to make an offer to stage the event, to see if any other participants were willing to take it on.

There were two other offers made, one from IBA (Israel) and the other from the BBC's commercial rival, ITV. There were concerns at this time that some countries wouldn't be prepared to accept Israel as the host broadcaster. Technologically speaking, the country was behind most of Europe, and still hadn't introduced a colour television service. In addition, geographically, Israel was quite a long way from the core of Western European countries participating in the contest at this time. Where ITV was concerned, the award of the contest to them would effectively exclude the BBC. Rather than risk that, the BBC made its own offer on 5 June 1973, and this was accepted on 7 June. Publically Bill Cotton stated: 'What gets some of the smaller countries is the hassle of organising it all. But if the winning country is unwilling to take on the task, the BBC will always do its duty.'

The BBC then had to start finding a suitable venue. Initially they considered the Royal Opera House in London, but this proved to be unavailable, as did the Royal Albert Hall, which had already been used to stage the 1968 contest. The final choice of venue was announced in July 1973 as the Dome in Brighton.

Michael Hurll was chosen by Bill Cotton to produce and direct the show. 'I think it was because I was quite good at doing live television,' recalls Hurll, 'and I actually picked the venue in Brighton to do it. We didn't have much money in those days, and I got the venue for nothing I think from the Brighton Corporation. When I look back at it, the stage seems terribly small in comparison with what they have now.'

The concert hall of the Dome could normally seat up to 2,102 people, but for the contest some seating would be removed in the circle to create space for the commentator booths, and other seating would be removed for technical equipment, cameras etc, so the audience present in the hall would be just over 1,000.

Both TVE (Spain) and CLT (Luxembourg) had been keen to see the contest staged in a TV studio, and RTP (Portugal) favoured the idea of having the juries at the venue, though the BBC very much wanted a return to national juries in each country. NOS (Netherlands) felt that to have juries seeing the rehearsals that were invariably interrupted for technical reasons was distracting and that they should see only the actual Final, though they should be allowed to listen to the songs twice on audio only.

Some of the press had felt that bringing the juries to the host country could have an impact on the outcome. Depending on how well they had been looked after, the jurors could be subconsciously biased one way or the other towards the host nation.

There had been considerable dissatisfaction with the closeness of the voting in 1973. At a meeting held on 30 August 1973, discussions took place about changes for the forthcoming contest. One consideration was a wish to avoid any country receiving 'nil points'; and for added suspense, a lottery element was proposed to decide the voting order. A new voting system was thus devised that incorporated elements from the two most recently used.

Each jury would be based in their own country and comprise ten members of the public, each of whom could award between one and five votes for each song (apart from their own country's), with no abstentions allowed. Therefore each country could award a maximum of 50 votes to any other country's song (i.e. 10 x 5 votes) and a minimum of ten votes (i.e. 10 x 1 vote). If 18 countries were participating, the highest possible score would be 850 (i.e. 17 x 50), and the lowest possible score 170 (i.e. 17 x 10).

The order of the voting would be decided by a lottery, which would take place on stage during the contest. A card would be drawn to decide which country voted first, and the votes would be announced in presentation order. It was pointed out that with this random order there could be a drop in the sound quality on the various international lines.

There was also a procedure put in place should there be a tie, with the countries not involved in the tie having one vote each to determine the winner. The new voting system was then approved by the EBU. There were concerns expressed about the reliability of the adding up on the night, and executive producer Bill Cotton investigated the possibility of using a computerised system, but this was subsequently ruled out on the basis of being prohibitively expensive.

Also raised in September 1973 was the possibility of the juries being able to see the final dress rehearsal, and Cotton looked into the possibility of providing vision circuits. It was said that if it involved no extra cost then there would be no objections. However, the script shows that the final rehearsal was eventually done via sound only for the juries.

Eighteen countries had expressed an intention to enter the contest: the same 17 that had participated the previous year, plus new entrants Greece. On 9 November, Turkey expressed an interest in entering too, but they were informed this wasn't possible as the scoreboard for the contest had already been ordered and constructed, which had cost about £3,000. One innovation in this regard was that the name of the country voting would be lit up from behind on the scoreboard. The draw for the running order in the contest was made on 5 December 1973. No song could be published prior to 4 March 1974; the only acceptable public performances were for national Finals.

On 10 December, IBA (Israel) then declared it had a problem with the 6 April date of the Final. As this fell on the eve of the Jewish Passover, they might not be able to transmit the programme live. They suggested delaying until 7 April, or possibly locating the Israeli jury in the UK or elsewhere in Europe. There was a feeling amongst other countries that as Israel had known about the date for some time no exceptions should be made regarding a live transmission. Ultimately though it was only Italy that didn't take the broadcast live. This was because it coincided with a referendum taking place there on divorce laws, and with a song titled '*Sì*' ['Yes'] as its entry, RAI (Italy) didn't want to be seen as trying to influence the outcome.

1974 EUROVISION SONG CONTEST

One other very late development altered the line up in the contest. The French President, Georges Pompidou, died unexpectedly on the evening of Tuesday 2 April, and his funeral was arranged for 6 April. As a mark of respect, ORTF (France) pulled out of the contest. With the French delegation already in Brighton, their singer, Dani, had to be content with watching the show from the audience. Her backing vocalists were also accompanying the entries of Luxembourg and Monaco, which had coincidentally been drawn back to back. France would have performed in position 14 in the running order.

Katie Boyle returned to present the contest for a fourth time; 'I was told to have her,' says Hurll, 'because she could speak French.'

Security was tight for the contest. British conductor Nick Ingman recalls seeing tanks in the streets of Brighton, while Boyle remembers being ferried in bullet-proof coaches from the hotel to the venue, each time taking a different route.

Rehearsals started at the Dome on Tuesday 2 April from 14:30. These involved producer and director Hurll choosing his shots, working in the stalls and selecting appropriate camera lenses. At the same time, the orchestra microphones were tested; the fold-back facilities for the backing tracks were tried out; and the scoreboard verification was also checked … but there was found to be a major problem with the latter.

After just 20 minutes it became evident that there had been a gross misjudgment of the time it would take to arrive at the totals. With scores into three digits for every country, it looked as if the voting would go on for almost an hour. The scoreboard also started to look like a 'European bank statement,' and if a query arose on the adding up it could exacerbate the mounting problems. Eventually Bill Cotton took the unilateral decision that the new scoring system would have to be abandoned and that the only alternative was to revert to the one last used in 1970. The various national representatives and Heads of Light Entertainment protested at this decision, but it was the only practical alternative, and it still allowed a role for each country's ten jury members, who were no doubt already booked for the task ahead. Although the juries would still vote in a random order, for timing and sound quality reasons this would be determined by a draw being made by EBU Scrutineer Clifford Brown before the contest.

Camera rehearsals with the various acts commenced on Wednesday 3 April at 10.30, starting with Finland. Each act had 50 minutes scheduled on stage with the orchestra for their first rehearsal, without costumes, and the United Kingdom had their slot from 11.40 to 12.30. The first full day of rehearsals finished at 19.25 for the competitors with the conclusion of Sweden, although a further 35 minutes was set aside for the orchestra to rehearse the interval act.

Thursday 4 April saw all the remaining countries have their first rehearsal. There was also a commentators' briefing from 19.30, scheduled for an hour.

'What I used to do was rehearse it once with cameras,' says Hurll, 'and then get the delegations in, and ask them what they didn't like, and to tell me and I'd change it. But after the second rehearsal it was a case of "That's it," and if they came up after the second rehearsal and said something they hadn't mentioned when they had the opportunity earlier, then it was too late for them.'

The second rehearsals took place on Friday 5 April, this time in costume, starting again at 10.30. This time there was just 20 minutes allocated to each country, with the United Kingdom scheduled from 11.20 to 11.40. The second rehearsals concluded at 18.40. After notes were given to the production and technical staff, there was a dinner break. Then at 20.00 came a complete run-through of the whole show, with all artists in costume, plus dummy voting using lines from Television Centre.

Terry Wogan broadcast his Radio 2 show on the morning of Friday 5 April from the Outside Broadcast caravan at the Dome, remarking that the music would be in mono as opposed to the usual stereo. It was thought that this might have been best left unsaid, but both Wogan and his producer had felt it was necessary. The reason it was in mono was that Radio 2 couldn't justify the extra manpower and cost of providing stereo lines for just the one programme, which was coming from Brighton only because of the *Eurovision Song Contest*.

1974 EUROVISION SONG CONTEST

The BBC1 lunchtime magazine show *Pebble Mill at One* on 5 April featured a filmed interview with Olivia Newton-John with presenter Donny McLeod. This still exists in the BBC archives.

Nationwide on the same evening featured humorist Richard Stilgoe singing his 'ideal song' that couldn't fail to win the contest, and presenter Andrew Harvey reporting on the contest with a 4'00" feature.

Also on the same day, BBC local radio broadcast a special programme, which went out nationally, including interviews with all the singers and playing the songs.

On the evening of 5 April, BBC1 showed a trailer for the contest, featuring '*Te Deum*' voiced over by Simon Bates. Two further trailers followed on the Saturday, including, after *Clunk-Click*, one of 1'05" duration using both 'Long Live Love' and '*Te Deum*'.

In Brighton, meanwhile, there was a problem with the outfit for presenter Katie Boyle, as she recalled in her autobiography *What This Katie Did*: 'My dress was made of a glorious salmon-pink satin, and was meant to be trimmed with matching ostrich feathers. But the feathers were delayed, and when they turned up at the eleventh hour they were a horrifying clashing bright purple!' Costume supervisor Joyce Mortlock dyed the feathers overnight, dried them out with a hair dryer and straightened them with a comb, thus achieving a perfect match for the dress. However, there was then a further problem, as Boyle also explained in her book: 'When I put the dress on, due to some ghastly misunderstanding, it wouldn't meet over my bust, and my bra and pants showed through blatantly; the lines would have been picked up a thousand times or worse on screen. There was no alternative, I had to strip and be sewn into the dress, so when I walked out in front of the audience, there was merely a layer of satin between us.'

Work on Saturday 6 April started at 10.30 with technical rehearsals involving Boyle, EBU Scrutineer Brown and the scoreboard operators. From around 12.15 the jury spokespersons were lined up from each participating country on sound circuits.

In the afternoon, from 14.30 to 16.30, there was a full dress rehearsal of the whole show, this time using the jury spokespersons for the dummy voting. Each country recorded this rehearsal on sound only. As the rehearsal also acted as a back-up for the programme itself, a car was waiting to take the videotape recording back to BBC Television Centre in London in case of any emergency.

The hall was cleared for security between 17.30 and 19.45, before the audience was admitted in readiness for the live transmission at 21.30.

Bookmakers were offering the following odds: United Kingdom 7/2 favourite, Luxembourg 5/1, Netherlands 6/1, Italy and Sweden 7/1, Norway 8/1, Greece and Ireland 10/1.

Radio Times had a colour cover photo of Newton-John alongside Cliff Richard, with the headline 'Congratulations?' Inside there was a four page feature incorporating interviews with some past contestants, composers and music professionals. The programme pages gave a checklist of the entrants, including translations of the song titles.

As previously mentioned, the programme was broadcast live in all participating countries except Italy, who took it on deferred transmission. It was also broadcast live in Austria, Hungary, Czechoslovakia, Bulgaria and the Soviet Union, while France, Poland, Tunisia, Morocco and Algeria recorded it for later transmission. Other countries that took the programme were Iceland, Cyprus and South Korea (all in black and white) and Japan and Jordan (in colour). Apart from in the UK, the programme was broadcast on radio in Belgium, Sweden, Norway, Switzerland, Ireland, Spain, Germany and Finland and on BFBS.

The total audience for the programme was expected to be around 500 million according to the script, but the EBU were later to put the figure at a more modest 231 million.

1974 EUROVISION SONG CONTEST

EUROVISION SONG CONTEST 1974
Saturday 6 April at 21.30.00 (Duration 108'40")
From The Concert Hall, The Dome, Brighton, United Kingdom
Presented by Katie Boyle

David Vine provided the BBC1 commentary, with Terry Wogan fulfilling that role for Radio 1 and Radio 2 and Richard Astbury for British Forces Radio.

'Our commentary would take a pro-British stance,' says Astbury, 'very much so, and we would build it up with and "Here comes the United Kingdom". There was the odd bit of mickey-taking, but not nearly as much as say Terry Wogan did. In all the contests I was involved with, I very much had my favourites, and it would be reflected in my commentary as to which ones to watch out for.'

Astbury would not only commentate on the contests, but he would also use the opportunity to record interviews for his weekly *Pop Around Europe* radio show: 'It was in my own interest to get as much material as possible from artists that I would never normally have met, and to play some of their entries, which I had being doing in the weeks leading up to the contest.'

| Finland | 'Keep Me Warm' (2'51") | Sung by Carita. | Words by Heikki Harma and Frank Robson. Music by Eero Koivistoinen. | Conducted by Ossi Runne |

SONGS FOR EUROPE VOLUME TWO

United Kingdom	'Long Live Love' (2'42")	Sung by Olivia Newton-John (with Maggie Stredder, Marian Davies, Joan Baxter, Ingrid Thomas and Ann Simmons).	Composed by Valerie Avon and Harold Spiro.	Conducted by Nick Ingman.

Olivia Newton-John later told the press, 'I knew all along [the song] was unsuitable. It was very frustrating having to go through those rehearsals when the song wasn't right. I wouldn't have chosen it. I'd have preferred a ballad. I don't think it was a suitable song for me or the contest. I wasn't the only one who didn't particularly like our song. All of us felt very frustrated. But we couldn't do anything about it. It was the viewers' choice and we all had to accept that.'

'We had no input at all into the way the song was presented,' says composer Val Avon. 'I had to make my own way to Brighton, pay for my own hotel. When I watched the rehearsals, I thought it was sad that no-one came up to speak to us, everything was centred on the artist.

'I was aware that Olivia Newton-John didn't like the song. I'd met her couple of times since *A Song for Europe*, and she was very lukewarm, and also when we were in Brighton. I thought she shouldn't have given the interviews directly after the show. She gave an interview, which I overheard, and said, "Well I didn't like the song anyway." I thought, "If you are representing the United Kingdom, it doesn't matter whether you like the song or not." Many artists have had hit records with songs they didn't like. You don't knock the success they bring you. But I don't think she liked coming fourth and not winning.

'Considering she sang at number two [in the running order], I think she did well to get into the top four, and maybe if it had been on later it might have done better. But she just didn't like it, she didn't want to do it, and she had to do it, and to me she just didn't give it anything. But it would never have won anyway,' concludes Avon. 'I knew that ABBA were going to win.'

'Because Ronnie Hazlehurst virtually ran the BBC music department, he was always wary of monopolising everything,' says conductor Nick Ingman, 'so I think he stood back and looked at it as two separate jobs. He was the musical director for the whole show, and it was deemed that I should conduct the UK entry, as I'd been involved with the whole arrangement of the song.'

Knowing that millions of people would be watching, how had Ingman felt just before he conducted? 'It was a very tense atmosphere, because it was live, there was no room for slip-ups. I was very nervous, in case I screwed up. There was nothing much that could have gone wrong, but you never knew. In the green room afterwards it was electric, and with the camera crews in there as well, it was pretty intrusive, and everybody was on a nervous high.'

The *Daily Express* wrote in advance of the contest: 'Olivia would have preferred to sing a ballad, but she is landed with a bouncy Eurovision computerised song "Long Live Love". Although it's climbing high in the charts, I believe she will have to give it all the projection she can to win. Obviously a lot of people believe she will.'

The *Sun* gave the entry a rating of 8/10, the same mark it awarded Sweden. Only the Netherlands was rated higher by the newspaper with 9/10.

SONGS FOR EUROPE VOLUME TWO

Spain	*Canta Y Sé Feliz* (2'50")	Sung by Peret (with Tersesa Pubill, Consuelo Pubill, Juan Calabugh, Pedro Reyes and Antonio Valenti).	Composed by Pedro Pubill Calafat Moya (Peret).	Conducted by Rafael de Ibarbia.

Norway	'The First Day Of Love' (2'57")	Sung by Anne-Karine Strom and Bendik Singers (Anne-Lise Gjostol, Bjørn Kruse and Philip Kruse).	Words by Philip Kruse. Music by Frode Thingnæs.	Conducted by Frode Thingnæs.

Anne-Karine Strom had been part of the Bendik Singers when they sang 'It's Just A Game' for Norway in the 1973 contest, finishing in seventh place.

1974 EUROVISION SONG CONTEST

Greece	'Krassi, Thalassa Ke T'Agori Mou' (3'00")	Sung by Marinella (with Theoni Vassilaki, Stamatis Gioujelis, Mitsa Routi and Damianos Serefoglou).	Words by Pythagoras. Music by George Katsaros.	Conducted by George Katsaros.
Israel	'Natati La Khaiai' (2'55")	Sung by Poogy (Dani Sanderson, Alon Oleartchik, Meir Fenigstein, Itzhak Klafter, Ephraim Shamir and Gideon Gov).	Words by Dani Sanderson and Alon Orteartchik. Music by Dani Sanderson.	Conducted by Yonathan Rechter.
Yugoslavia	'Generacija 42' (2'57")	Sung by Korni (Kornelije Kovač, Zlatko Pejakovic, Bojan Hreljac, Josip Bocek and Vladimir Furduj).	Composed by Kornelije Kovač.	Conducted by Zvonimir Skerl.

SONGS FOR EUROPE VOLUME TWO

Sweden	'Waterloo' (2'40")	Sung by ABBA (Agnetha Fältskog, Anni-Frid Lyngstad, Benny Andersson and Björn Ulvaeus) (with Ola Brunkert and Rutger Gunnarsson).	Words by Stikkan Anderson. Music by Benny Andersson and Björn Ulvaeus.	Conducted by Sven-Olof Walldoff.

The group ABBA had formed in Stockholm in 1972. They were originally known as Björn, Benny, Agnetha and Anni-Frid, but formally adopted the acronym in late 1973. They had entered the Swedish heat for the *Eurovision Song Contest* in 1973 with the song 'Ring, Ring', which finished in third place. The song was given an English lyric by Neil Sedaka and Phil Cody and went on to become a hit in several European countries. In the UK, it received considerable airplay on Radio 1, but failed to chart. The group once again entered the Swedish heats for the contest in 1974, and this time they were victorious with the Swedish-language version of 'Waterloo'.

For the performance in the *Eurovision Song Contest*, the song was sung in English. The group also recorded French and German versions for the international market.

'Waterloo' spent nine weeks in the UK charts, reaching number one in May, where it spent two weeks at the top. Their appearance from the contest was shown again on *The Afternoon Programme* on BBC1 on Wednesday 10 April. ABBA performed the song on *Top of the Pops* on the 11 April edition, which still exists in the BBC archives. On the 18 April edition, 'Waterloo' was used in audio only over shots of the audience dancing and for the chart rundown, although this programme and that of 25 April, in which the group also appeared, no longer exist. A further appearance by the group came on the edition broadcast on 2 May, by which time 'Waterloo' had reached number one in the charts, and this exists in the BBC archives. However, their appearance on the following week's edition has been wiped. As one of the top-selling singles of 1974, 'Waterloo' was also included in the Christmas Day edition of *Top of the Pops*, which still exists.

The song charted again in 2004, when re-released to mark its thirtieth anniversary, this time peaking at number 20 in May of that year.

ABBA went on to huge international success, achieving many number one singles in the UK charts, including '*Mamma Mia*', 'Dancing Queen', 'Fernando', 'Take A Chance On Me' and 'The Winner Takes It All'. Their last public performance as a group was in December 1982 on BBC1's *Late, Late, Breakfast Show*. Despite many offers, they have declined to reform, although in July 2008 they appeared together in public at the Swedish premiere of the movie *Mamma Mia*, which is based around their music.

'I never thought ABBA were going to be as big,' says Michael Hurll. 'I thought they were good, and when I look back at that performance now, I think the costumes look a bit cheap. I actually did their very last show as well on the BBC, and I had always kept in touch with them throughout. Any time they were over in the country they would come and do something like *Seaside Special* when I was producing that.'

'I knew they were going to win,' comments conductor Nick Ingman, 'almost before they opened their mouths. They came on in ridiculous blue sequined outfits, but their energy level was so extraordinary, and then it was still quite unusual to have a two boy, two girl group, so a combination of that plus the opening bars of the music … we knew it was all over. I remember meeting their conductor briefly, and he felt rather embarrassed at having to dress as Napoleon, wearing a silly hat, but it was all in the spirit of the show, and that was another string to their bow.'

BFBS commentator Richard Astbury was also confident of an ABBA win, as he had known of the group for some time: 'Because of my acquaintances with record companies, I and Peter McDonagh were invited by Polydor records to host and compère a record fair near Düsseldorf in 1973. We played Polydor records to all the retailers attending from the North Rhine-Westphalia area in Germany. There was a band there that they had invited from Sweden, called Björn, Benny, Agnetha and Anni-Frid. They were wonderful, and I said to Peter, "This band is absolutely fantastic", and we sat at a long table afterwards, having supper, and got to know them. They had "Ring, Ring" out, which they actually performed that night to punctuate our disc jockey antics, and they did another song called "Nina, Pretty Ballerina", another catchy song, and I just loved them.

'Then, in the early part of 1974, I was sent a white label promo from this band, now called ABBA, and it was "Waterloo" [sung in Swedish], and again I thought it was wonderful, and I played it to death on the radio, right up until the *Eurovision Song Contest*.

'Dick Norton, who was my boss, suggested we go over to Brighton to do the contest. I knew in my mind that they were going to win. I remember very well being driven from the hotel to the Dome, and Dick saying to me "Do you want to put a bet on?". I replied that I was too nervous and said, "I can't stop at a betting shop now". They were at 14/1 or something, and much to my astonishment, at that time, they did win; but I had felt very confident they would. I met them afterwards and they remembered me from the record fair in Düsseldorf, so they gave me preferential treatment when it came to talking to them in their hotel.

'I kept in touch with ABBA afterwards through Polydor, and I subsequently went up to Polar records in Sweden and interviewed [composer] Stikkan Anderson, and kept in touch with them for years afterwards'.

Luxembourg	'Bye, Bye, I Love You' (3'00")	Sung by Ireen Sheer (with Martine Lejeune, Catherine Bonevay, Francine Chabaut and Domenique Poulain).	Words by Michael Kunze and Horst Ibach. Music by Ralph Siegel.	Conducted by Charles Blackwell.

1974 EUROVISION SONG CONTEST

Ireen Sheer was born in Basildon, Essex in February 1949. She had been a member of the group the Family Dogg in the late 1960s, before she concentrated on a solo career, mainly in Germany. Conductor Charles Blackwell had previously conducted the song 'Never Goodbye' in *A Song for Europe* 1962.

Monaco	'Celui Qui Reste Et Celui Qui S'En Va' (2'56")	Sung by Romuald (with Martine Lejeune, Catherine Bonevay, Francine Chabaut and Domenique Poulain).	Words by Michel Jordan Music by Jean Pierre Bourtayre.	Conducted by Raymond Donnez.

Romuald had previously represented Monaco in the 1964 contest, finishing in third place, and Luxembourg in the 1969 contest, finishing in eleventh place.

Belgium	*'Fleur De Liberté'* (2'55")	Sung by Jacques Hustin (with Doreen Chanter, Irene Chanter, Vicky Brown, Lisa Strike and Margo Newman).	Words by Frank F Gérald. Music by Jacques Hustin.	Conducted by Pierre Chiffre.

SONGS FOR EUROPE VOLUME TWO

Netherlands	'I See A Star' (2'54")	Sung by Mouth and MacNeal (with Piet Souer, Ronald Westerbeek, Jan Vermeulen and Johann Huisdens).	Words by Gerrit den Braber. Music by Hans van Hemert.	Conducted by Harry van Hoof.

'I See A Star' spent eight weeks in the UK charts, reaching number eight in the week ending 8 June. Mouth and MacNeal appeared on *Top of the Pops* on the editions broadcast on 16 and 30 May, the latter performance being a repeat of the former. Neither edition exists in the BBC archives.

Ireland	'Cross Your Heart' (2'53")	Sung by Tina Reynolds (with John Curran, Pat Reilly and Ann Bushnell).	Composed by Paul Lyttle.	Conducted by Colman Pearce.

1974 EUROVISION SONG CONTEST

| France (Withdrawn) | 'La Vie À Vingt-Cinq Ans' | Sung by Dani (with Martine Lejeune, Catherine Bonevay, Francine Chabaut and Domenique Poulain) | Composed by Christine Fontaine. | Conducted by Jean-Claude Petit. |

Despite France's song being withdrawn from the contest, an English language version was subsequently recorded and released as 'That Old Familiar Feeling' with a lyric by Lynsey de Paul.

| Germany | 'Die Sommermelodie' (2'52") | Sung by Cindy and Bert (with Hans van Hall, Horst Mand, Brigitte Witt and Hanna Dolitzsch). | Words by Kurt Feltz. Music by Werner Scharfenberger. | Conducted by Werner Scharfenberger. |

SONGS FOR EUROPE VOLUME TWO

Switzerland	'Mein Ruf Nach Dir' (2'58")	Sung by Piera Martell (with Athina Amperiadou, Sylvia Pyka, Gerd Gudera, Angelo Saati and Irene Schwendimann).	Composed by Pepe Ederer.	Conducted by Pepe Ederer.

The English version of the song, 'My Ship Of Love', was written by Tony Isaacs. He was a British clarinet player who was well known for being the main lyric writer behind the group the Swingle Singers.

Portugal	'E Depois Do Adeus' (2'38")	Sung by Paulo de Carvalho.	Words by José Niza. Music by José Calvário.	Conducted by José Calvário.

Italy	'Si' (3'02")	Sung by Gigliola Cinquetti (with Mirella Bossi, Paola Francia, Silvia Annichiarico and Paola Orlandi).	Composed by Mario Panzeri, Daniele Pace, Lorenzo Pilat and Corrado Conti.	Conducted by Gianfranco Monaldi.

1974 EUROVISION SONG CONTEST

Gigliola Cinquetti had previously won the *Eurovision Song Contest* in 1964 for Italy with '*Non Ho L'Età*'. '*Sì*' was subsequently given an English lyric by Norman Newell and released as a single under the title 'Go (Before You Break My Heart)'. This spent ten weeks in the UK charts, reaching number eight in the week ending 1 June. Cinquetti appeared on *Top of the Pops* on the editions broadcast on 9 and 23 May, though neither exists in the BBC archives. However, her appearance on BBC2's *They Sold A Million*, broadcast on 14 July, where she performed 'Go (Before You Break My Heart) with the backing group Three's a Crowd, does exist.

THE VOTING

The voting system was the same as had been used in 1970, with ten jury members each awarding one vote to their favourite song. On the United Kingdom jury were Viviene Thurston, Arthur Stringer, Ian Burchell, Basil Herwald, Sheila Delaney, Robert Walker, James Williams, Phyllis Jeans, Catherine Woodfield and Juliet Hiller. The United Kingdom spokesperson was Colin-Ward Lewis.

SONGS FOR EUROPE VOLUME TWO

	Finland	Luxembourg	Israel	Norway	UK	Yugoslavia	Greece	Ireland	Germany	Portugal	Netherlands	Sweden	Spain	Monaco	Switzerland	Belgium	Italy	TOTAL	POSITION
Finland	■		2		1			1										04	13TH
United Kingdom	1				■	4	1	1	2					1	1	3		14	4TH=
Spain		1		2					1	2	1		■		3			10	9TH=
Norway				■								1		1		1		03	14TH=
Greece							■			1	4	2						07	11TH
Israel			■	2				1		2	2	1					3	11	7TH=
Yugoslavia	1					■				1		1				1	2	06	12TH
Sweden	5	1	2	2		1		1	2	1	3	■	1		5			24	1ST
Luxembourg		■	2		2	1	3	1					1	1		1	2	14	4TH=
Monaco		2	1	1				1	2	1		1	2	■	1	2		14	4TH=
Belgium		3		2			5									■		10	9TH=
Netherlands	1		1	1		3	2	1	1	1	■	3				1		15	3RD

1974 EUROVISION SONG CONTEST

Ireland		2	1	2	1		▓			2	2	1			11	7ᵀᴴ=
Germany						1	▓				1	1			03	14ᵀᴴ=
Switzerland				1			1					▓	1		03	14ᵀᴴ=
Portugal									▓	1		2			03	14ᵀᴴ=
Italy	2	1	1		5		1		1		2	4	1	▓	18	2ᴺᴰ

Analysis: Sweden took the lead right from the opening round of voting, and never lost it, though it was by no means a runaway victory. When the United Kingdom failed to award Sweden any votes and Italy five, it brought the Italians to within a point of the lead; Belgium too was only one vote behind after Greece had voted. It was slow and steady progress for Sweden, and after Monaco had voted, Italy were back to just two votes behind. The Swiss jury's votes proved to be decisive. When they awarded five to Sweden it opened up a seven-point lead over the Italians with only two rounds of voting to go, which included the Italian jury themselves.

Mathematically the voting went to the final round, but it would have required the Italians to award all of their votes to the Netherlands or even Monaco to change the result, and neither looked particularly likely to happen. The Italians did though award three votes to the United Kingdom, who had been well down the scoreboard, and this lifted them into joint fourth place in the final round, enabling the country to maintain a record of always finishing in the top four since 1967. The highest number of votes for the United Kingdom had been four, which had come from Yugoslavia.

It was the first time that Sweden had won the contest, though with just 15% of the maximum possible vote they had one of the lowest winning scores; only the four joint winners in 1969 had had a lower percentage.

SONGS FOR EUROPE VOLUME TWO

WINNING REPRISE

| Sweden | 'Waterloo' (2'40") | Sung by ABBA. | Words by Stikkan Anderson. Music by Benny Andersson and Björn Ulvaeus. | Conducted by Sven-Olof Walldoff. |

CREDITS
Executive Producer: Bill Cotton
Assistant to Executive Producer: Queenie Lipyeat
Producer: Michael Hurll
Film Sequences Director: Brian Whitehouse
Designer: John Burrowes
Design Assistant: Jan Spoczynski
Sound Supervisor: Chris Holcombe
Lighting: Tommy Thomas
Costume Supervisor: Joyce Mortlock
Make-Up Supervisor: Judith Clay
Vision Mixer: Tony Rowe
Music Director: Ronnie Hazlehurst
EBU Scrutineer: Clifford Brown

1974 EUROVISION SONG CONTEST

The contest was watched by an audience of 36.00% of the population (18.18 million) from the start of the programme at 21.30, rising to 38.90% (19.64 million) from 22.30.

A total of 345 viewers were surveyed for the BBC's Audience Research Report on the contest, and many of them thought it had been the best for years, being both entertaining and well presented. However the songs had been considered no more than moderately enjoyable, and some respondents had even described them as a pretty poor selection, including the United Kingdom entry. Only just over 20% had enjoyed them very much, and 10% had dismissed them, finding little to choose between them. Opinions had been divided on the result, 45% agreeing on the winner, 41% not entirely agreeing and 14% definitely disagreeing, feeling that the Swedish winner was 'just gimmicky'. Others had preferred the entries of the United Kingdom, the Netherlands and Italy, and some thought that Olivia Newton-John had deserved more votes. A sizeable minority were happy with the final outcome and generally agreed that the best song had won, and that Sweden deserved their victory. There was praise for both Katie Boyle and David Vine. The former was said to have combined glamour and competence, and the latter to have given helpful and interesting descriptions. A few thought that Boyle was losing her appeal, and that someone younger should be sought. On the whole the respondents thought that the contest was pleasant once-a-year viewing and that the voting was intriguing and exciting; though some felt that it was in need of a face-lift.

The BBC has retained an incomplete copy of its broadcast version of the contest, with the voting sequence missing, though the complete programme exists in other European archives. The BBC's budget for the show was £97,250.

The BBC subsequently expressed its regret for the late change to the voting system, and thanked the EBU for its cooperation. It was indeed fortunate that at least the objectives of the abandoned new voting system had been met, in that 1974 had produced a clear-cut winner and no country had received '*nul points*'. A sub-group was set up to look at another possible new voting system, with representatives of ARD (Germany), SR (Sweden) and

YLE (Finland), who had intimated they had a possible proposal, as well as the BBC.

Some countries, notably Greece, wanted an increase in the number of permitted performers, from six to 12, so that dancers could be included. YLE however felt that this would involve acts too far removed from the original intentions of the contest. SR, who were the likely organisers of the 1975 contest, felt it would be difficult given the size of the stage and the orchestra to have that many performers. So the consensus was to leave the limit at six.

THE NEW VOTING SYSTEM

In September 1974, ARD and YLE both put forward similar proposals for the voting in future contests. ARD suggested that each country's jury should identify its top nine songs and award them points ranging from 1 to 10, but didn't elaborate. YLE suggested having a 17-member jury for each country, with each member marking the songs from 1 to 5 as had been proposed for the abandoned 1974 system. In this way, each jury would identify its top eight songs, and these would then receive that country's votes, with 14 going to the first-placed song, then 10, 7, 5, 4, 3, 2 and 1 to the others in succession. As an alternative, YLE suggested a compromise voting pattern of 10, 8, 7, 6, 5, 4, 3, 2 and 1. The idea of having an uneven number of jurors was that although the points total could still produce a tie, in that event a show of hands would determine the outcome. The BBC suggested, based on the above ideas, having a voting pattern of 12, 10, 8, 7, 6, 5, 4, 3, 2 and 1. It was the latter suggestion that found favour, and has been used in all subsequent contests.

BUDGETING FOR THE FUTURE

The BBC had met the costs of the 1972 and 1974 contests mainly at its own expense, but couldn't necessarily afford to do the same if a similar situation were to arise again, especially as inflation was running at around 20% at the time. A new method had to be devised to finance the contest for the future.

In 1974 Jack White, the Controller of Programmes at RTÉ, headed an Executive Group that came up with a draft proposal to solve the problem. This would eventually be adopted as a template for the future. It worked on the principle of active participation and broadcasters committing in advance, so that if they withdrew at a late stage they would still be liable for a fee.

Using the example of the 1974 budget, the additional cost to the host broadcaster had been around £89,880. That was the £97,250 it had cost the BBC in total, less what it would have spent anyway (i.e. on artist fees, conductor, commentators, costumes, hotel bills, transport etc). If all 18 countries in 1974 had divided that cost equally, each would have had to pay £4,988. However, there was also a remit not to deter the participation of smaller countries or broadcasters with more limited budgets, so a share-per-unit system was proposed. If applied in 1974, this would have produced the following outcome:

Broadcaster	Country	Units	Total Cost *
ARD	Germany	40	£12,840
BBC	United Kingdom	40	£12,840
ORTF	France	33	£10,593
RAI	Italy	32	£10,272
TVE	Spain	22	£ 7,062
NOS	Netherlands	17	£ 5,457
SR	Sweden	15	£ 4,815
JRT	Yugoslavia	14	£ 4,494
RTB	Belgium	13	£ 4,173
SRG	Switzerland	11	£ 3,531
YLE	Finland	10	£ 3,210
NRK	Norway	8	£ 2,568
RTP	Portugal	6	£ 1,926

RTÉ	Ireland	6	£ 1,926
EIPT	Greece	6	£ 1,926
IBA	Israel	5	£ 1,605
CLT	Luxembourg	1	£ 321
RMC	Monaco	1	£ 321
TOTAL		280	£89,880

*Total cost based on 1974 budget figures.

Based on the budget of around £40,000 proposed by SR (Sweden) for the 1975 contest, the BBC's share would have been £5,442, while SR itself as host broadcaster would have paid £2,041. With a different line-up of countries, the total number of units would change. In 1975 the total would have equated to 294 units. So, for example, Luxembourg and Monaco would have paid £136 each based on a £40,000 budget.

In the event, it would appear that these ideas weren't actually adopted until the Executive Group met in Milan in 1975 ahead of the 1976 contest, and then they were somewhat simplified, in that broadcasters would be placed into groups according to the level of financial contribution they would be required to make. It was also decided that there should be a share paid by passive broadcasters, i.e. those countries taking the programme but not actually competing. For 1976 it was proposed that the active participants would be split into the following groups.

Group One Countries: United Kingdom, Germany, France, Italy and Spain
Group Two Countries: Netherlands, Belgium, Austria, Norway, Finland, Switzerland, Yugoslavia,
Group Three Countries: Luxembourg, Ireland, Monaco, Greece, Israel and Portugal

There would be some variations, with different countries moving in and out of the contest around this era, but Sweden, Denmark and Turkey would fall into Group Two in the years when they were active participants. The 'big five' Group One countries between them would generally be responsible for paying 50% of the budget.

Radio Times Cover: 24 January edition featuring Mary Hopkin and *A Song For Europe* 1970.

Sheet Music: 'I'm Going To Fall In Love Again' featuring Mary Hopkin. Second place in *A Song For Europe* 1970.

Sheet Music: 'Knock, Knock, (Who's There?)' featuring Mary Hopkin. Winner of *A Song For Europe* 1970.

Radio Times Cover: 21 March edition featuring Mary Hopkin and the *Eurovision Song Contest* 1970.

Radio Times Cover: 27 February edition featuring Clodagh Rodgers and *A Song For Europe* 1971.

Sheet Music: 'Jack In The Box' featuring Clodagh Rodgers. Winner of *A Song For Europe* 1971.

Record Cover: 'Pupazzo' featuring Clodagh Rodgers. Italian version of 'Jack In The Box'.

Radio Times Cover: 3 April edition featuring Clodagh Rodgers and the *Eurovision Song Contest* 1971.

Record Cover: 'Caja De Sorpresa' featuring Clodagh Rodgers. Spanish version of 'Jack In The Box'.

Record Cover: 'Jack In The Box' (German issue) featuring Clodagh Rodgers. Winner of *A Song For Europe* 1971.

Sheet Music: 'Beg, Steal Or Borrow' featuring the New Seekers. Winner of *A Song For Europe* 1972.

Record Cover: 'Beg, Steal Or Borrow' (Dutch issue) featuring the New Seekers. Winner of *A Song For Europe* 1972.

Record Cover: 'Oh, Ich Will Betteln, Ich Will Stehlen' featuring the New Seekers Rodgers. German version of 'Beg, Steal Or Borrow'.

Radio Times Cover: 25 March edition featuring the New Seekers and the *Eurovision Song Contest* 1972.

Record Cover: 'Beg, Steal Or Borrow' (Japanese issue) featuring the New Seekers. Winner of *A Song For Europe* 1972.

Radio Times Cover: 13 January edition featuring Cliff Richard and *A Song For Europe* 1973.

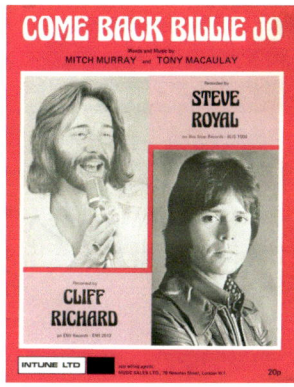

Sheet Music: 'Come Back Billie Jo' featuring Cliff Richard. Second place in *A Song For Europe* 1973.

Record Cover: *Eurovision Special* featuring Cliff Richard. Includes the songs from third to sixth place in *A Song For Europe* 1973.

Record Cover: 'Ashes To Ashes' and 'Days Of Love' featuring Cliff Richard. Sixth and fifth place in *A Song For Europe* 1973.

Sheet Music: 'Help It Along' featuring Cliff Richard. Third place in *A Song For Europe* 1973.

Sheet Music: 'Power To All Our Friends' featuring Cliff Richard. Winner of *A Song For Europe* 1973.

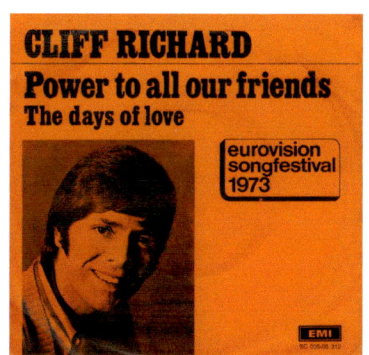

Record Cover: 'Power To All Our Friends' (Dutch issue) featuring Cliff Richard. Winner of *A Song For Europe* 1973.

Record Cover: 'Il Faut Chanter La Vie' featuring Cliff Richard. French version of 'Power To All Our Friends'.

Record Cover: 'Todo El Poder A Los Amigos' featuring Cliff Richard. Spanish version of 'Power To All Our Friends'.

Sheet Music: 'Long Live Love' featuring Olivia Newton-John. Winner of *A Song For Europe* 1974.

Record Cover: 'Long Live Love' (French issue) featuring Olivia Newton-John. Winner of *A Song For Europe* 1974.

Radio Times Cover: 6 April edition featuring Olivia Newton-John and the *Eurovision Song Contest* 1974.

Official Programme Cover: featuring the *Eurovision Song Contest* 1974.

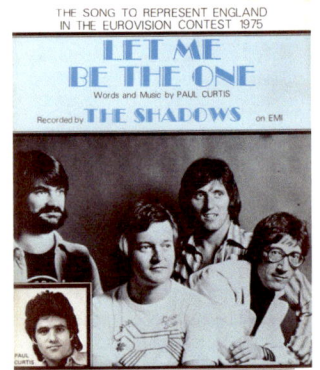

Sheet Music: 'Let Me Be The One' featuring The Shadows. Winner of *A Song For Europe* 1975.

Record Cover: 'Let Me Be The One' (Spanish issue) featuring The Shadows. Winner of *A Song For Europe* 1975.

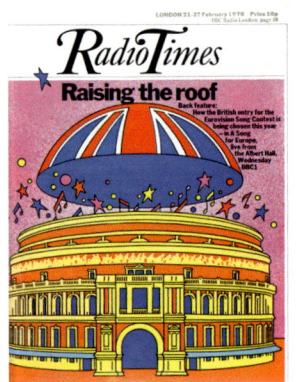

Radio Times Cover: 21 February edition featuring *A Song For Europe* 1976.

Record Cover: 'Wake Up' featuring CoCo. Second place in *A Song For Europe* 1976.

Sheet Music: 'Save Your Kisses For Me' featuring Brotherhood of Man. Winner of the *Eurovision Song Contest* 1976.

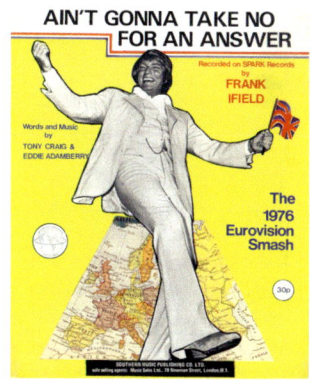

Sheet Music: 'Ain't Gonna Take No For An Answer' featuring Frank Ifield. Twelfth place in *A Song For Europe* 1976.

Record Cover: 'Maria, Maria Wann Kommst Du Zu Mir' featuring Sunshine. German version of 'Maria'. Seventh place in *A Song For Europe* 1976.

Sheet Music: 'Love's A Carousel' featuring Tammy Jones. Sixth place in *A Song For Europe* 1976.

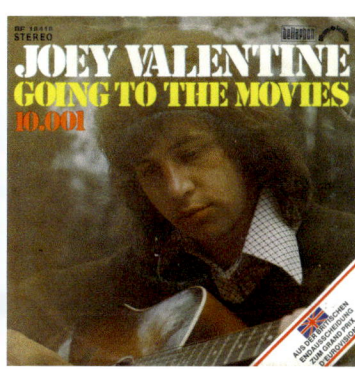

Record Cover: 'Going To The Movies' featuring Joey Valentine. Eleventh place in *A Song For Europe* 1976.

Record Cover: 'Love, Kiss And Run' featuring Sweet Dreams. Fourth place in *A Song For Europe* 1976.

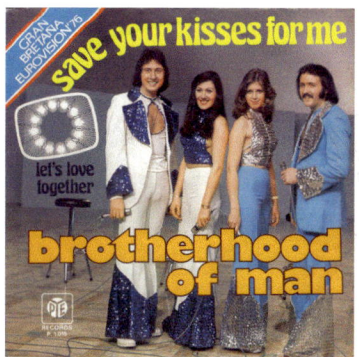

Record Cover: 'Save Your Kisses For Me' (Spanish issue) featuring Brotherhood of Man. Winner of the *Eurovision Song Contest* 1976.

Record Cover: 'What Do You Say To Love?' featuring Mary Mason. Second place in *A Song For Europe* 1977.

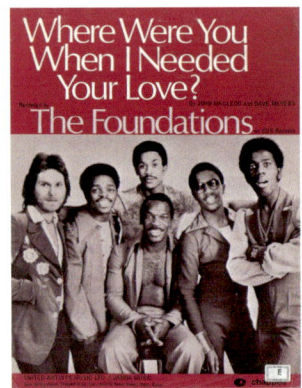

Sheet Music: 'Where Were You When I Needed Your Love?' featuring The Foundations. Third place in *A Song For Europe* 1977.

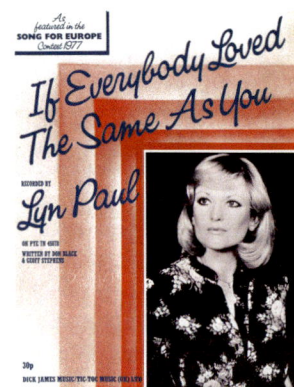

Sheet Music: 'If Everybody Loved The Same As You' featuring Lyn Paul. Sixth place in *A Song For Europe* 1977.

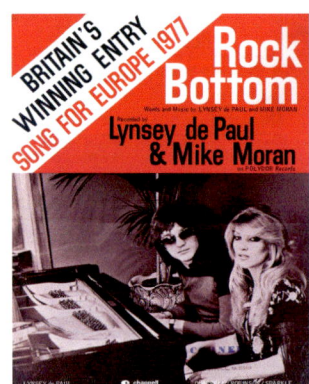

Sheet Music: 'Rock Bottom' featuring Lynsey de Paul and Mike Moran. Winner of *A Song For Europe* 1977.

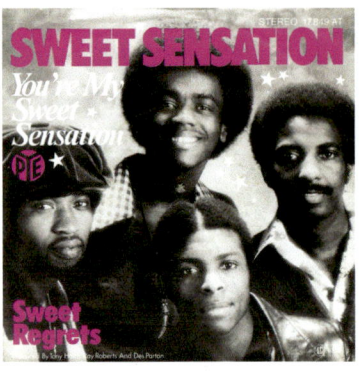

Record Cover: 'You're My Sweet Sensation' featuring Sweet Sensation. Eighth place in *A Song For Europe* 1977.

Record Cover: 'Everybody Knows' featuring Beano. Eleventh place in *A Song For Europe* 1977.

Record Cover: 'Promises, Promises' featuring Rags. Fourth place in *A Song For Europe* 1977.

Record Cover: 'Rock Bottom' (Spanish issue) featuring Lynsey de Paul and Mike Moran. Winner of *A Song For Europe* 1977.

Radio Times Cover: 2 April edition featuring Angela Rippon and the *Eurovision Song Contest* 1977.

Record Cover: 'Für Immer' featuring Lynsey de Paul and Mike Moran. German version of 'Rock Bottom'.

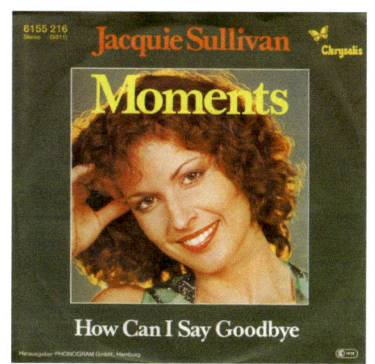

Record Cover: 'Moments' featuring Jacquie Sullivan. Sixth place in *A Song For Europe* 1978.

Record Cover: 'Lonely Nights' featuring Ronnie France. Ninth place in *A Song For Europe* 1978.

Record Cover: 'One Glance Nights' featuring the Jarvis Brothers. Third place in *A Song For Europe* 1978.

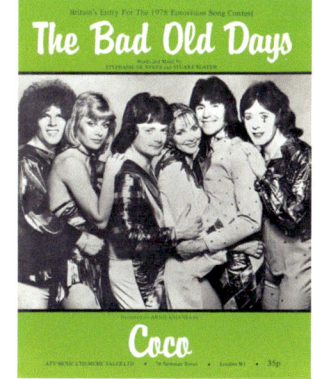

Sheet Music: 'The Bad Old Days' featuring CoCo. Winner of *A Song For Europe* 1978.

BBC Trophy: Awarded to 'The Bad Old Days' written by Stephanie De-Sykes and Stuart Slater. Winner of *A Song For Europe* 1978. Photo (c) Gordon Roxburgh.

Record Cover: 'Don't Bother To Knock' featuring Midnight. Second place in *A Song For Europe* 1978.

Record Cover: 'Mary Ann' featuring Black Lace. Winner of *A Song For Europe* 1979.

Record Cover: 'You Are My Life' featuring Lynda Virtu. Entrant in *A Song For Europe* 1979.

Record Cover: 'Miss Caroline Newley' featuring M Squad. Eleventh place in *A Song For Europe* 1979.

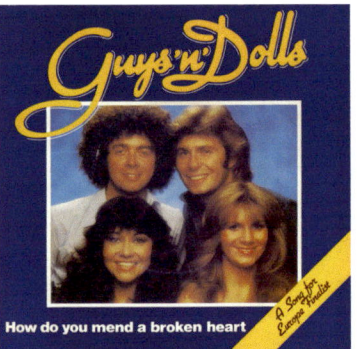

Record Cover: 'How Do You Mend A Broken Heart?' featuring Guys 'n' Dolls. Tenth place in *A Song For Europe* 1979.

Record Cover: 'Home Again' featuring Monte Carlo. Entrant in *A Song For Europe* 1979.

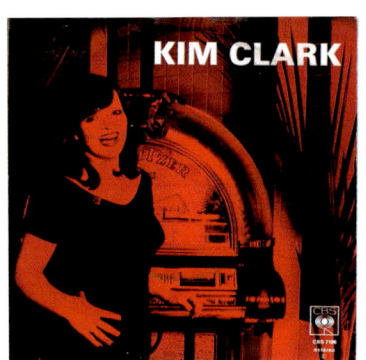

Record Cover: 'Fantasy' featuring Kim Clark. Second place in *A Song For Europe* 1979.

Cover: Publicity folder for 'Mary Ann' featuring Black Lace. Winner of *A Song For Europe* 1979.

Radio Times Cover: 31 March edition featuring the *Eurovision Song Contest* 1979.

Sheet Music: 'Mary Ann' featuring Black Lace. Winner of *A Song For Europe* 1979.

1975 UNITED KINGDOM

There were rumours that quite a few artists, including Slade, David Essex and Gary Glitter, had turned down the offer of representing the United Kingdom in the 1975 contest. However, Bill Cotton succeeded in persuading the Shadows to accept the opportunity.

The Shadows had been the backing group to Cliff Richard in the late '50s and early '60s, and with their distinctive guitar sound they went on to have a number of instrumental hits in their own right, including 'Apache' and 'Dance On'. The group have had several changes of line-up throughout the years, but key members Bruce Welch, Hank Marvin and Brian Bennett have maintained a pretty constant involvement throughout. In 1969 they disbanded, but as it turned out only for a few years. Marvin and Welch continued their careers as part of Marvin, Welch and Farrar, a trio including Australian John Farrar who joined as a third vocalist. In 1973 the group reformed along with their former drummer Bennett. It was this line-up of Marvin, Welch, Farrar and Bennett that was in place when they were invited to do *A Song for Europe*. They were joined for the performances by bassist and keyboard player Alan Tarney, though he wasn't to feature in the named line-up or in publicity photographs. Farrar and Tarney had both been backing performers for Richard when he sang in the 1973 competition.

The songs were initially previewed weekly on the *Lulu* show, from 4 January through to 8 February. The group had recorded all six performances for this in one session, to be edited into the weekly editions. Each song was introduced by the *Eurovision* logo and the same fanfare as had featured in 1974. The title of the song would then be displayed in the centre of the logo, followed by the names of the composers. There was a slow fade and expanding of the *Eurovision* logo as the song began.

The recording for the Final took place on Sunday 9 February. An orchestra of 26 musicians was conducted by Alyn Ainsworth. The *Radio Times* for the week of transmission included a photograph of the Shadows on

SONGS FOR EUROPE VOLUME TWO

their Saturday programme pages, along with details of the song titles and composers.

A SONG FOR EUROPE 1975
Saturday 15 February at 19.31.13 (Duration 44'40")
Presented By Lulu

The programme opened with the James Bond-influenced title sequence for the *Lulu* show, the title music being an instrumental version of Lulu's hit 'The Man With The Golden Gun' from the Bond film of the same name, composed by John Barry and Don Black and arranged on this occasion by John Coleman. There followed an opening dance routine to a medley of songs from the movie *Doctor Doolittle*, with Lulu and the dancers choreographed by Nigel Lythgoe. Amongst the dancers were Veronica (Ronnie) France, Ludovico (Lud) Romano and Kenneth Warwick. Lulu was dressed like a circus ringmistress for this routine.

Following this, still in the same outfit, Lulu introduced *A Song for Europe*, and the *Eurovision* logo appeared, with 1975 written in the middle, to the accompaniment of the fanfare. Lulu then introduced each song with details of the title and composers. After the first song she changed outfits, into a long white dress. The Shadows also changed their outfits for each song.

Song One	'No No Nina' (2'53")	Sung by the Shadows.	Composed by John Farrar and Peter Best.

John Farrar was born in Melbourne, Australia in 1946. He was a songwriter, arranger, guitarist and singer and had worked extensively with fellow Australian Olivia Newton-John. He moved to Britain after he was invited to join the trio Marvin, Welch and Farrar. He performed as a backing guitarist and vocalist when Cliff Richard

1975 UNITED KINGDOM

sang in *A Song for Europe* 1973. He then teamed up with Marvin, Welch and Brian Bennett to reform the Shadows. In 1974 he produced the single and the album of 'Long Live Love' for Olivia Newton John. So 1975 was the third year in a row that he had had an association with the contest.

Peter Best was another Australian, born in Adelaide in 1943. This was his only contribution to *A Song for Europe*. He went on to work mainly as a film composer, on film such as *Crocodile Dundee* and *Muriel's Wedding*.

The 4 January edition of *Lulu* in which the song was previewed was watched by 23.10% of the population (11.67 million) and scored an RI of 53.

| Song Two | 'This House Runs On Sunshine' (2'22") | Sung by the Shadows. | Composed by Brian Bennett and Mike Redway. |

Brian Bennett was another composer who was also a member of the Shadows. He had co-composed with Mike Hawker the entry 'Tomorrow Rising' for the 1973 contest, finishing fourth. A prolific writer, Bennett would go on to compose many television themes, including for *Birds of Feather*, *New Tricks* and *Ruth Rendell Mysteries* and for the BBC's coverage of golf and rugby matches. He is also an orchestral conductor, and still performs with the Shadows on tour. In 2004 he was awarded the OBE.

Mike Redway was a singer and songwriter, and had deputised for Frank Sinatra on a Tony Hatch-produced recording that sadly never saw the light of day. Like Lulu, he can claim to have recorded a James Bond theme song: the one for the original *Casino Royale*, composed by the legendary Burt Bacharach. However it is the instrumental version of that theme that is best remembered, and Redway didn't even get a credit for his vocal version.

Redway admits that he had tried for *A Song for Europe* several times before, including in 1974 with a song called 'Rock And Roll You're Beautiful'. 'That didn't get in,' he says, 'though it got to number one in Ireland, and has had seven cover versions so far, so it didn't work out too badly.'

How had the song with Bennett come about? 'Well, I knew Brian Bennett, and my son one morning was reading the newspaper and he said "This is a good title for a song, Dad: 'This house runs on sunshine.'" It was the heading of an article all about solar power, and I thought, "Great idea," so I mentioned it to Brian and we wrote the song. It was a bit of both when it came to words and music.'

As Bennett was a member of the Shadows, had this made the selection of the song easier? 'No, it didn't help at all. In those days the artists were allowed to pick a couple of songs to go forward into the final selections, and they didn't care for it …. I won't say who didn't care for it. So we had to go the long route, and we still got in, which was encouraging.'

Had he been happy with achieving third place then? 'No, not really. If you do these things, you've got to win. Because if you don't win, that's the end of that recording more or less, unless you get covers. But I did think "Let Me Be The One" was a good song.'

The 11 January edition of *Lulu* in which the song was previewed was watched by 20.30% (10.25 million).

| Song Three | 'Don't Throw It All Away' (2'56") | Sung by the Shadows. | Composed by Gary Benson and David Mindel. |

This was the second year in a row that Gary Benson and David Mindel had a song in the Final. Normally Mindel would put forward two songs, sometimes three, in the hope of getting one through. He recalls: 'The Shadows were my heroes. When I used to play in bands, we played their songs. I had done a lot of commercials over the years, so I was very used to writing to a specific brief, and I can write in any style. With "Don't Throw It All Away", I remember we had the verse and it took about six months to get the chorus, so I don't think it

1975 UNITED KINGDOM

was specifically written with the Shadows in mind. It can take months to do a song. Where a lot of writers sometimes fall down is that they get a great chorus or a great verse and, in their desire to finish the song, they hurry it. You really need to get everything as good as it can be.

'The funny thing was, I had no idea where "Don't Throw It All Away" had finished in the contest. I was away on my honeymoon at the time, and Gary had to get hold of me on the phone to tell me. That song though has done so well for us; we've had numerous covers on it, a country hit with it, a rhythm and blues hit with it, and a reggae hit. Barry Manilow and Olivia Newton-John recorded it as well.'

The 18 January edition of *Lulu* in which the song was previewed was watched by 20.20% (10.20 million).

| Song Four | 'Cool Clear Air' (2'49") | Sung by The Shadows. | Composed by Guy Fletcher and Doug Flett. |

The songwriting duo of Guy Fletcher and Doug Flett were back, having composed the winning song 'Power To All Our Friends' in 1973. Had they tried in the intervening year for Olivia Newton-John? 'I think we probably did try with Olivia,' says Fletcher, 'because one of my closest friends is Bruce Welch, and he was, at the time, her boyfriend, so we saw a lot of Olivia, she was a friend of ours, so we would have tried for her.'

'Cool Clear Air' did not achieve one of their best results, but Fletcher says: 'It was one of our better songs. As far as songs written for *Eurovision* go, it was probably the best, and the Shadows performed it really well. I didn't think "Let Me Be The One" would win it, but I was fairly blinded by our own song; it was a great song, I loved it. I recorded it myself with my own group, Rogue, and that was quite successful for us. I love that Marvin, Welch and Farrar-type sound.'

The 25 January edition of *Lulu* in which the song was previewed was watched by 17.30% (8.74 million) and scored an RI of 55. The programme also included a *Eurovision* medley, comprising 'Puppet On A String', 'Knock, Knock (Who's There?)', 'Boom Bang-A-Bang' and 'Congratulations'. There was an Audience Research Report undertaken for this edition of *Lulu,* recording the opinions of 203 viewers. Few had much enthusiasm for 'Cool Clear Air', and some felt that there was little chance of the United Kingdom winning the international event, based on the songs heard so far. The Shadows were considered a pleasant and accomplished group, but those surveyed were not convinced they were the right choice for the *Eurovision Song Contest.*

| Song Five | 'Stand Up Like A Man' (2'53") | Sung by The Shadows. | Composed by Ben Findon and Michael Myers. |

Ben Findon had co-written with Geoff Wilkins the entry 'Hands Across The Sea', which had finished third in the 1974 competition. This was the first contribution to the competition for Michael Myers.

The 1 February edition of *Lulu* in which the song was previewed was watched by 18.30% (9.24 million) and scored an RI of 58.

| Song Six | 'Let Me Be The One' (2'45") | Sung by The Shadows. | Composed by Paul Curtis. |

Paul Michael Curtis, to give him his full name, was from London, and was a singer, songwriter and record producer. This was his first entry to make the Final of *A Song for Europe*. He had previously been a member of groups called the Narcotics and Union Express. 'When I first started,' he says, 'my parents, who are a bit straitlaced, just thought I was a yobbo who didn't want to work, but of course they are proud of me now.' Curtis had originally planned to record the song himself, but recalls: 'When in the studio, it just didn't sound right. So at the last minute I put it in for the song contest.'

The 8 February edition of *Lulu* in which the song was previewed was watched by 22.70% (11.46 million) and scored an RI of 58.

All the songs were shown again from a recording done during the main session. Then Lulu ran through the song titles once more and gave the address to which votes should be sent and the deadline of the last post on Wednesday 19 February. She also reminded viewers that they could listen again to the songs on Terry Wogan's morning show on Radio 2 on Monday 17 February. She then thanked the Shadows for all their hard work, and joined them on stage during the closing credits. This *A Song for Europe* edition was watched by 16.00% (8.08 million).

THE CONDUCTOR

Alyn Ainsworth was born in 1924, and was initially a singer when he was signed up at the age of 14 to join the dance band of Herman Darewski. When his voice broke he learned to play guitar and later joined Oscar Rabin's orchestra, where he learned about arranging. In 1951 he joined the BBC Northern Variety Orchestra, first as an arranger and then as a conductor. He was briefly engaged to Teddie Beverley of the Beverley Sisters fame, but that was later cancelled. He left the BBC in 1960 to work freelance. He conducted several times the orchestra at the *Royal Variety Performance*. This was his first contest as musical director for *A Song for Europe*.

THE PRODUCER

This was the first and only time that John Ammonds was in charge of *A Song for Europe*. Born in 1924 in London, he started his career at the BBC in 1941 as a sound effects operator. In 1953, while working for the

SONGS FOR EUROPE VOLUME TWO

BBC in Manchester, he met comedians Eric Morecambe and Ernie Wise for the first time. In 1958 he became a producer, and his early successes included programmes with comedian Harry Worth and singer Val Doonican. In 1968 Bill Cotton asked him to produce *The Morecambe and Wise Show*, and he turned the pair into huge stars. He is also credited with coming up with the silly dance that they did at the end of each show, after seeing Groucho Marx do something similar in the film *Horse Feathers*. He also produced shows for Les Dawson, Marti Caine and Frankie Howerd and in 1975 was made an MBE.

THE RESULTS

The results were announced one week later, on the *Lulu* show of Saturday 22 February, which was recorded on 20 February. The programme started at 19.31.27. Bill Cotton made the announcement of the votes, and revealed them in order of presentation.

Song	Title	Votes	Result
1	'No, No Nina'	1,261	Sixth
2	'This House Runs On Sunshine'	10,451	Third
3	'Don't Throw It All Away'	3,099	Fourth
4	'Cool Clear Air'	1,601	Fifth
5	'Stand Up Like A Man'	14,294	Second
6	'Let Me Be The One'	17,477	First

Analysis: The total number of postcard votes was the lowest since the system was introduced in 1965. It could be that just the postal prices had been enough to deter people from voting, or maybe they hadn't been able to see an obvious winner. The deadline had also allowed about a day less for voting than in previous years, due to the results programme being recorded two days ahead of transmission rather than one, meaning that second class postcards weren't a reliable option for posting as they could well be delivered late. The actual number of votes separating the first- and second-placed songs was the smallest yet, nearly 3,200. In terms of percentages, however, 'Let Me Be The One' had a comfortable 36.30% of the total, which stood up pretty well in comparison with other winners. This was the fourth occasion that the song that was last in the running order had won the contest.

Bill Cotton presented the awards to composer Paul Curtis and to the Shadows. They then performed the winning song, 'Let Me Be The One'. The programme concluded with Lulu, accompanied by the orchestra, performing 'Waterloo'.

CREDITS
Producer: John Ammonds
Director: Stanley Appel
Designers: Brian Tregidden and Robin Tarsnane
Costume Designer: Linda Martin
Make-Up Designer: Pauline Gyertson
Sound Supervisor: Hugh Barker
Lighting: Dickie Higham
Production Assistant: Michael Cager
Script: Eric Davidson
Musical Director: Alyn Ainsworth

The 22 February edition of *Lulu* that included the results was watched by 21.80% of the population (11.01 million) and scored an RI of 55. The BBC's archives hold recordings of all the *Lulu* shows from 1975, including the *A Song for Europe* edition.

SONGS FOR EUROPE VOLUME TWO

The winning song was as usual released on a single with the runner-up on the B-side. The song reached number 12 in the British charts. The Shadows made two appearances on *Top of the Pops* with 'Let Me Be The One', on 27 February and a month later on 27 March. The 27 February edition is held in the BBC archives. A video performance of the song was included in the edition of the Granada ITV series *Shang A Lang* broadcast on 20 May, which is held in their archives. All the songs were also released on the Shadows' album *Specs Appeal*.

Gary Benson recorded his own version of 'Don't Throw It All Away', the song he had co-written with David Mindel. It reached number 20 in the UK charts in August 1975, and Benson made two appearances on *Top of the Pops*, on 7 August and 21 August, though neither edition exists in the BBC's archives. However his appearance on the *Twiggy* show broadcast on 19 November 1975 has been retained.

EUROVISION SONG CONTEST PREVIEWS

The BBC declined to undertake the preview presentation co-ordination this year for the EBU, citing pressure of work and a desire not to appear too dominant.

The previews had to be ready by 1 March, and were transmitted over the Eurovision Network on 6 March, for broadcast (supposedly) between 10 and 17 March. As usual, the rules allowed for them to be shown only once.

Presented by Pete Murray
Recorded: Saturday 8 March 1975

Part One: Sunday 9 March at 16.24.57 (Duration 31'58"). Audience 5.20% (2.63 million), RI 50.

Part Two: Sunday 16 March at 15.57.15 (Duration 28'23"). Audience 5.00% (2.53 million), RI 55.

1975 UNITED KINGDOM

The songs were presented in the same order as they would appear in the *Eurovision Song Contest* itself, except for the United Kingdom entry, which was shown at the end of Part Two. The United Kingdom preview of 'Let Me Be The One' was taken from the *Lulu* edition transmitted on 15 February. The preview of the Turkish video was in black and white. The BBC has not retained the preview programmes in its archives, though copies exist on audio.

1975 EUROVISION SONG CONTEST

There had been an initial reluctance by the Swedish broadcaster SR (Sveriges Radio) to stage the 1975 contest, due to the huge expense of the event, and disquiet about this from the left wing in Sweden. However, it was tactfully pointed out that if a small country like Luxembourg could stage the contest, then it shouldn't be a problem for a larger one like Sweden. SR had wanted all competing countries to share in the cost of the event, but talks broke down and SR was left to foot the bill. This did though lead to the aforementioned review of the way that the contest would be financed in future, where there would be cost sharing, with the host country having to pay only about 20% of the total.

Aside from France returning, after their unfortunate absence in 1974, Turkey made an application to join, Malta wanted to return, and Austria were considering participating again, and for a while it looked as if there would be 21 countries in the contest this year. A limit of 20 countries had been set in 1972, as the Executive Group at that time had foreseen the possibility of more countries wishing to enter. In the end, Austria decided not to go ahead with their return in 1975, and Greece withdrew at a late stage, but this still left a record 19 countries in the contest. The draw for performance order took place on 24 January 1975 in Geneva.

The Shadows flew out to Stockholm on Wednesday 19 March, on the same date that rehearsals commenced at the venue. Rehearsals had started at 09.30. Each country had 50 minutes, and rehearsals were in the following order: Netherlands, Ireland, France, Germany, Luxembourg, Malta, Belgium, Israel, Turkey and Monaco. On Thursday 20 March, rehearsals started later, at 10.35, with Norway, Switzerland, Yugoslavia, United Kingdom (in the 14.40 to 15.30 slot), Finland, Portugal, Spain, Sweden and Italy.

On Friday 21 March, camera rehearsals started at 09.50, with each country having 20 minutes. All the artists were now in costumes, and the songs were rehearsed in presentation order. In the evening, from 21.00, the programme was rehearsed in full, along with dummy voting, finishing at 23.00.

During the day of Saturday 22 March, there were technical rehearsals in the morning from 10.30 with presenter Karin Falck and the scoreboard. In the afternoon there were rehearsals for some of the artists as required, before a final full dress rehearsal from 17.00 to 19.00. The live transmission followed at 21.00 local time.

The Dutch entrants, Teach-In, were given an additional rehearsal shortly before the live transmission, according to Dick Bakker, the composer of their entry. He informed the website www.andtheconductoris.eu: 'We felt we had a major problem …We had been drawn first. No country performing first had ever won the festival … We were always first to rehearse as well. In all rehearsals, I noticed the sound for [our song] "Ding-A-Dong" was awful. The sound technicians needed time to get their equipment right, and they more or less used our rehearsal time to do that. Being a sound freak by profession, I thought the situation was unacceptable. We made our complaints heard to the entire organisation, even to the big boss, the producer of the show. I suggested to him allowing Teach-In to perform the song 15 minutes before the start of the live broadcast on Saturday evening to get the audience in the concert hall in the mood and to give the sound technicians the opportunity to adjust their equipment correctly. Though initially there was not much enthusiasm from the Swedish organisation for our demand, in the end it was honoured.'

Apart from the participating countries, 34 others took the broadcast. According to an EBU press release, these included countries in Eastern Europe and the Soviet Union, the Mediterranean area, Chile, Hong Kong, Iceland, Japan, Jordan and Korea. Some countries took it on a deferred transmission, and several were expected to take the BBC commentary rather than provide their own.

Bookmakers had Italy at 6/1 favourite, the United Kingdom at 7/1, the Netherlands and Spain at 8/1, Ireland at 12/1 and Luxembourg and Germany at 14/1.

Radio Times for the week of transmission had a four-page article on the history of the Shadows, and the programme pages for the Saturday included a score chart.

SONGS FOR EUROPE VOLUME TWO

BBC1 promoted the contest with a specially-made trailer of 1'12" duration voiced-over by John Leeson. This used clips from the previews and 1'00" of 'Let Me Be The One'. It was broadcast just before *Dixon Of Dock Green* and, when giving details of the time of the contest, finished up using the lyric 'tonight' from 'Let Me Be The One'.

Radio 2 had a programme called *Gateway to Europe* presented by Tony Brandon at 20.30 on the Saturday night, looking back at some of the hits from the contest with the help of Brian Fahey and the Scottish Radio Orchestra.

EUROVISION SONG CONTEST 1975
Saturday 22 March at 21.00.01 (Duration 132'19")
From the St Eriks Massan Alvsjo, Stockholm, Sweden
Presented by Karin Falck

Pete Murray provided the commentary on BBC1, and Terry Wogan on Radio 2. Murray remembers the occasion well: 'You had to wear black tie, and unfortunately I had forgotten my trousers. I remember that more than anything from doing the contest.'

Richard Astbury had been scheduled to be the commentator for British Forces Radio, but things didn't go according to plan for him either, as he recalls:

'With the engineering budget, they used to sigh a little bit, because we used to have to book lines in those days with the Deutsche Bundespost, and to book a studio-quality line cost many thousands of Deutschemarks. The engineers had booked the line, but half an hour before the contest we were told that we hadn't got it. So I had to go to Terry Wogan, who was a few commentary boxes down, to say, "I've come all the way to Stockholm, we've been here for two or three days, staying in a very nice hotel, but I'm sorry to say no-one is going to hear me. We'll have to tune into the BBC [as we often did anyway] and take your commentary. Would you be so kind as to mention BFBS a few times?" – which he did. So we went all that way without saying a word.

'However, it did mean I could get backstage straight away, and get interviews with most of the contestants, and therefore I had a slightly expanded *Pop Around Europe* to do when I got back. There would be just a two-man team that would go out from BFBS; a commentator and a producer, that was it. We did all our own recordings of interviews, and it was *de rigueur* every year that we would interview the British representatives.'

Netherlands	'Ding-A-Dong' (2'26")	Sung by Teach-In.	Words by Eddy Ouwens and Will Luikinga. Music by Dick Bakker.	Conducted by Harry van Hoof.

The group Teach-In had been formed in 1969, and had gone through several changes of line-up over the years. At the time of the contest it comprised Getty Kaspers (lead singer), John Gaasbeek, Chris de Wolde, Koos Versteeg, Ard Weeink and Rudi Nijhuis. Their winning song reached number 13 in the UK charts, and the group appeared on *Top of the Pops* on 27 March, 10 April and 1 May. Only the edition of 10 April still exists in the BBC's archives.

Ireland	'That's What Friends Are For' (2'47")	Sung by the Swarbriggs.	Composed by Jimmy and Tommy Swarbrigg.	Conducted by Colman Pearce.

SONGS FOR EUROPE VOLUME TWO

France	'Et Bonjour À Toi L'Artiste' (2'59")	Sung by Nicole Rieu.	Composed by Pierre Delanoë and Jeff Barnell.	Conducted by Jean Musy.

The song was given an English lyric by Lynsey de Paul and recorded by Nicole Rieu as 'Live For Love'.

Germany	'Ein Lied Kann Eine Brucke Sein' (2'48")	Sung by Joy Fleming.	Words by Michael Holm and Fred Jay. Music by Reiner Pietsch.	Conducted by Reiner Pietsch.

Luxembourg	'Toi' (2'45")	Sung by Géraldine.	Words by Pierre Cour, Bill Martin and Phil Coulter. Music by Bill Martin and Phil Coulter.	Conducted by Phil Coulter.

There were two familiar composers involved with the Luxembourg entry, Bill Martin and Phil Coulter, who previously had been responsible for 'Puppet On A String' and 'Congratulations'. Martin relates the story behind their third entry: 'Phil and I were splitting up [our writing partnership], and I had no idea he was involved with [this singer], a girl called Géraldine. He wrote "*Toi*" with Pierre Cour, and we spent a lot of money on it, and she couldn't sing. I had no interest at all. I didn't even help to promote it; it meant nothing to me. I went to the contest because I was friends with the Shadows and I loved the atmosphere.'

Norway	'Touch My Life (With Summer)' (2'49")	Sung by Ellen Nikolaysen.	Words by Johnny Sareussen. Music by Svein Hundsnes.	Conducted by Carsten Klouman.

Ellen Nikolaysen had been a member of the Bendik Singers, who represented Norway in 1973.

Switzerland	'Mikado' (2'54")	Sung by Simone Drexel.	Composed by Simone Drexel.	Conducted by Peter Jacques.

British actor Bill Owen provided the lyric for the English version release of 'Mikado'.

Yugoslavia	*Dan Ljubezni* (2'54")	Sung by Ashes and Blood.	Words by Dušan Velkaverh. Music by Tadej Hrušovar.	Conducted by Mario Rijaveć.

SONGS FOR EUROPE VOLUME TWO

United Kingdom	'Let Me Be The One' (2'52")	Sung by the Shadows (Bruce Welch, Hank Marvin, John Farrar and Brian Bennett with Alan Tarney).	Composed by Paul Curtis.	Conducted by Alyn Ainsworth.

In advance of the contest, *Daily Mail* journalist Roderick Gilchrist wrote: 'They've wrung every ounce of appeal out of a song that even Mick Jagger couldn't make exciting. Presentation's dated. Gallant fourth or fifth.'

Brian Wesley, writing in the *Sun*, said: 'Possibly our weakest entry for years. Repetitive, unexciting. Rating 6/10.'

Ken Irwin of the *Daily Mirror* concurred: 'The boys don't expect to win. And they probably won't.'

Despite Bruce Welch infamously tripping over his words at the start of the song, the Shadows did much better than expected, finishing second. Afterwards, Hank Marvin told the *Daily Mail*: 'We are delighted to finish second, and that's the truth. Because of all of the press criticism we were scared we would finish well down. We were in with a chance of winning right until the end.' Bill Cotton, defending his choice of the Shadows to represent the country, said: 'We feel we have been vindicated.'

In light of this success, Bruce Welch told another interviewer: 'We will now be working together again as the Shadows.' Of his slip-up over the words to the song, he recalled: 'When they were setting it all up, my microphone fell on the floor, and I had to pick it up, and this made me nervous. I could remember the first line, as it was the title of the song, but on the second I messed up the words, and I turned to the lads and said "I knew it." I just forgot a line of the song. It was as silly as that. There was nothing I could do but have a laugh about it. Fortunately the other guys are not holding it against me. I don't think it made any difference to the result.

1975 EUROVISION SONG CONTEST

We thought the Dutch song was great. Naturally we're disappointed at not winning, particularly as we came so close. But it was very exciting backstage watching the scores come in.'

Paul Curtis also composed the Shadows' follow-up single, 'Run Billy Run', which was in a similar style to 'Let Me Be The One', but it failed to chart. The group did achieve several more chart hits, including 'Don't Cry For Me Argentina' in 1978, 'Theme From The Deer Hunter (Cavatina)' in 1979 and 'Riders In The Sky' in 1980. However it is sales of their albums that have consistently maintained their high profile over the decades, and they have continued to tour, including with Cliff Richard.

| Malta | 'Singing This Song' (3'04") | Sung by Renato. | Words by M Iris Mifsud. Music by Sammy Galea. | Conducted by Vince Tempera. |

| Belgium | *Gelukkig Zijn*'/ 'Could It Be Happiness' (2'48") | Sung by Ann Christy. | Composed by Mary Boduin. | Conducted by Francis Bay. |

| Israel | *'At Ve' Ani'* (2'47") | Sung by Shlomo Artzi. | Words by Ehud Manor. Music by Shlomo Artzi. | Conducted by Eldad Shrem. |

SONGS FOR EUROPE VOLUME TWO

Turkey	'*Seninle Bir Dakika*' (3'04")	Sung by Semiha Yanki.	Words by Hikmet Münir Ebcioğlu. Music by Kemal Ebcioğlu.	Conducted by Timur Selçuk.

Monaco	'*Une Chanson C'est Une Lettre*' (2'50")	Sung by Sophie.	Words by Boris Bergman. Music by André Popp.	Conducted by André Popp.

Finland	'Old Man Fiddle' (2'34")	Sung by Pihasoittajat.	Words by Arthur Spencer and Hannu Karlsson. Music by Kim Kuusi.	Conducted by Ossi Runne.

Portugal	'*Madrugada*' (2'30")	Sung by Duarte Mendes.	Composed by José Luis Tinoco.	Conducted by Pedro Vaz Osório.

Spain	'*Tú Volverás*' (2'56")	Sung by Sergio and Estibaliz.	Composed by Juan Carlos Calderón.	Conducted by Juan Carlos Calderón.

1975 EUROVISION SONG CONTEST

| Sweden | 'Jennie, Jennie' (2'55") | Sung by Lars Berhagen. | Composed by Lars Berhagen. | Conducted by Lars Samuelson. |

The EBU had to send out a memo to all broadcasters to point out that the Swedish entry would be sung in English and not French as had been earlier stated. (This was probably just a clerical error, and it is unlikely that the Swedish entry was ever going to be sung in French.)

| Italy | 'Era' (2'45") | Sung by Wess and Dori Ghezzi. | Words by Andrea Lo Vecchio. Music by Shel Shapiro. | Conducted by Pier Natale Massara. |

Composer Shel Shapiro was born in London in August 1943 and was a singer, record producer and actor. In 1963 he made his debut in Italy as a singer with the group Shel Carson Combo, which eventually changed its name to the Rokes. He worked with many Italian artists, including Gianni Morandi, Mia Martini and Luca Barbarossa.

THE VOTING

Each country had a jury of 11 people, with a recommendation that there should be a balance between the sexes, and that around half should be under 25 years old. There was a minimum age of 16 and a maximum of 60. Each jury member could award between one and five votes to each song, immediately after the performance, with no abstentions allowed, and of course they could not vote for their own country's entry. In line with the newly-agreed system, the song gaining the highest number of votes was awarded 12 points, the second ten points, the third eight points, and then from seven down to one point for the song gaining the tenth highest number of votes. Any ties would be decided by a show of hands.

One small procedural change that was not strictly implemented in its first year was that the jury spokesperson and presenter should use the term 'points' instead of 'votes' when announcing what each jury had decided, as these were no longer the marks of any one individual, but the result of combined scores. The points were announced in presentation order, and the scoreboard was in English.

Ray Moore was the United Kingdom spokesperson. On the British jury were Mrs C Carmichael, Mrs J Pritchard, Mrs M Ingham, Miss S Lamb, Mr D Evans, Mrs S Johnston, Mr S Morris, Mr J Foster, Mr D Brodie Lowe, Miss D Jackson and Mr D Nightingale.

1975 EUROVISION SONG CONTEST

	Netherlands	Ireland	France	Germany	Luxembourg	Norway	Switzerland	Yugoslavia	UK	Malta	Belgium	Israel	Turkey	Monaco	Finland	Portugal	Spain	Sweden	Italy	TOTAL	POSITION
Netherlands		8	5	8	10	12	6	8	12	12	3	12	4	10	10	7	12	12	1	152	1ST
Ireland	6		6		4	7	1	6	4	12				1	4	3	10	4		68	9TH
France	8	12					3		8	7	2	7	1	7			12	8	8	8	91	4TH
Germany					8				3								4			15	17TH
Luxembourg	12	10	3				7	3	5		6	5		5	8	6	4	10	84	5TH
Norway	2											2						7	11	18TH
Switzerland	7	2	10	6	2	1		5	6	8		7	5	4	2			12	77	6TH
Yugoslavia	3	4		2					5					1		7		22	13TH=
United Kingdom	4	3	12	10	12	7	8	12		8	10	10		12	7	5	10	5	3	138	2ND
Malta	1		8		5	2	4	2			7	1	2					32	12TH
Belgium	5			7			3										2		17	15TH

SONGS FOR EUROPE VOLUME TWO

Israel	10	1	1	1	1	5	2		1		1		6		3			6	2	40	11ᵀᴴ
Turkey															3					03	19ᵀᴴ
Monaco				3	4			2	1		2			2	3				5	22	13ᵀᴴ=
Finland		5		12	6	10	12	5	4			8		8			1	3		74	7ᵀᴴ
Portugal			2										12				2			16	16ᵀᴴ
Spain		7		5		3	5	4		4	4	3	4	8				6		53	10ᵀᴴ
Sweden			7		7	8	1	6	7	2		3	8	6	6	6	5			72	8ᵀᴴ
Italy		6	4	4	3	6	10	10	10	10	6	5	10	1	12	10	7	1		115	3ᴿᴰ

Analysis: Despite co-writer Bill Martin's total lack of interest in '*Toi*', it was Luxembourg who got off to a great start and took the early lead. The United Kingdom got off to a slow start with the first couple of juries, and then picked up a succession of high marks to take over the lead. They lost this advantage by giving their nearest challengers the Netherlands the maximum 12 points. For the next few rounds it was extremely close, as the leaders swapped places. The Netherlands and the United Kingdom were level after Israel voted, but the following few rounds saw the Netherlands start to build up a lead as the gap widened between the top two. Once Sweden voted it was all over, and the Dutch couldn't be caught. The United Kingdom picked up top marks from France, Luxembourg, Yugoslavia and Monaco, with Turkey being the only country not to award it any points.

This was the first time that a song had won the contest from being first on in the running order. It gave the

1975 EUROVISION SONG CONTEST

Netherlands their fourth win in total, matching France and Luxembourg. The United Kingdom had its ninth second-place finish.

WINNING REPRISE

Netherlands	'Ding-A-Dong' (2'26")	Sung by Teach-In.	Words by Eddy Ouwens and Will Luikinga. Music by Dick Bakker.	Conducted by Harry van Hoof.

CREDITS
Executive Producer: Roland Eiworth
Production: Bo Billten
Designer: Bo-Ruben Hedwall
Music Director: Mats Olsson
EBU Scrutineer: Clifford Brown

The contest was watched by 37.60% of the British population (18.99 million) from the start of the programme at 21.00, rising to 40.70% (20.55 million) from 22.00.

A BBC Audience Research Report found that about 30% of the 409 viewers who were consulted had found the programme pleasing. They had thought the songs for the most part enjoyable, as they all had something of their own, and a swing about them, and were easy on the ear. They complimented the artists on how hard they must have worked and noted that they had performed competently in a difficult atmosphere. The postcard idea of using the artists painting portraits was also considered most welcome.

The remainder of the panel had enjoyed the show only moderately, or not at all. They felt that the songs were aimed at what would appeal to the judges, rather than at achieving a high quality, and had tended to be mediocre and more suited to the 1950s. Only Finland and Switzerland, they remarked, had dared to be different.

The new voting system was thought to be fair and easy to follow, and the respondents were in general accord with the points given, feeling that the Netherlands, albeit with a typical *Eurovision* song, deserved to win.

When the United Kingdom and the Netherlands had been neck and neck in the voting, the viewers had found it to be very tense, although there had seemed to be some politically-motivated high and low marks being awarded. Some were concerned over the low marks for Turkey on their first ever appearance and genuinely felt they had deserved more. Other countries whose entries were favoured were Spain and Italy. There were some frustrations expressed about the slowness of the scoreboard, and some comment to the effect that the voting still went on too long.

Pete Murray was considered to have coped adequately with a thankless task, and to have been pleasant and informative, despite difficulties caused by faults of the organisation. (Several times he had expected songs to be sung in English, when they were not.) He did though seem to be most interested in the United Kingdom receiving enough votes to win, and had given no praise to the Netherlands at all, according to some on the panel.

The BBC has retained a copy of the broadcast version in its archives.

1976 UNITED KINGDOM

There was a big change in approach for selection of the 1976 United Kingdom entry. Having found it increasingly difficult to attract well-known artists who were prepared to take a risk in entering a competition, the BBC decided to let the composers choose the artists to sing their songs. Something like 300 songs were submitted for consideration, and 12 would contend the live Final, the largest number since 1962. There would also be a return to juries selecting the winner on the night. The first time the viewing public would see or hear the songs was in the actual live show, and strict rules were put in place to ensure none of them had been performed in public or released on record before the contest. Lots were drawn to determine the running order.

The Royal Albert Hall was the prestigious venue chosen, and camera rehearsals started there on Tuesday 25 February at 10.00. Each act had 40 minutes with the orchestra, which comprised of 28 musicians under the direction of Alyn Ainsworth. They were scheduled to rehearse in the same order as they would perform on the night. There was a 20 minute break after the first two songs. At 13.00 there was not only a lunch break, but also a photo call in the foyer for all the artists. At 14.00 rehearsals resumed, and the group Champagne should have been next, but they were delayed in arriving, and had to be rescheduled for a later slot. Probably everybody else was brought forward by one place, and Tammy Jones would have finished rehearsing at 16.00, after which there was a short break. At 16.30 the next three acts had their opportunity on stage, before a dinner break at 18.30. The final two acts, probably Tony Christie and the rescheduled Champagne, rehearsed in the evening from 19.30. Then, from 20.50 until 22.00, there were camera rehearsals for the opening and closing sequences.

On Wednesday 25 February from 09.00 there was a rehearsal for the interval act, comprising a performance by 26 members of the cast of the hit West End musical *Ipi Tombi*. Then from 10.00 until 13.00 there was the first full run-through with all the artists, the orchestra, interval act and scoring.

SONGS FOR EUROPE VOLUME TWO

After lunch, at 14.00, there was a full dress run-through, going on until 17.30, with testing of the regional lines from 16.30. Dinner took place from 17.30 and then, with an hour to go, the sound and vision were lined up and the audience took their seats ready for the live transmission.

The programme was promoted with a *Radio Times* cover. It featured colour artwork of the Royal Albert Hall with a Union Flag roof. Inside there was an article spread over five pages, with colour photos of all the artists, featuring interviews with some of the artists and composers taking part, and a roll-call of previous British entries.

A SONG FOR EUROPE 1976
Wednesday 25 February at 19.29.47 (Duration 84'03")
Presented by Michael Aspel

The broadcast started with the orchestra playing the '*Te Deum*' music (0.33"), as a title caption for the programme was shown over a live camera shot of the stage. Michael Aspel was played on to the stage by a 10" piece of music composed by Alan Roper.

Aspel gave a brief explanation of the proceedings before it was on to the first song.

Song One	'Wake Up' (3'00")	Sung by Co-Co (Terry Bradford, Keith Hassler, Cheryl Baker, Peter Pereira and Kay Langfield).	Composed by David Hayes and Phil Dennys. (Alan Merrill and Jake Hooker.)	Backing Vocal: Leigh Aspinal (OOV). Plus Orchestra.

1976 UNITED KINGDOM

Terry Bradford was the lead singer of Co-Co, a group formerly known as Mother's Pride. 'We were very much moulded in that first one,' he says of the 1976 contest, 'and we understood that. We thought if we'd had a little bit more input perhaps we might have had more chance, but in truth the Brotherhood of Man was the right act to win it. We were very new to it all, very naive in different ways, but we'd done a couple of television shows under the name Mother's Pride, and we were getting a bit of interest.'

For singer Cheryl Baker (aka Rita Crudgington) this was her first appearance in the contest. 'Ever since I watched Sandie Shaw win with "Puppet On A String", all I wanted to do was to be in it. If I couldn't be an Olympic runner (because I loved sport), then this was the music equivalent, and that was my dream. But I never thought it would actually happen. At the time, they were asking all these big names, and there was I living in east London … How was that ever going to happen to me? So my dream was the *Eurovision*, my ambition was to sing in a band, and probably in those days in something like a Mecca dance hall. I used to go to these dance halls and watch the bands and think how amazing it would be to be in a band like that, doing all the harmonies.'

Baker explains how she joined her first group, Mother's Pride: 'I was working in an office for an Israeli guy; just the two of us, that was the entire company. He was called back suddenly to Israel, as a reservist in the army. I went in to work and there was a note on the typewriter saying, "Rita. Gone to war. See you when I get back. Joshua." I had to think what I could do next. I'd always bought the *NME* and *Melody Maker* every week, and looked through the adverts for singers wanted, but I'd never rung any of them. So I was sitting in the office, bored, and saw an advert for a girl singer required, must have experience, for recording contract, TV and radio. I was a bit nervous about ringing them, and the only reason I did was that it was a London number; if it had been anywhere else, I would never have called. I rang the number and it was for Slim Miller at his agency. He took my details, and when I said my name was Rita Crudgington, he said "That will have to go!" He gave me the number of the band, who at that time were in a summer season in Blackpool, and I was a bit disappointed as I'd only rung because of the London number. Eventually, after a lot of thought, I rang the number. It was Terry

Bradford who answered, and when I said my name, he laughed and said "I'm ever so sorry, but I've just put the phone down on an Agnes Smedley. How can I have an Agnes and a Rita in the same group?"

'Fortunately they were actually based in Leyton, so very handy for me, and that Sunday they came back from Blackpool and held auditions. There were hundreds of girls, as it had been a very good advert. I heard some really good singers next door while I was waiting, but the one thing I knew I could do well was harmonies, and it was a harmony band. So I was called in and they gave me a few harmony lines to do, which was easy for me, and then I did a solo number; it was "You've Got A Friend". They said they would let me know by Wednesday, and I went home, and as soon as I got home, I had a phone call asking me straight back. I got in the car, went straight back, and sang some more with them, and again they said they would let me know by Wednesday. I got home again, and they rang and said "You've got the job". That was the Sunday night, so I didn't even need to wait.

'Fortunately Joshua had come back to the office by the Tuesday, and he gave me his blessing to go straight off and join the group on the Wednesday. That was in the summer of 1975. I thought they were fantastic, and within weeks of my joining them, we were asked to sing our first *A Song for Europe* entry, which was "Wake Up". So my first gig with them was in the October, and just a few months later, in the February, I was going to be appearing at the Royal Albert Hall, which was just amazing. I'm glad that we lost, though. We wouldn't have won the *Eurovision Song Contest*, as Brotherhood of Man were amazing, and had a fantastic song, and I wasn't ready for it either. I wasn't hugely disappointed when we lost; in fact I was thrilled that we came second, and only by two points. The voting was very nerve-wracking and exciting, but I had no reason to think we would win, as I was in an area in my life and career that I'd never experienced before. I remember a few weeks later we were appearing at some small club, and we watched Brotherhood of Man winning the *Eurovision Song Contest*. I was thrilled for them, and we announced to everybody at the venue that the UK had won the contest.'

Although the song was credited to David Hayes and Phil Dennys, it emerged years later that 'Wake Up' was actually composed in 1974 by Alan Merrill and Jake Hooker of the group the Arrows and recorded by them, but not released at the time. It would appear that Hayes was in fact David Most, brother of record producer Mickie Most. Terry Bradford, who had no idea of the song's history back in 1976, says: 'We had a publishing deal with RAK at the time, with David Most, and we had been given this song and asked if we wanted to sing it in *A Song for Europe*. It was a good song, a good idea … but looking back, I don't know quite how they got away with that one. There is no doubt about it now; it's absolutely incredible that it is the same song. I don't know what would have happened had we won.'

The Arrows had had a couple of hits in 1974 and 1975, including the classic 'I Love Rock 'n' Roll', written by Merril and Hooker and produced by Mickie Most on RAK Records. In an interview with Carl Wiser of the website songfacts.com, Merill explained what happened with 'Wake Up': 'Around 1975, the Arrows changed gears. We had put three singles out, two were hits, and we were feeling [full of ourselves]. That came across in the way we strutted into the office, and Mickie did not like that. He liked humility. He liked people being one of the lads. That's what put Mickie off of the band; the pomposity. We thought our management could force his hand to put our records out, but our management was cowed by Mickie and his partner, Peter Grant. Our management was impotent against Mickie, and as a result we had a TV series but no records out. People would go, "They had their own TV series and they didn't have any hits." Well, you can't have any hit records if you don't have anything out. That was how Mickie told off the band for disrespecting him and taking on management when he said we shouldn't. I came up with a song called "Wake Up", which was almost the Arrows' second single. Mickie didn't think it was any good. To show how discerning he was, when David Hayes changed the lyrics and put it out with Co-Co in 1976, two years after we presented it to Mickie, it almost won *A Song for Europe*. It came in second by Co-Co. Exactly the same melody, same arrangement, same chorus, only Dave changed some of the lyrics. My name is nowhere on the credits. Ours was in 1974, theirs was in 1976. We were clearly first. That's the dirty music business.'

SONGS FOR EUROPE VOLUME TWO

Song Two	'Do You Believe In Love At First Sight?' (2'43")	Sung by Polly Brown.	Composed by Ron Roker, Gerry Shury, Chris Rae and Frank McDonald.	Backing Vocals; Joy Yates, Stevie Lange and Val Stokes (in vision). Plus Orchestra.

Polly Brown (aka Polly Browne) was born in April 1947 in Birmingham. She had been a member of the group Pickettywitch, who were best known for their number five hit in 1970, 'That Same Old Feeling', and had two further top 30 hits the same year. As a solo artist she recorded the song 'Up In A Puff Of Smoke', which reached a modest number 43 in the charts in 1975 but received a great deal of airply on Radio 1. 'Do You Believe In Love At First Sight?' was the first of two songs she would perform in the 1976 contest, as she was also one half of the duo Sweet Dreams.

Ron Roker, one of the song's four writers, says: 'It was a much bigger break then than it appears to be now. *A Song for Europe* was not only a vehicle for the artists to launch a career, but for the writing teams as well. We met because we were all working for publishers, and the publishers we were assigned with were ATV Music and Northern Songs. Everybody knew everybody else; it was a small big business. We eventually ended up with writers like Guy Fletcher, Roger Greenaway, Stephanie De-Sykes, Lynsey de Paul and Kenny Lynch. You were in each other's pockets, and it was a great fun time and very creative.

'Polly Brown was a fabulous singer. We were blessed with a lot of talent in those days. We had just done a record for Dick Levy at GTO Records, and we hadn't got anything for *A Song for Europe* that year, and he said we ought to put "Do You Believe In Love At First Sight?" in for the contest. I said it was nothing like a *Eurovision* song and was more a Dionne Warwick-, Diana Ross-type song, and it suited Polly. Anyway he disagreed and put it in, and of course it got through to the Final.'

The song was later covered by Dionne Warwick.

1976 UNITED KINGDOM

Song Three	'Save Your Kisses For Me' (2'58")	Sung by Brotherhood of Man (Lee Sheriden, Martin Lee, Nicky Stevens and Sandra Stevens).	Composed by Tony Hiller, Lee Sheriden and Martin Lee.	Plus Orchestra.

Brotherhood of Man was a group created by songwriter and producer Tony Hiller. After a number ten hit in 1969 with 'United We Stand', the group had undergone a number of changes in personnel before the current line-up came together. 'I knew Sandra, so I introduced her to the group,' explains Martin Lee. 'Lee and I were already writing together, and Nicky came in from a guy called Eric Hall. We all gelled together very well, writing songs, singing songs.'

'We were originally session singers,' notes Lee Sheriden, 'as well as writers. We used to do the Brotherhood of Man sessions – the group had been around for a few years – but the various members were all off doing other work, so we started to *become* the Brotherhood of Man. We had more success initially in Europe, with songs like "Lady" and in 1975 "Kiss Me Kiss Your Baby". The latter was a million seller, it was a number three in France, it went gold in Belgium and the Netherlands, and was a good forerunner for us for *Eurovision*.'

'We had tried a little bit before for *Eurovision*,' recalls Lee, 'but never really got into it. Then they changed the format – because previously the songwriters had to give the song to a specified artist, but then it changed so that the songwriters could nominate the artist, and of course we nominated ourselves, so then we really got into it more.

'We were just writing loads of songs, but you could maybe enter only one or two for the contest, so it was a case of which ones stuck in your head. They had to be very commercial and instantly likeable, and in that era the songs were stories. It was "Save Your Kisses For Me" that stood out, and we decided to make it about a child, as it's what people dote upon. There were also the language problems, as not so many Europeans spoke English then as they do now, so we had to be very careful, and it had to be very obvious. We bantered loads of ideas around, and we picked what we thought was best.'

'We heard a rough recorded version of the song first,' recalls Nicky Stevens. 'We would get together and allocate the parts, the harmonies, rehearse, and then Lee would go off and do the arrangements for the orchestra, and then off into the studio.'

'We loved the song from the first moment,' adds Sandra Stevens. 'It had that bit of magic.'

'I was singing the lead first of all,' states Sheriden. 'It was going to be a song for the album for me. Then there was a silence, and I could see them all chatting, and then they said, "Lee, can you come up?", and I went up and Tony said, "Lee, we think Martin should sing the lead on this song." And thank god they did, because it worked.'

When it came to the contest, what had the group thought of their chances?

'I just lived on hope, praying,' says Nicky Stevens.

'Paul Curtis had a good song with Hazel Dean, a great singer,' was the verdict of Sandra Stevens.

'And of course Co-Co, who came second, were good,' adds Lee.

The last round of voting was very tense, with just three points between Brotherhood of Man and Co-Co going into it. 'I couldn't watch or listen,' says Nicky Stevens. 'I just went "la la la" loudly and covered my ears so as not to hear … Next minute they are screaming, and I'm going "Have we won? Have we really won?"'

'I thought on that last vote from London, that Co-Co would win,' recalls Lee. 'They were a London based band, so I thought they would definitely get it, because sometimes it doesn't come down to the song, but who people know and are familiar with, so other things can come into play.'

1976 UNITED KINGDOM

Sandra Stevens slightly disagrees. 'A good song will always come through and win. The collective public always pick the right one.'

Manager and composer Tony Hiller reflects: 'Whenever the Brotherhood of Man went on tour, I would go along with them, basically to write songs. One time they were appearing at the Cloud Nine club in Preston, and we sat down and wrote a couple of songs specifically with *Eurovision* in mind, and everything about it felt right. When songwriters agree to sit down to work together, whatever happens, there is equality. You can be on a roll and do nine tenths of a song, and you still share the credit. Someone could come in with just the title and another word. In this case it started with Lee Sheriden having an idea – in fact, to be honest, I wasn't too sure about the title at the beginning – and we tried various things, and gradually it came together. As I knew I was going to cut it, in my head I could hear the arrangement, the line-up of brass etc. On all the songs we did, I was more the lyricist, and I came up with that final line "Even though you're only three." The trick about writing songs is that the chorus has got to be so easy, and I'd put in words like "kiss" and "honey" because it's happy, but you do write to a formula.

'I called in Guy Lutman [who had been the choreographer with the dance troupe Feet on the *Lift Off With Ayshea* series] and said we needed some movement, and he did a fabulous job. They were one of the first groups to incorporate choreography.'

Had Hiller felt confident about winning? 'The thing about writing a song is that after you have sung it about 20 times it becomes commercial in your own mind, as you've heard it and heard it, so you think you have a chance. Then you get there and hear a group perform another song and you think they are going to walk it. Sometimes you don't even know why, it's just that commerciality, but everything was right with the two boy, two girl line-up for us. It was very nerve-wracking, the Final at the Royal Albert Hall; I was dead scared, especially going into that last round of voting.'

SONGS FOR EUROPE VOLUME TWO

Song Four	'Couldn't Live Without You' (3'09")	Sung by Hazel Dean.	Composed by Paul Curtis.	Backing Vocals: Joan Baxter, Laura Lee and Nick Curtis (OOV). Plus Orchestra.

Hazel Dean was from Chelmsford, and had started singing in her school choir. She would later make a small change to her name, becoming Hazell Dean.

'I'd watched the contest before in the '60s and '70s,' says Dean. 'It was a serious competition with credibility, a grand affair with an orchestra. I probably did have an ambition to do it; not a burning desire, but it was a good thing to do. I had sung with Paul Curtis in a band called Union Express. Paul loved my voice, and was the first person ever to record me, so it was a natural choice for me to perform the song. It was my first television appearance. To debut at the Royal Albert Hall was absolutely nerve-wracking, but what a place to make a debut. My parents were there, and so very proud of me.'

Composer Paul Curtis had written the previous year's winning song, 'Let Me Be The One', which had gone on to be runner-up in the *Eurovision Song Contest*. He told *Radio Times*: 'My girl will walk it. When she gets out there in front of the nation they'll say "What a fantastic star." I thought right at the beginning we would get through to the Final, because this girl is a sensational singer and it is a real quality song.'

'Of course Paul's comments put me under pressure,' adds Dean, 'but Brotherhood of Man had a fantastic song. Had I not been competing against them, then yes, this girl should have walked it! I did watch the voting, I didn't hide away. I had a lovely time, as it was all so new to me. Of course I was disappointed with the outcome, but that's life. I was so young, and actually relieved it was all over.'

Record Mirror reviewed the song as follows: 'Powerful ballad that Hazel sings well, but at the moment there

1976 UNITED KINGDOM

doesn't seem to be a lot of room in the charts for songs like this. Maybe with a different song …'

Song Five	'A Love For All Seasons' (2'38")	Sung by Champagne (Norman Smeddles, Valerie Smeddles, Phil Thompson, Jan Michelle and Derek Marl).	Composed by Wayne Bickerton and Tony Waddington.	Plus Orchestra.

'The contest was one of those things you did as a writer,' states composer Wayne Bickerton. 'We were having a lot of success with acts like the Rubettes and Mac and Katie Kissoon, and we thought "Let's have a go at *Eurovision*," as there was a pot of gold, in those times, if you hit it off.'

Bickerton recalls his early career: 'I got involved in the very early 1960s, when I was a musician playing in bands in Liverpool, and I met someone who was going to become my creative partner: Tony Waddington. We ended up in a band with Pete Best and went to New York with him, and spent some time there, and had a record in the charts, a cover of "Boys", with me singing on it. Tony and I started writing when we came back from the USA around 1965/66. I ended up getting a job with Decca Records as a songwriter and producer, which was quite something.

'When, many years later, I asked Dick Rowe [A&R man at Decca Records], who was my immediate boss, how I came to get the job, he said, "Very simple. Edward Lewis [Head of Decca Records] asked us all up to his office and said, 'Look, we are not doing very well in the charts, and what's happening with our repertoire?' I said, 'I've just seen a young man from Liverpool …,' and I got as far as the word 'Liverpool' and [Lewis] just pointed a pencil at me and said 'Hire him!'" So that is the story of how I got my break. By 18 months later I was made the label manager at Deram, which was the contemporary side of Decca, and I had a lot of success with people like Cat Stevens.

'But during all this time Tony and I were writing, and we had success in the '60s in America with the Flirtations, and had quite a lot of hits that got into the Billboard charts. One song in particular has become an R&B classic, called "Nothing But A Heartache". Another song was "Can't Stop Loving You", which was recorded by the Flirtations first, and then by Tom Jones. It was probably the one song that took us the longest time to write, and was around for a couple of months, as we just couldn't get the right chorus. We had a great lyric story, but we needed to get a hook. We were out together, with my wife, out in the country, staying at our cottage, which had a very old piano. We were just going over a few things, and one of us, I can't remember who it was, suddenly went, "Bang, can't stop loving you, bang," and that was it. "Sugar Baby Love", which was our biggest hit, took far less time.'

On the subject of the division between words and music, Bickerton declares, 'We've never sat down between us and said "You write this and I'll write that," and allocated who does what in the studios. It's just something that happens. It would be fair to say that Tony can spend some time working on words, and I'll spend a lot of time working on music, doing the arrangements, getting the recordings made; but at the end of the day it doesn't matter who does what, the end result is what matters.'

'Val and I had been in a band going back to the '60s,' explains Norman Smeddles. 'We were in a Liverpool group called Petticoat and Vine, which was a two boy, two girl group. We had a fair bit of success in the early '70s, with some television work; we appeared on *The Benny Hill Show*. The band progressed and changed its name to Champagne in 1974. We then did *Opportunity Knocks*, which we won five times, and that led on to other work.

'When we won *Opportunity Knocks*, Wayne Bickerton and Tony Waddington offered us a recording contract in 1975 with their company State Records. However, for reasons best known to themselves, our managers decided not to take State Records' offer, but put us with a virtually unknown company called Thunderbird Records, which was a bit of a waste of time as we had only a couple of singles released by them. However Wayne Bickerton was still interested in us when *A Song for Europe* came up, and he approached our managers and said he would like us to do the contest, and we signed for State Records around that time.'

Bickerton points out: 'Having your own record label gives you artistic control, otherwise you are in the hands of the company's A&R guys, and if you don't see eye to eye, then it's a nowhere road.'

'I remember going to State's offices and listening to the song, so I don't think we did the demo,' recollects Smeddles. 'I think that was probably done by session singers. We thought it was a decent song, and we liked it, and wanted to do it right away. We had been on a crest of a wave since winning *Opportunity Knocks*, and had done quite a bit of television, so we were under the illusion it would only be a matter of time before we got a hit record. So we wanted to do *A Song for Europe*.

'We'd done theatres before, and had some experience behind us, so we weren't overawed by it, but the Royal Albert Hall was probably the biggest venue we had done. We were working in cabaret in the West Country up until a few days before rehearsals, when the two girls in the group fell ill. We had planned to stay in the West Country and then go straight to London to do the contest. However, because they had been ill, we decided to go back to Liverpool, so they could see the doctors and have a couple of days at home. On the Tuesday morning of the band call and rehearsal, we travelled down from Liverpool, and on the journey the windscreen shattered on our car. So we were about three or four hours late in getting to London, and we missed the sound check and the band call. We did eventually get it done out of sequence, but Wayne Bickerton and our managers weren't too happy with us. After our final rehearsal, Wayne Bickerton handed us a new lyric for the second verse and asked us to learn it for the show. There was some heated discussion as to whether it was wise to change the song at such a late stage. Common sense eventually prevailed and we left the song unchanged. Wayne wasn't happy. I think he felt we'd have done better in the voting if we'd changed it.

'Maybe as a ploy to make us feel confident, we had been told by our managers and other people like Wayne and Tony that we were the favourites, and that we were going to win. Our costumes, to be honest, were probably a mistake. The girls had always worn quite risqué gear; low cut and sexy costumes. But when it came to *A Song for Europe*, our managers and Wayne, for whatever reason, decided we needed to be more sophisticated, so they had the dresses made by [top designer] Ken Brophy. They were long evening gowns, and although the song was "A Love For All Seasons", they seemed to think that all seasons were autumn, as they were in all autumn colours. I think the dresses were a mistake. They were totally the opposite of everything we had done up until then.

'We hadn't heard the other songs until the final dress rehearsal, as we had missed them the day before. But I do remember watching Brotherhood of Man, and thinking theirs was a really catchy song.'

As for the live broadcast, Smeddles says: 'I seem to remember it being a bit chaotic backstage. There were only two dressing rooms, one for the girls, and another for the guys, so we were all thrown in together. It was all very quick, and we were a bit nervous. I remember we had to get onto the stage quickly as Michael Aspel was announcing us. In the rehearsals we had four microphones and the drummer. Although we were miming the guitars, we were singing live. Off camera they had to get four microphones on plus the full drum kit. There were a lot of stage hands who raced on, and as we got into position and lined up, there were only three microphones. I think it was Derek, our bass player, who didn't have a microphone, so we were trying to attract attention really quickly, and one of the guys realised we were one microphone short, and he ran up and put a microphone on … but at the wrong end, so we all had to quickly change positions, and by that time we were being counted in and had to launch into the song before we really had time to catch breath.'

'I looked at Brotherhood of Man,' adds Bickerton, 'and could see that they had been obviously carefully choreographed, and I thought "Wow". You could see it was a very catchy song, simple, and you could see on the night that it was all going to happen for them.'

Champagne were asked to compete again the following year, as Norman Smeddles explains: 'We were

1976 UNITED KINGDOM

offered a number of songs, and I hate to say that one of them was [the eventual winner] "Rock Bottom". I remember listening to the demo of it, done by Lynsey de Paul and Mike Moran. We had two managers, Kevin O'Brien and Tommy Murray, and I recall Tommy was quite set on us doing the song, but we didn't feel it was a song for Champagne. We didn't like it, and didn't actually think it was a *Eurovision* song. Kevin agreed with us, so we basically rejected it. A decision that, of course, with hindsight we regretted.'

The group carried on with television work, appearing with David Nixon, Ken Dodd and Jim Davidson and on *The Morecambe and Wise Show*, *Tom O'Connor's Big Night Out*, and various all-winners shows for *Opportunity Knocks*, including a satellite show that went out live to Australia. They also toured with Shirley Bassey and Mike Yarwood. The group finished professionally in 1981, as Norman and Val Smeddles decided to concentrate on having a family and came out of the music business for a while. Now with a grown-up family, the Smeddles have resumed working as a duo on a semi-professional basis, and still use the name Champagne.

Song Six	'Ain't Gonna Take No For An Answer' (3'05")	Sung by Frank Ifield.	Composed by Tony Craig and Eddie Adamberry.	Backing Vocals: Vicky Brown, Margo Newman and Lisa Strike (in vision). Plus Orchestra.

Frank Ifield had sung before in the contest in 1962, with 'Alone Too Long', finishing in second place. Shortly after that appearance he had several number one hits over the 1962/63 period, including 'I Remember You',

SONGS FOR EUROPE VOLUME TWO

'Lovesick Blues', 'Wayward Wind' and 'Confessin' (That I Love You)'. He continued to be a prolific recording artist through the rest of the '60s, and several further singles of his reached the top 30 in the charts. He was arguably the best-known contestant in the 1976 contest.

Speaking to *Radio Times*, Ifield said: 'I think it's the song, not the singer that counts. The whole reason I am here is that I liked the song and wanted to record it. As far as I'm concerned, I really love things like the *Eurovision Song Contest*. It's one of the highlights of the year, and a great escape for the public. It's something the whole country gets involved in, and that I like.'

In the 1980s, after a bout of pneumonia, Ifield was rushed to hospital with collapsed lungs. Following an operation he was told that he wouldn't be able to sing again. He then made a career as a television and radio host back in his native Australia. He made one further return to the charts as Frank Ifield featuring the Backroom Boys with 'She Taught Me How To Yodel', reaching number 40 in 1991.

The songwriting team of Tony Craig from London and Eddie Adamberry from Gibraltar had been together for about three years.

A *Record Mirror* review of Ifield's later single version of the song said: 'Poor old Frank came bottom in the *Eurovision* vote, but in all honesty it ain't that good. Ever so average ballad with a bit of a lift now and then.'

| Song Seven | 'Maria' (2'47") | Sung by Sunshine (Rod McQueen, Drew Ross, Alistair MacBean, Joy Rose and Jean Hawker). | Composed by Rod McQueen and Eva McQueen. | Plus Orchestra. |

1976 UNITED KINGDOM

Lead singer and composer Rod McQueen told *Radio Times*: 'Normally, I would not have bothered to enter, because it is so limiting to have to write songs for a particular singer. Now everyone has the same chance. You can't tell me there wasn't favouritism before. It makes me sick when people suggest we are writing down to the *Eurovision* contest. That's rubbish. I might have put in a little bit of extra beat, but all I want is for the song to be enjoyed.'

McQueen's wife and fellow composer Eva wasn't present in the Royal Albert Hall, as she had just given birth to a baby boy an hour before the show.

The group recorded a German-language version of their entry as '*Maria, Maria Wann Kommst Du Zu Mir*' with lyrics by Michael Kunze. In addition they recorded a disco version of the song.

Song Eight	'Love's A Carousel' (3'20")	Sung by Tammy Jones.	Composed by Harold Spiro.	Plus Orchestra.

Tammy Jones was born Helen Wyn Jones in March 1944. She shot to fame through her appearances on *Opportunity Knocks* in 1975, when she recorded the highest ever number of votes received. Her single 'Let Me Try Again' was a number five hit in April 1975.

'I didn't choose my stage name,' says Jones. 'I was auditioning for a BBC television show for producer Ernest Maxin, still as Helen, and he decided that he would have me on the show, but that we needed to do something about my name. At that time I looked very much like Tammy in the Debbie Reynolds film of that title, so that's where the Tammy came from. Because Tom Jones was doing so well at the time, they decided to keep the Welsh surname Jones. So I became Tammy Jones.

'I'd actually auditioned three times before for *Opportunity Knocks*, twice in Wales, once in Liverpool, and failed. Then I decided to give it one more try in London, and I sang "Let Me Try Again". I had a round of applause from all the other contestants, so [presenter] Hughie Green was impressed and booked me straight away. I won for five weeks, and then did various all-winners shows. I did 12 shows altogether.'

Having been in one show that was a competition, how had Jones ended up in another with *A Song for Europe*? 'I had actually thought about the contest before,' she says, 'when there had been some talk about whether Wales would ever get its own entry. I was even asked years earlier on an interview for BBC Wales what sort of song I would sing if I ever represented Wales. So that was at the back of my mind when Harold Spiro approached my manager about me singing the song, and I had to go for it. In the past sometimes my manager had made me sing songs I didn't want to sing, but when I heard "Love's A Carousel" I was impressed.

'I'd not performed in venues as big as the Royal Albert Hall before, though I had done the London Palladium, and I had a lot of experience of working with orchestras. All day though during rehearsals I thought I would be nervous, but when I look back and watch it now, I don't think I was nervous at all. I was used to being out there performing on my own.

'I think I chose my own outfit in the end. We tried to find something to blend in with the song, a carousel type of dress, and that style was the in thing then.

'I never thought I would win the contest, but all day I was the favourite to win, in all the talk going round, and a lot of the papers were tipping me to win, I think based on the sort of songs that had won in the past. I hoped I would win it, but I was up against a lot of strong competition, and having heard and seen Brotherhood of Man, I had a feeling they would take it. They were very strong in everything; not just the song, but the entire production.

'When it came to the voting, I was disgusted with Cardiff. How dare they give me such a low mark [of nine]? Since I was born and bred in Wales, they could have at least supported me better! It wouldn't have made any difference in the end, even if it had moved me up a place; it doesn't matter if you come second, third or last: it's academic. Unfortunately, afterwards, the record company, CBS, didn't promote the song enough and push it, as

1976 UNITED KINGDOM

I still feel I could have had a hit with it.'

Jones continued to perform in concerts and on cruise ships before she emigrated to New Zealand in the mid-'90s. There, she continues to perform in cabaret and still sings 'Love's A Carousel', as her audience will request it.

Harold Spiro (along with Val Avon) had had several entries in the contest before, going back to 1970. He had won *A Song for Europe* in 1974 with 'Long Live Love', sung by Olivia Newton John, which had then finished fourth in the *Eurovision Song Contest*.

| Song Nine | 'Going To The Movies' (2'48") | Sung by Joey Valentine. | Composed by Daniel Boone (aka Peter Lee Stirling). | Backing Vocals: Alex Keenan, John Carter, Neil Lancaster, Vicky Brown and Chas Mills (OOV). Plus Orchestra. |

Joey Valentine was from Lochgelly in Fife. He had been trying to be a full time professional singer for about 16 years. He had been an architectural draughtsman, a soldier, a chef, a bricklayer and a joiner. However in 1974 he landed himself a recording contract.

Daniel Boone (born Peter Charles Green) was otherwise known as Peter Lee Stirling and had been one of the composers behind the 1965 winning song 'I Belong', sung by Kathy Kirby, which had gone on to finish second in that year's *Eurovision Song Contest*. As Boone, he had a big success as a singer with the song 'Beautiful Sunday', which he co-wrote with fellow 1976 competitor Rod McQueen. It reached number 21 in the UK charts, but went higher in the USA, reaching number 15 in the Billboard Hot 100.

SONGS FOR EUROPE VOLUME TWO

Song Ten	'Love, Kiss and Run' (3'04")	Sung by Sweet Dreams (Polly Brown and Tony Jackson).	Composed by Barry Blue and Stephen Worth.	Backing Vocals: Clare Torry, Jill McIntosh and Stephanie De-Sykes (OOV). Plus Orchestra.

Sweet Dreams were the creation of producer and composer Ron Roker. They had already achieved chart success with a cover of the ABBA song 'Honey, Honey' in July 1974, reaching number 10. Curiously 'Honey, Honey' was in fact the follow up single by ABBA after 'Waterloo', but although released by them across Europe, the USA, Australia and New Zealand, it wasn't released in the UK at the time, and instead was covered by Sweet Dreams, making them the first artists in Britain to record an ABBA song. Roker recalls: 'About a year later, ABBA composer Stig Anderson came over and asked me when we were going to record another ABBA song, and I told him when ABBA recorded one of mine … but they never did!'

This was the second song in the 1976 contest to feature singer Polly Brown. However, she told *Radio Times* she wasn't happy about this, as she found song contests nerve-wracking: 'I don't really like competing and having people evaluate what you are doing. I'd much rather just sing. I was in a song contest before, in Majorca, and I suppose that's a help, because at least I know what to expect this time. But I didn't enjoy it. I couldn't talk to any of the other singers in the contest as they were all foreign.'

Tony Jackson (aka Anthony Norville) was born in Barbados in March 1944. At school he had formed a six man vocal group called the Opals. After leaving school he had been a drummer with the Telstars before moving to London. He had initially joined a reggae band called the Skatalites, then another group called Gulliver's

1976 UNITED KINGDOM

People. He possessed a distinctive high tenor voice and, in 1974, Roker had teamed him up with Brown to form Sweet Dreams. In 1975 he had released a solo single, 'As If By Magic'.

Barry Blue (aka Barry Green) was born in December 1940. He was a singer, producer and composer, and was best known for singing the hit songs 'Dancing (On A Saturday Night)' and 'Do You Wanna Dance', both top ten hits in 1973. He had written 'Kiss Me Kiss Your Baby', which was a million-seller for the Brotherhood of Man in 1975. He would go onto write hit songs for Diana Ross, Celine Dion and Andrea Bocelli. Fellow songwriter Stephen Worth was his brother-in-law. Sweet Dreams creator Roker produced the song.

The *Record Mirror* said: 'This one is co-written by Barry Blue that did quite well, and if enough people put their money where their votes went it could be a small hit. Catchy chorus and clap along beat.'

Song Eleven	'Take The Money And Run' (3'10")	Sung by Louisa Jane White.	Composed by Roger Saunders and Scott English.	Backing Vocals; Irene Chanter, Doreen Chanter and Margaret Smith. (OOV). Plus Orchestra.

'I got into singing when I was about six,' recalls Louisa Jane White. 'I was at dancing class, and my brother played piano for old people's homes, and I used to go and sing at the local homes, and I enjoyed it, and went into singing. I went into a local group and then got spotted by a London agent, and that was when I met my husband, who became my manager.'

White had previously been in a group called Bubbles, Bangles and Beads with Polly Brown, and had competed in the *International Song Contest* in Poland. She had made several appearances on the ITV series *Lift Off With Ayshea*, and had a lot of work abroad. She had also performed on several occasions for both Radio 1 and Radio 2, recording five songs that would then be stripped across various shows. 'I had a few singles out,' states White, 'and had a bit of a name in the business, but not any hit records. My husband got a call from a publishing company, saying that the composers would like to use me to sing their song for the contest, which I of course said yes to. But I could never see it as a *Eurovision* entry – it wasn't the type – and I don't think the writers did either as it was slightly reggae and a bit edgy, and was obviously about a hooker!

'I didn't know I was actually in the contest until I read it in the *Daily Mail*, and someone rang me up to tell me I was one of the final 12. I wasn't daunted by appearing at the Royal Albert Hall, I welcomed the opportunity, and what a fantastic place to perform in! I was with Pye Records at the time, and they sent me along to Ossie Clark, one of the great dress designers. I picked something, and I loved it. In fact I had it for many years, until it fell apart, but it was a little bit revealing, so we had to put in an extra little bit underneath, so the camera didn't catch anything.'

Speaking to *Radio Times* at the time, White said: 'I think now that the writers are choosing their own singers, the range will be much wider and probably the standard will be that much higher. I don't know how I will do. I like the song very much and obviously I would like to win.'

Reflecting back now on the contest, White comments: 'I think everybody was picking Brotherhood of Man to win, which was great, as it went on to win the whole thing. I was very surprised when the votes came in; I couldn't believe we had done so well. Everybody was so friendly, and it was a lovely night.'

The exposure on *A Song for Europe* led to further work for White both at home and abroad, but she was never asked again to do the contest. She worked into the '80s, until raising a family became her full time job. Nowadays she works in a nursing home as an activities person.

Roger Saunders, born in March 1947, had been a member of the three-man group Freedom, supplying vocals, guitar and keyboards. The group had been founded in 1967 by two former Procol Harum members.

1976 UNITED KINGDOM

However, by 1972, the band having failed to get the backing it had been promised, Saunders signed a solo deal with Warner Records and released an album. The group disbanded and Saunders became much in demand as a session guitarist. He also struck up a songwriting partnership with Scott English, but 'Take The Money And Run' was their only composition to make the Final of *A Song for Europe*. Throughout the '80s Saunders was a member of the Glitter Band. He died in early 2000 from cancer.

English was born in Brooklyn, New York and had worked with many top names, including Elvis Presley and Tom Jones. As a singer himself he had reached number 12 in the UK charts in 1971 with 'Brandy', which he wrote with Richard Kerr. The song was later reworked as 'Mandy' and became a huge hit for Barry Manilow. Another of English's most successful compositions was 'Bend Me, Shape Me', sung by Amen Corner.

Song Twelve	'Queen Of The Mardi Gras' (2'38")	Sung by Tony Christie.	Composed by Geoff Stephens and Tony Macaulay.	Backing Vocals: Lavinia Rodgers, Sue Martine, Eleanor Keenan, Scott Fitzgerald and Spencer Shires (in vision). Plus Orchestra.

Tony Christie was born Anthony Fitzgerald in April 1943. He was best known at the time for two chart hits in 1971: 'I Did What I Did For Maria', written by the Mitch Murray and Peter Callander team, and the memorable 'Is This The Way To Amarillo', which reached number 18 on its original release.

It was Christie's manager at the time, Harvey Lisberg, who spoke to the *Radio Times* journalist: 'The two writers got together and actually computed a song they reckoned would win. It's no good saying it wasn't calculated, because it was. We have no doubt that it will win.'

This was the only appearance in the contest for Christie, and while his profile in the UK took something of a dip for a while, he remained very popular in Europe, particularly in Germany. He recorded no fewer than nine albums for the German market.

When 'Is This The Way To Amarillo' was re-released in 2005, featuring comedian Peter Kay, it went to number one. Christie had also recorded the theme song to *The Protectors* television show, entitled 'Avenues And Alleyways'. This had reached only number 37 in 1972, but following his success in 2005, it was re-released and reached number 26. A further variation on his biggest hit, retitled 'Is This The Way To The World Cup', reached number eight in 2006. In 2010 he made his West End debut in the show *Dreamboats and Petticoats*.

Geoff Stephens had been one of the composers behind 'Knock, Knock (Who's There?)', sung by Mary Hopkin, which had won *A Song for Europe* and been runner up in the *Eurovision Song Contest*. Tony Macaulay had co-written the runners-up in both the 1973 and the 1974 *A Song for Europe* contests.

'I liked "Queen Of The Mardi Gras" a fraction more than some of the other ones,' said Macaulay. 'Again it was in that *Eurovision* feel. It was written as more of a project. Whenever I sat down and thought, "Let's write a *Eurovision* hit," it wasn't really the right way to start, not for me. Geoff Stephens was the best writer I have ever worked with, though he plays in one key – C. He is the most instinctive musician I've known, and has more natural melodies in his head. We would thrash the melody out in the greatest detail. He had been a schoolmaster before, and he worked in a clear-headed way. He was quite a calm fellow, but his tunes would have great passion. We sat down and we methodically worked the tune out. He would plonk away on the piano with his bass booming voice, and I would work on the guitar usually as it gave us more scope. Then we'd often get in the car or go for a long walk to get away from the musical instruments. We worked on the words away from the instruments. My collaboration with Geoff was the most instinctive by a long way. He is a brilliantly talented songwriter.

'Tony Christie was someone way down on our list of people that we wanted to work with us, and I can't remember exactly how that came about, but I think Geoff called around and Tony was keen to do something like that. Tony was good, and nice to work with; a very powerful singer. I remember I designed the green dresses that the three girls who did the backing vocals wore.'

'Queen Of The Mardi Gras' eventually finished in third place. '"Save Your Kisses For Me" was visually so impactful,' says Macaulay. 'I didn't think the lyric was that wonderful, but visually it was stunning, and we couldn't possibly compete with the Brotherhood of Man.'

THE INTERVAL ACT
The company of the West End musical *Ipi Tombi* performed a selection of songs from the show.

THE VOTING
Each jury consisted of 11 members of the public aged between 16 and 60, with a balance between the sexes. Five or six members in each jury were above the age of 25, and there had to be no less than a ten year age gap between the oldest member and the youngest. Each jury member could award between 1 and 5 votes for each song, with no abstentions. All votes had to be registered immediately following each song's performance. The votes were totalled up, and 12 points were awarded to the song that gained the highest number, 11 points to the second, and so on down to 1 point to the song in twelfth place. In the event of any tie, a show of hands would determine the order. If three or more songs tied for the same position, and there was still a further tie, then the jury foreman would have a casting vote. There were 14 regional juries in total. The points were announced in the same order as the presentation of the songs.

SONGS FOR EUROPE VOLUME TWO

THE SPOKESPERSONS

Bristol	Chris Denham
Bangor	Elfyn Thomas
Leeds	Brian Baines
Norwich	John Crowest
Newcastle	Mike Neville
Aberdeen	Gerry Davis
Birmingham	Tom Coyne
Manchester	Mike Riddoch
Belfast	Michael Baguley
Cardiff	Iwan Thomas
Plymouth	Donald Heighway
Glasgow	David Findlay
Southampton	Peter McCann
London	Ray Moore

1976 UNITED KINGDOM

THE RESULTS

	Bristol	Bangor	Leeds	Norwich	Newcastle	Aberdeen	Birmingham	Manchester	Belfast	Cardiff	Plymouth	Glasgow	Southampton	London	TOTAL	POSITION
'Wake Up'	11	11	11	12	9	9	11	10	9	10	12	7	5	11	138	2ND
'Do You Believe In Love At First Sight?'	2	3	8	9	3	2	12	8	4	4	6	3	2	5	71	10TH
'Save Your Kisses For Me'	9	9	12	8	12	12	5	11	11	11	10	12	8	10	140	1ST
'Couldn't Live Without You'	3	4	4	6	2	8	10	6	8	7	4	5	7	3	77	8TH=
'A Love For All Seasons'	8	5	2	5	11	3	6	5	7	5	5	2	4	9	77	8TH=
'Ain't Gonna Take No For An Answer'	4	1	1	1	1	1	1	3	2	1	2	1	1	1	21	12TH
'Maria'	6	6	5	4	5	11	4	1	6	3	11	8	6	4	80	7TH
'Love's A Carousel'	1	12	10	7	7	10	2	4	10	9	7	4	9	6	98	6TH
'Going To the Movies'	5	10	3	2	4	6	3	2	3	2	1	6	3	2	52	11TH
'Love, Kiss And Run'	12	2	7	11	8	4	8	7	5	8	8	9	12	8	109	4TH
'Take The Money And Run'	7	8	6	3	10	5	9	9	1	6	9	10	10	7	100	5TH
'Queen Of The Mardi Gras'	10	7	9	10	6	7	7	12	12	12	3	11	11	12	129	3RD

SONGS FOR EUROPE VOLUME TWO

Analysis: The decision to return to voting by juries would appear to have been vindicated, as it provided an extremely close and exciting competition for the viewers. 'Wake Up' led for most of the voting, until Glasgow pulled 'Save Your Kisses For Me' level, and it was only in the penultimate round that the latter song took the lead. 'Save Your Kisses For Me' eventually won by a margin of just two points over 'Wake Up', making it the closest British contest since 1961, when the margin had been a single point. 'Save Your Kisses For Me' gained the maximum score from four juries, as did 'Queen Of the Mardi Gras', whereas 'Wake Up' received only two sets of top marks. Altogether six songs gained at least one set of maximum points. 'Save Your Kisses For Me' achieved 83.33% of the maximum possible, ahead of 'Wake Up' with 82.14%. Leeds was the only jury to get the top two songs in order, and was close with 'Queen Of The Mardi Gras', placing it in fourth place rather than third. Birmingham was the only jury not to place the winner within the top five songs.

* There was an error made by the scoreboard operators following the Birmingham vote: 'Queen Of The Mardi Gras' should have had 56 points, but only 54 points was displayed. Thereafter it consistently showed two points lower than the actual total it had received.

The awards were presented by Brian Cowgill, Controller of BBC1, although originally Head of Light Entertainment Bill Cotton was down to do this. Tony Hiller received the award on behalf of the composers, and all the members of Brotherhood of Man came on stage to receive their award. Then Brotherhood of Man reprised the winning song, 'Save Your Kisses For Me'. The end credits had an arrangement of 'Congratulations' played over them.

1976 UNITED KINGDOM

CREDITS
Producer: Stewart Morris
Assistant: Lydia Spratt
Designer: Robin Tarsnane
Sound Supervisor: Chris Holcombe
Lighting: Tommy Thomas and Bob Jones
Costume Supervisor: Jane Nagy
Make-Up Supervisor: Pauline Gyertson
Vision Mixer: Mike Turner
Production Assistant: Marcus Plantin
Assistant Floor Manager: David Warne
Floor Assistants: Richard Cox, Richard Boden and Cliff Pinnock
Juries/Scoreboard PA: Geoff Jowitt
Musical Director: Alyn Ainsworth

Immediately following the live transmission there was a photo call on stage for the winning artists. The programme – which still exists in the BBC archives – had actually run about five minutes shorter than planned, so the BBC aired a five minute *Tom and Jerry* cartoon to take the time up to 21.00. The contest was watched by 28.10% of the population (14.19 million) from the start of the programme at 19.30 rising to 30.10% (15.20 million) from 20.15. It scored an RI of 56.

    The reaction to the programme from the 296 viewers sampled for the BBC's Audience Research Report was moderate rather than enthusiastic. Viewers tended to like the new method of choosing the entry, although a number were bored by the yearly ritual. There were complaints however that the singers were largely unknown.

SONGS FOR EUROPE VOLUME TWO

There were also some complaints that the cameras were a long way from the stage and that the scoreboard couldn't be easily seen.

Only about 40% agreed with the choice of the winning song, although most of the others would have placed it in the top three and thought it was a lively, catchy song, well presented by the Brotherhood of Man, which could do well in the *Eurovision Song Contest*.

Michael Aspel was thought to have done well, though some disliked his jokes and the way he repeated the scores, and some said he had seemed bored by the whole thing. But there were tributes to his pleasant, relaxed and thoroughly professional manner, and it was said that he had kept the programme running smoothly.

Nicky Stevens says: 'I remember that after the Royal Albert Hall show, we all headed back to our manager's house. We were going up the Edgware Road in taxis, and our manager was leaning out of the window shouting "We've just won *A Song for Europe*," and cars were beeping their horns. We got back, and I don't think we had a lot of sleep, as first thing in the morning we were at a hotel in London for a big press conference. After that the work just flooded in; it was manic.'

All the songs were released on 7" singles but only 'Save Your Kisses For Me' made the charts, reaching number one, a position it held for six weeks. 'Save Your Kisses For Me' featured on the editions of *Top of the Pops* broadcast on 4, 18 and 25 March and 1, 8, 15, 22 and 29 April. The performances from 4 March and 25 March exist only on a domestic video format, while the edition of 18 March no longer exists at all in the BBC archives. All the other editions exist in broadcast quality. The 25 March and 22 April editions featured repeats of earlier studio performances. The 15 April edition used the promotional preview video.

Brotherhood of Man went on to appear on *Miss England* on 19 March and on the *Cilla* edition broadcast on 20 March, both of which shows have been retained in the BBC archives, and on ITV's *Tiswas* on 1 May, which no longer exists. As 'Save Your Kisses For Me' became one of the biggest hits of the year, further performances followed on *Seaside Special* broadcast on 7 August and on a Christmas edition of *Top of the Pops* broadcast on

1976 UNITED KINGDOM

26 December, which also exist in the BBC archives.

Champagne appeared on *The Morecambe and Wise Show* broadcast on 19 April with 'A Love For All Seasons', and this edition has likewise been retained in the BBC archives.

On ITV, Hazel Dean appeared on *Supersonic* broadcast on 13 March with 'Couldn't Live Without You', while Louisa Jane White appeared on *The Arrows Show* on 27 April performing 'Take The Money And Run'. Both of these programmes still exist in the Granada TV archives.

EUROVISION SONG CONTEST PREVIEWS

The previews had to be ready by 14 March, for transmission on international circuits on 19 March, to be broadcast nationally between 23 and 30 March. Once again the BBC broadcast Part One before the first of the permitted dates.

Presented by Michael Aspel
Recorded on Saturday 20 March.

Part One: Sunday 21 March at 16.54.25 (Duration 30'18"). Audience 8.10% (4.09 million). RI 53.
Part Two: Sunday 28 March at 16.56.52 (Duration 27'36"). Audience 6.00% (3.03 million).

The songs were previewed in the order in which they would be performed in the contest, except for the United Kingdom's, which as usual was shown at the end of Part Two. For the first time, the BBC specially shot a preview video. This featured the Brotherhood of Man filmed in Holland Park.

The preview video of Finland's entry was sung in Finnish, but would be sung in English in the Final, while the Austrian entry featured some different English lyrics than those used in the version in the Final.

SONGS FOR EUROPE VOLUME TWO

CREDIT
Television Presentation by: Stewart Morris

These programmes exist in the BBC archives.

'We had watched the previews,' says Sandra Stevens of Brotherhood of Man, 'and we saw France as a threat. Also Waterloo and Robinson for Austria…until the song got to the middle eight. If it had had a hook then it would have been a danger, but it just went down and down and died, and it wasn't good enough. But the French song was very good.'

1976 EUROVISION SONG CONTEST

There was never any doubt that the Dutch broadcaster NOS would stage the 1976 event, although there were disagreements over the financing. The Dutch considered it illogical that under the new rules they should have to pay their active participant's fee as well as meet their costs as organisers. As a result it was decided in exceptional circumstances to waive their active participant's fee. However, from 1977, the hosts, whoever they might be, would be expected to pay their share of the overall contribution. This meant that the winners might have to declare as early as June 1976 whether or not they could afford to stage the 1977 contest.

At several stages it looked as if there was going to be a full house of participants this year, with the maximum of 20 countries permitted at the time. RTM (Radio Television Marocaine) Morocco was interested in entering, and was listed in telexes in September 1975. So too was Turkey, although it had withdrawn by October 1975. SR in Sweden too had withdrawn, following fears about the costs of staging the event again, although a different Swedish broadcaster, Channel Two, was considering taking its place. Greece and Austria both decided to return to the contest, and by the provisional deadline it appeared that 19 countries would be participating. RAI (Italy) was not fully confirmed, as it had had a change of Head of Light Entertainment, but felt it was 99% certain it would be there. Malta was subsequently to withdraw from the contest, bringing the final number down to 18 countries.

The financing was agreed at a meeting in Milan in 1975. The Group One broadcasters – United Kingdom, France, Germany, Spain and Italy – would contribute 50% of the total, amounting to 27,825 Swiss Francs each.

Group Two broadcasters – Belgium, Austria, Norway, Finland, Switzerland and Yugoslavia – would contribute 33%, or 3,118 Swiss Francs each, less *pro rata* deductions from the input of the passive participants. The Netherlands' contribution would also be paid from the latter.

Group Three broadcasters – Ireland, Luxembourg, Monaco, Greece, Portugal and Israel – would pay 7,884

SONGS FOR EUROPE VOLUME TWO

Swiss Francs each.

The passive broadcasters – Morocco, Turkey, Iceland, Tunisia and Algeria – would pay 4,038 Swiss Francs each. Amongst other countries, a deferred relay of the contest was possibly going to be taken by Hong Kong.

The draw for the running order was made in Hilversum on 7 January 1976. All national selections had to be completed by 8 March, with no transmissions of the songs except for the actual national Finals allowed before 1 March. The rules originally stated that no sheet music could be published or record versions released before 8 March. However, the BBC successfully argued that as their Final was on 25 February it would be unrealistic to hold back any releases for 12 days.

Rehearsals commenced on Tuesday 30 March at 14.00 with each country having a 40-minute slot. All the countries rehearsed in the same order as the draw, with the United Kingdom having the 14.00 to 14.40 slot. The first day's rehearsals concluded with Israel coming off stage at 17.10.

On Wednesday 31 March rehearsals kicked off at 10.00 with Luxembourg, and concluded at 17.10 with Finland.

Thursday 1 April saw all the remaining countries have their first rehearsal, between 10.00 and 17.10.

The second rehearsals were of only 20 minutes' duration for each country, and went on throughout the day on Friday 2 April, with the United Kingdom first on stage from 09.30 until 09.50. The final country, Yugoslavia, finished their second rehearsal at 18.00.

A full dress rehearsal of the show took place later that same evening, from 20.30 until 23.00.

On Friday 2 April, TRT (Turkey) sent the following telex to EBU President Sir Charles Curran:

Dear Sirs. From the English and French translation of the text of the Greek entry to the *Eurovision Song Contest* 1976 we noticed a clear and strong political accent and evident allusions to the recent Cyprus events. This we believe is contrary to the spirit and aims of the EBU and *Eurovision* and will no doubt constitute a precedent to such detrimental activities in future. We strongly believe that you have unintentionally overlooked the text of the song, which contains a strong dose of provocation. As a member of EBU's administrative council we sincerely want to draw your attention to this case and we are sure that you will take all the necessarily steps to prevent telecasting of this song during the finals of the *Eurovision* 1976. Thank you in advance. I remain sincerely yours. Dr Saban Karetes, Director General of TRT.

A reply was sent on Saturday 3 April:

Dear Sir. We have received your telex about the Greek entry to the 1976 *Song Contest* and are very sorry indeed for the concern that the text of their song is causing you. We must however state that the contest rules have no provision for any control over the texts on any grounds whatsoever. In addition we must draw your attention to the fact that the host organisation is not entitled, and we are sure that nobody else within the EBU would be entitled, to prevent telecasting of any song entered into the contest that is in accordance with the current rules. Apart from this, in our opinion, the text of the Greek song has not necessarily the political implication that you are reading into it. We would be very grateful if you could accept this factual situation, as it is absolutely impossible to accede to your demand. In doing so you would greatly help in enabling our union as such to maintain its strictly non-political character. Sincerely yours, Erik Jurgens Chairman NOS.

In the event, TRT cut transmission of the Greek entry, a fact that was reported in the *BBC News* broadcasts of 4 April. The EBU decided to take no action, although the Greeks were told that it had been wrong for them to be put in that position. It was also noted that the North African countries had cut out the Israeli entry, so although TRT had broken the rules, it was thought best not to press the issue, as they could have cut the whole transmission.

There was a further rehearsal of the show on Saturday 3 April from 17.00 until around 19.00 before the live transmission, which was at 21.00 local time.

The BBC delegation included Bill Cotton, producer Stewart Morris, production assistant Lydia Vine, Ann Rosenberg from BBC Publicity and George Howard from the BBC Board of Governors.

The bookmakers had the United Kingdom as the 3/1 favourite to win, Netherlands at 5/1, Finland at 7/1, Monaco and Germany at 8/1, France and Italy at 10/1 and Norway at 12/1.

Publicity in *Radio Times* was fairly minimal, with just a small black and white photograph of Brotherhood of Man accompanying a list of the songs in the programme pages. BBC1 aired a trailer on Saturday 3 April following that evening's edition of *Jim'll Fix It*. This lasted 1'16" and used a mixture of footage from *A Song for Europe* and from the preview video, voiced over by John Braben.

'I remember Michael Aspel and Terry Wogan both had their own radio programmes at the time,' says Lydia Vine. 'Michael I think was on Capital Radio and Terry of course on Radio 2. They had to have radio facilities at the contest so that they could both do their shows. I seem to remember Terry having to follow on from Michael in this radio box at the venue, and Terry saying something like "Good grief, he works off scripts!"'

The Congresgebouw venue had an audience of around 2,000 spectators. The worldwide audience figures were announced as totalling 450 million in 30 countries, with a further 80 million listening via radio in 11 countries. An orchestra of 42 musicians accompanied the 18 entries.

EUROVISION SONG CONTEST 1976
Saturday 3 April at 21.00.01 (Duration 130'41")
From the Congresgebouw, The Hague, The Netherlands
Presented by Corry Brokken

1976 EUROVISION SONG CONTEST

Michael Aspel was the commentator for BBC1, with Terry Wogan fulfilling that role for Radio 2 and Andrew Pastouna for British Forces Radio, with Richard Astbury acting as the latter's producer.

'As a producer, you have to make sure that the presenter has enough information to talk,' explains Astbury, 'in case something goes wrong, or gets delayed. All the preparation was done in exactly the same way each year. We would take a hotel three or four days before the contest. We would go to all the rehearsals, we would make notes, and then we would sit at a little portable upright typewriter, typing index cards for each act. We would also have separate cards for the history of the contest, the host city, and little bit about the preparations for the contest. These were cards that our commentator could draw on whenever he wanted to speak a little bit longer, or edit down as required, and they were in list form. We would attend the rehearsals, the commentators' briefing, and the really important one, the dress rehearsal, after which there is no going back. You ran the dress rehearsal on the afternoon as if it was for real. Then you went back to the hotel, did what you had to, and try to stay calm.

'It was, at the time, very nerve-wracking in many ways, particularly for us, as we didn't do this sort of thing every day; it was a one off for us, and it was something very, very special to do. What we told the forces to do in Germany, and elsewhere, was to turn the television on, turn the sound down, and listen to us on the radio, although our commentary was very much for a radio audience. I never knew how many people listened, but it was very important to John Russell that BFBS was seen and heard by other broadcasting organisations. He wanted us to have this international approach, and that's really how it all started. I believe.

'We were treated with a lot of respect from the other broadcasters, and a lot of the radio stations in Germany knew who we were … because we had pinched a lot of their listeners. In 1975, Polydor records – Deutsche Grammophon in Germany – did a survery as to how many people listened to BFBS. Now, in those days there must have been, I suppose, with families and servicemen, around 180,000 forces personnel based in Germany. Deutsche Grammophon came back with the results of their research, which revealed that every day between five and eight million Germans were listening to us.'

SONGS FOR EUROPE VOLUME TWO

United Kingdom	'Save Your Kisses For Me' (2'55")	Sung by Brotherhood of Man (Lee Sheriden, Martin Lee, Nicky Stevens and Sandra Stevens).	Composed by Tony Hiller, Lee Sheriden and Martin Lee.	Conducted by Alyn Ainsworth.

'There were a lot of functions you got invited to,' says singer Nicky Stevens, 'receptions and the like, and of course there were loads of photographers there. We were very good; we didn't go to too many, and we wanted to be rested, and to make sure that when we went on stage we were watertight and did the best we could do. I remember thinking, with the choreography at the start, "We've all got our backs to the audience and Martin has to turn round first to sing that first line. Thank god I haven't got the lead on this!"'

'It did worry us being first on stage,' states Martin Lee. 'With 18 songs on, how were the juries going to remember us? We had to make an enormous impression so that we stood out from the others, and obviously we did. The whole orchestra had been saying that we were the winners, and just about everybody we met said we were going to win, which just added to the pressure. We knew we were in with a very good shot, because there weren't that many great songs in it, but there were the odd one or two, and you just never know on the night.'

'I was relieved when we came off stage,' adds Sandra Stevens, 'but I was really proud of everybody that we had done it. I was worried about Martin. He was shattered, as he had been up all night. He was anxious and saying "What happens if we don't win?" We were number one in the UK, everybody had put us there and everybody wanted us to win. I told him not to worry about it, because we were going to win!'

'At rehearsals I was watching the performance of every song,' says composer Tony Hiller, 'and looking at the strengths of them, the clothes, the movement and the attitude of the artists as well; and to me, honestly, we had the winner. Most songs you hear in that situation you hear three or four times, and they all become commercial, so anyone could do it. The thing for me that did it was the dance – it was different. The lyric I knew was great, although whether it was too clever for a European audience, with the '… only three' line, I wasn't so sure. But after several plays I felt it would work, and it did!'

Nicky Stevens is at pains to point out that the group are not being big-headed when they say they knew they had the winner: 'We watched the other songs and tried to be totally non-biased, and we all agreed that with the exception of France and Austria, the rest weren't as good as ours. But there was something inside me that said we were going to win.'

How had Hiller felt during the voting? 'I was dying every minute. It was an amazing situation, and from about the last three countries, I knew we were going to win it. Unless we got a run of zeros, we were home and dry.'

Unlike in the UK event, Nicky Stevens was able to watch the voting this time. 'It was different this time … I had moved onto alcohol,' she jokes. 'I must have drunk a load of brandy, trying to stop this adrenalin rush. It was like drinking water, and the feeling of winning that night, nothing will ever compare to it.'

Prior to the show, Roderick Gilchrist of the *Daily Mail* gave his verdict on the UK's entry: 'Straight out of the *Eurovision* formula factory, bright, jolly, with a repetitive catchline that stays in your head like a nursery rhyme. Also meets the winning ingredients of the past two years. It's topped the charts in Britain and has already sold a million records throughout Europe. Can it lose? Most of the other competitors think not. One problem, they're drawn first, which isn't good.'

The *Daily Mirror* wrote: 'It must win, otherwise there's no justice.'

However, Brian Wesley, writing in the *Sun*, said: 'Typical inoffensive Euro-fodder. Will our bridesmaid finally be the bride? I doubt it. Rating 7/10.'

SONGS FOR EUROPE VOLUME TWO

Apart from being number one in the UK, the song topped the charts in Belgium, France, Ireland, the Netherlands and Norway, and was a top ten hit in Austria, Germany, New Zealand, South Africa, Sweden and Switzerland. It also charted in Italy, and reached number 27 in the USA on the Billboard Top 100. It was the biggest-selling single in the UK in 1976 and, with total sales in excess of five million copies, is one of the biggest-selling *Eurovision* entries ever.

The Brotherhood of Man went onto have further chart success with songs including 'My Sweet Rosalie', 'Oh Boy', 'Beautiful Lover', 'Angelo' and 'Figaro', with the last two reaching number one. Apart from a few years between 1982 and 1984 when Barry Upton replaced Lee Sheriden in the line-up while Sheriden was studying for a music degree, the group have remained together. They still perform regularly on the cabaret circuit and on television shows.

Switzerland	*'Djambo, Djambo'* (2'45")	Sung by Peter, Sue and Marc.	Composed by Peter Reber.	Conducted by Mario Robbiani.

The entry was sung in English. Peter, Sue and Marc had represented Switzerland in the 1971 contest with '*Les Illusions De Nos Vingt Ans*', which had finished in twelfth place.

Germany	'Sing, Sang, Song' (2'57")	Sung by Les Humphries Singers.	Words by Kurt Hertha. Music by Ralph Siegel.	Conducted by Les Humphries.

Les Humphries was born John Lesley Humphries in August 1940 in Croydon. The group was formed in Hamburg in 1969 and usually performed a mixture of pop and gospel covers. There were normally some 20 plus

1976 EUROVISION SONG CONTEST

singers in the group, but only six of them could perform on stage at the contest under the rules. Les Humphries died in December 2007.

'Sing, Sang, Song' wasn't in fact the winner in the German national Final. It had been been runner-up to 'Der Star', sung by Tony Marshall and composed by Detlef Petersen, but that song had been disqualified when it was discovered it had been previously performed in public.

Israel	'Emor Shalom' (2'42")	Sung by Chocolate Menta Mastik.	Words by Ehud Manor. Music by Matti Caspi.	Conducted by Matti Caspi.
Luxembourg	'Chansons Pour Ceux Qui S'Aiment' (2'56")	Sung by Jürgen Marcus.	Words by Vline Buggy and Fred Jay. Music by Jack White.	Conducted by Jo Plée.
Belgium	'Judy Et Cie' (2'50")	Sung by Pierre Rapsat.	Words by Eric van Hulse. Music by Pierre Rapsat.	Conducted by Michel Bernholc.
Ireland	'When' (3'00")	Sung by Red Hurley.	Composed by Brendan Graham.	Conducted by Noel Kelehan.

SONGS FOR EUROPE VOLUME TWO

| Netherlands | 'The Party's Over' (3'00") | Sung by Sandra Reemer. | Composed by Hans van Hemert. | Conducted by Harry van Hoof. |

Sandra Reemer had sung as part of the duo Sandra and Andres at the 1972 contest, when their entry *'Als Het Om De Liefde Gaat'* had come fourth for the Netherlands.

| Norway | 'Mata Hari' (2'55") | Sung by Anne-Karine Strom. | Words by Philip Kruse. Music by Frode Thingnæs. | Conducted by Frode Thingnæs. |

Anne-Karine Strom had sung 'The First Day Of Love' for Norway in 1974, and had also represented her country in 1973 as part of the Bendik Singers.

| Greece | *'Panaghia Mou, Panaghia Mou'* (3'00") | Sung by Mariza Koch (with Dimitris Zouboulis). | Words by Michael Fotiades. Music by Mariza Koch. | Conducted by Michalis Rouzakis. |

1976 EUROVISION SONG CONTEST

| Finland | 'Pump-Pump' (2'52") | Sung by Fredi and Friends. | Words by Vexi Salmi and Pertti Reponen. Music by Matti Siitonen (Fredi). | Conducted by Ossi Runne. |

Fredi had represented Finland in the 1967 contest, finishing twelfth with *'Varjoon-Suojaan'*.

| Spain | *'Sobran Las Palabras'* (2'53") | Sung by Braulio. | Composed by Braulio Bautista. | Conducted by Juan Barcons. |

| Italy | 'We'll Live It All Again'/ *'Noi Lo Rivivremo Di Nuovo'* (3'00") | Sung by Al Bano and Romina Power. | Words by Albano Carrisa and Romina Power. Music by Detto Mariano. | Conducted by Maurizio Fabrizio. |

| Austria | 'My Little World' (2'41") | Sung by Waterloo and Robinson. | Composed by Gerhard Heinz. | Conducted by Erich Kleinschuster. |

SONGS FOR EUROPE VOLUME TWO

Portugal	'Um Flora De Verde Pinho' (2'50")	Sung by Carlos do Carmo.	Words by Manuel Alegre. Music by José Niza.	Conducted by Thilo Krassman.

Monaco	'Toi La Musique Et Moi' (2'25")	Sung by Mary Cristy.	Words by Gilbert Sinoué and Andre Barse. Music by Georges Costa.	Conducted by Raymond Donnez.

France	'Un, Deux, Trois' (2'18")	Sung by Catherine Ferry.	Words by Jean-Paul Cara. Music by Jean-Paul Cara and Tony Rallo.	Conducted by Tony Rallo.

British composer Jack Fishman provided the lyrics for the English version, 'One, Two, Three'.

Yugoslavia	'Ne Mogu Skriti Svoju Bol' (2'41")	Sung by Ambassadori.	Words by Slobodan Durasović. Music by Slobodan Vujović.	Conducted by Esad Arnautalić.

1976 EUROVISION SONG CONTEST

THE VOTING

The voting system introduced in 1975 was used again. On the British jury were Miss G Barrett, Mrs M Andrew, Mr D Hornsby, Mr M Robinson, Miss M J Abraham, Mr C Young, Mr F Martin, Mr K Sammons, Mrs F Owel, Miss M Kynnersley and Miss P Green. Ray Moore was the United Kingdom spokesperson.

'It was very well run in The Hague,' recalls Lydia Vine. 'It was the first one I'd been to abroad, and I was quite impressed by them. I think it was BBC Governor George Howard who, during rehearsals, saw this enormous scoreboard with all the names of the countries, and said, "That's got to change," because although they were all in Dutch, it clearly said "Gr. Brittannie". He said, "We can't have that, it must say 'United Kingdom' in Dutch ['Verenigd Koninkrijk'], otherwise it will alienate Northern Ireland." There was a lot of fuss over that issue. The Dutch argued that they just couldn't fit that all in, but to him it was a big deal. We hadn't even noticed it.' The Dutch won the day and it remained as 'Gr. Brittannie'. It was the last time that the scoreboard would be shown in a language other than English or French.

SONGS FOR EUROPE VOLUME TWO

	UK	Switzerland	Germany	Israel	Luxembourg	Belgium	Ireland	Netherlands	Norway	Greece	Finland	Spain	Italy	Austria	Portugal	Monaco	France	Yugoslavia	TOTAL	POSITION
United Kingdom		12	8	12	8	12	3	10	12	12	10	12	4	10	12	10	7	10	164	1ST
Switzerland	12		5	4	1	7	1	6	10	2	7	4		8	7	4	6	7	91	4TH
Germany		2			2	1					2					2	3		12	15TH
Israel	6	7	3		7	5	4	2	7		8	1	10	6	2	1		8	77	6TH
Luxembourg						6	6	5											17	14TH
Belgium	7	6		1				4	6		12		8	3	8	8	5		68	8TH
Ireland	10		1	3	3				8		5	12	2		6	3	1		54	10TH
Netherlands		4	4	8	4	4	2		1	7		3	2	4	6	2		5	56	9TH
Norway							3							4					07	18TH
Greece						2					4		5		1		8		20	13TH
Finland	2		6	6			5	1	4			6		7		7			44	11TH
Spain	3									1			3			3	1		11	16TH

1976 EUROVISION SONG CONTEST

Country																			Total	Place
Italy	1	8		2			12		3	10	6		▨	1	10		10	6	69	7TH
Austria	4	3	10	10	5	3	10	7	2	6	5	8		▨		5		2	80	5TH
Portugal					6				4	1		1		▨			12		24	12TH
Monaco	5	5	7	7	12	8	8	8	5		2	7	7	5	3	▨		4	93	3RD
France	8	10	12	5	10	10	7	12	8	5	3	10	6	12	5	12	▨	12	147	2ND
Yugoslavia		1	2								3					4	▨		10	17TH

*On the night, the French jury omitted to announce that their four points had gone to Yugoslavia. However, this was revealed after the contest, and so has been included here.

Analysis: Apart from the opening round of voting, when Switzerland received the top mark from the United Kingdom jury, there were only two countries in real contention for the Grand Prix. From the very early stages it quickly became a contest between France and the United Kingdom. France took a good early lead, helped by the fact that they hadn't yet voted, while Monaco and Austria also scored well to keep them in outside contention throughout the first half of the voting. The turning point came just after the half-way mark, with both Greece and Finland awarding high marks to the United Kingdom and low marks to France, putting the United Kingdom into a clear lead. With France still to vote, the tide turned in favour of the United Kingdom.

There were a couple of low scores awarded to the United Kingdom by Ireland and Italy, but France couldn't capitalise on this, as they received only a handful more points rather than the high scores they needed from these juries. France was the only other country not to place the United Kingdom amongst the top three songs. Their jury awarded top marks to Portugal – making up half the entire total that Portugal received. With 164 points, the Brotherhood of Man ended up taking a whopping 80.4% of the maximum possible – an achievement that at the time of writing has still not been beaten under the present scoring system – and it gave the United Kingdom their third victory in the contest.

The Brotherhood of Man and Tony Hiller were presented with their awards by Getty Kaspers, lead singer of the 1975 winning group Teach-In.

The winning reprise was memorable for Hiller conducting from the side of the stage. 'It was just spontaneous,' says Hiller. 'Normally I realised that camera shots were important, but I was just on such a high, they couldn't pull me down for days. It was a tremendous feeling.'

WINNING REPRISE

| United Kingdom | 'Save Your Kisses For Me' (2'55") | Sung by Brotherhood of Man. | Composed by Tony Hiller, Lee Sheriden and Martin Lee. | Conducted by Alyn Ainsworth. |

1976 EUROVISION SONG CONTEST

CREDITS
Producer: Fred Oster
Director: Theo Ordeman
Designer: Roland de Groot
Music Director: Jan Stulen
EBU Scrutineer: Clifford Brown

The contest was watched by an audience of 43.60% of the British population (22.02 million) from the start of the programme at 21.00 rising to 49.70% (25.09 million) from 22.00 and scored an RI of 61. The BBC has retained a copy of its broadcast version in its archives. The Brotherhood of Man's winning performance of 'Save Your Kisses for Me' was given an unscheduled repeat broadcast on BBC1 just before the close-down on Saturday night/Sunday morning at 00.32.44.

1977 UNITED KINGDOM

After the success of 1976, it was inevitable that the BBC would retain the same format for selection of its entry in 1977. 332 songs were submitted for the competition; amongst them was 'The Night The Circus Came To Town' composed by the 1976 winners, Tony Hiller, Lee Sheriden and Martin Lee.

The final selection was decided by a panel consisting of Bill Cotton, Derek Chinnery (Head of Radio 1), Jeff Owen (Head of Radio 2), Stewart Morris (producer of *A Song for Europe*), Robin Nash (producer of *Top of the Pops*), plus two representatives from the MPA and two from the Songwriters' Guild. The running order of the final 12 songs was determined by the drawing of lots.

All the orchestrations for the finalists had to be submitted by Monday 28 February, and none of the songs could be publicly performed before 10 March. The BBC also required three copies of the recorded version of each song, and if instrumental backing tapes were to be used, a BBC representative had to be present at the recording session. Artists had to provide their own backing vocalists if required.

There was a change of venue, to the New London Theatre in London. This was also the year that Terry Wogan made his debut as the presenter of *A Song for Europe*. He had been involved with the contest before, having been the radio commentator for the *Eurovision Song Contest* in 1971 and 1974 to 1976 and the BBC1 television commentator in 1973.

The New London Theatre had opened in 1973 and seated around 900 people on two levels. From 1976 it had hosted a number of television events, including the *Masters Snooker* competition.

Rehearsals commenced on Monday 7 March at 14.00 with the orchestra setting up. The first performer on stage in costume was Mary Mason at 14.30 to have a band call and camera rehearsal. Each act had a 45-minute slot allotted for their rehearsal. The Foundations came next at 15.15. Following a 30-minute tea break at 16.00,

1977 UNITED KINGDOM

Tony Monopoly and Lyn Paul were the next two acts on.

After a dinner break at 18.00, High Society rehearsed at 19.15 and Carl Wayne at 20.00. The final act to rehearse on the Monday was the duo of Lynsey de Paul and Mike Moran, finishing at 21.30.

Tuesday 8 March started at 10.00 with the orchestra set up. Sweet Sensation commenced their rehearsal at 10.30. Val Stokes and Beano concluded the morning rehearsals, the latter finishing at 12.45, when there was a break for a lunch.

A photo call was the held during the lunch break for all the artists at 13.00 in the foyer of the New London Theatre. The final two acts to rehearse were Wesley, Park and Smith at 14.00 and Rags at 14.45.

After a short break, from 16.00 until 18.30, there was a rehearsal for the voting sequence and for the scoreboard operators. A dinner break took place after this. Then there was a run-through of the whole show from 19.45 until around 21.00.

On Wednesday 9 March, camera rehearsals, along with the orchestra as required, took place from 10.00 until the lunch break at 13.00.

From 14.00 there was a full dress rehearsal of the show until 17.30, with the regional lines being rehearsed from 16.30. There then followed a dinner break for an hour, before the line-up of cameras, which was scheduled between 18.30 and 19.30.

The programme was due to be broadcast live at 19.30 on 9 March on BBC1, however it was hit by industrial action by cameramen, as part of a pay dispute over their demand for an extra £3.00 per week, and the television broadcast couldn't go ahead.

Production assistant Lydia Vine recalls: 'There was a horrible feeling with the cameramen that industrial action was going to happen. We knew there was a chance they were going to pull the plug. I think everyone was hoping that it wouldn't happen – including the cameramen themselves, who had no power over the decision. They had worked hard, and it was the last thing they wanted to do, to walk out. I don't remember there being a lot of talk about the idea that if it happened we would do it on radio. That all seemed to happen at the last minute. Having rehearsed it visually for several days, including the Lynsey de Paul and Mike Moran song, which had been very difficult to shoot, to suddenly have nothing much to do on the night was strange. I think we had one picture in the gallery so that we could watch the show, but for the floor crew, sound and lighting, and everyone else, they had to do it exactly as it had been rehearsed – though they didn't need to worry about getting the performers in shot! So it made it a very strange experience, from the high tension, to a terrible feeling of deflation for everybody.'

Arrangements were made for the show to be broadcast in sound only on Radio 2's 1500m longwave service. This went out by deferred transmission at 21.02. Radio 1 and Radio 2's VHF service broadcast the scheduled programme of *Command Performance* presented by Ian Wallace.

Because the show wasn't broadcast on television, there is less information retained regarding it, in particular details of backing vocalists.

A SONG FOR EUROPE 1977
Wednesday 9 March at 21.02 (Duration 79'14")
Presented by Terry Wogan

The programme opened with '*Te Deum*', with the orchestra conducted by Ronnie Hazlehurst, followed by a fanfare to introduce Terry Wogan.

| Song One | 'What Do You Say To Love?' (2'56") | Sung by Mary Mason. | Composed by Nick Ryan and Robin Slater. | Backing Vocals: (3). Plus Orchestra. |

1977 UNITED KINGDOM

Mary Mason was from Cambridge and had started singing from the age of 13. She was a former Royal Ballet dancer, and turned professional when she was 18. She had taken three weeks off from her cabaret show to learn the dance routine for the contest, and her outfit had been designed by Yuki at a cost of some £2,000. This was her only appearance in the contest. She later expressed her disappointment at the show's intended television broadcast having been blacked out, as she had been relying on visual impact. 'Lots of people were running around the theatre in tears,' she recalled. Later on in 1977 she had some success with the song 'Angel Of The Morning', reaching number 27 in the charts.

Nick Ryan was a semi-professional composer who usually worked in an advertising agency. He was also a choirmaster and played bass for a local band in Leigh-on-Sea, where he met Robin Slater. Slater was also semi-professional, and worked as an estate agent and chartered surveyor when not songwriting.

| Song Two | 'Where Were You When I Needed Your Love?' (2'50") | Sung by the Foundations (Clem Curtis, Georges DeLanbanque, Valentine Pascal, Leroy Carter and John Savile). | Composed by John MacLeod and David Myers. | Plus Orchestra. |

The Foundations were a British soul group, predominantly known for two big hits, 'Baby, Now That I've Found You', a number one song in 1967, and 'Build Me Up Buttercup', which reached number two the following year. The group had undergone numerous changes of line-up, and lead singer Clem Curtis had had a period working in the USA, but on his return had reformed the group.

'It was John MacLeod and our manager who came up with the idea that we should try to do the *Eurovision*,' recalls Curtis. 'So they came up with "Where Were You When I Needed Your Love?", and we went through the whole process, which was something new for us. The thought of representing our country was great fun, and we wanted people to know that we were still around. We did this song, which we thought was very good, and thought we had as good a chance as anyone else. At that time the studios we were working in, and the musicians we were playing with, had us about 10/1 on to win … and then just five minutes before the show was due to go out live on television, the cameramen went on strike! So, as it was on the radio, people couldn't see the way we were dressed and no-one saw the act. If I remember rightly we had lots of sequins, blue suits, everybody looked really good.

'I think everybody thought it had affected their chances. I think Lynsey de Paul was one of the front-runners who said we shouldn't actually go on, because everybody had spent so much money to get all the artists to look right for the show. I think Bill Cotton was a little bit put off by everybody suggesting that … but he gave us an appearance on the children's show *Crackerjack* in response to it. I don't think it was because Lynsey de Paul and I were better known, but it was such a shock, as everything had being going perfectly fine, rehearsals were good, and then we had this bombshell with five minutes to go. It was such a disappointment.

'We had hoped the song might become a hit, but it didn't win, and no-one was pushing it as hard as if it had won … Had it gone anywhere it would have been great. But the fact is that it was Lynsey de Paul and Mike Moran who had won, and they got the exposure; there is little in it for the runners-up. I never tried to enter the contest again; it was a definite one off.'

Shortly afterwards the group went off to Australia to tour. Curtis still tours today as Clem Curtis and the Foundations.

John MacLeod was the only grandfather amongst all the composers in the 1977 competition; his successes included 'Let The Heartaches Begin' by Long John Baldry and 'Baby, Now That I've Found You' by the Foundations. He had written a number of songs with Tony Macauley, who also had an entry in the contest.

David Myers was one of the composers behind the 1971 entry 'Jack In The Box'.

1977 UNITED KINGDOM

| Song Three | 'Leave A Little Love' (2'50") | Sung by Tony Monopoly. | Composed by Alan Hawkshaw and Ray Cameron. | Backing Vocals: (5). Plus Orchestra. |

'I thought Tony Monopoly might be right for "Leave A Little Love",' said composer Alan Hawkshaw. 'I'd met him on a recording session for one of his albums.'

Monopoly's full name was Antonio Rosario Monopoli, and he was originally from Adelaide in Australia. As a teenager he spent five years in a Carmelite monastery. When he left, he went into showbusiness, and soon became a big star in his native country. In 1975 he came to the UK, appeared on the talent show *Opportunity Knocks* and won six successive editions, which helped to establish him as a singer in this country. This was his only appearance in *A Song for Europe*, and later his career went through some highs and lows. From performing in cruise ships and night clubs in Majorca, he was headhunted for a lead role in the West End production of *Moby Dick*, though the show closed after only a few months. He then went on to have the role of Old Deuteronomy in a national tour of *Cats*. Tony Monopoly died in March 1995.

This was the final *A Song for Europe* entry that had the names of Hawkshaw and Cameron as composers. Their first had been in 1969 in the form of 'Are You Ready For Love' for Lulu, and they had followed this up with songs for Mary Hopkin and Clodagh Rodgers in their respective years. Hawkshaw had also had a co-composed entry in 1973 with 'Days Of Love'.

'Don Black turned to me during the voting,' recalls Hawkshaw, 'and said "Isn't this exciting, we're neck and neck ..." Unfortunately we were both lying about ninth at the time!'

Hawkshaw has composed songs for Barbra Streisand, Tom Jones and Olivia Newton-John. Amongst his television themes are *Grange Hill* and the famous *Countdown* clock music. He received an Ivor Novello award for his score for the film *The Silent Witness*, and has been nominated for a BAFTA award. He also set up a

SONGS FOR EUROPE VOLUME TWO

foundation that supports talented but underprivileged music students in Britain.

Ray Cameron passed away some years ago. His son is the comedian Michael McIntyre.

| Song Four | 'If Everybody Loved The Same As You' (2'44") | Sung by Lyn Paul. | Composed by Geoff Stephens and Don Black. | Backing Vocals: (5). Plus Orchestra. |

Lyn Paul (aka Lynda Susan Belcher) was the only performer who had sung for the United Kingdom before in the *Eurovision Song Contest*; she had been lead vocalist for the New Seekers on 'Beg, Steal Or Borrow' in 1972. In 1973 she had also performed at a US Presidential Inauguration for Richard Nixon. In 1974 she had left the New Seekers to pursue a solo career, and the following year had a top 40 hit with 'It Ought To Sell A Million'. This was her last association with the contest, and she went on to further success, including as Mrs Johnstone in the popular musical *Blood Brothers*; a role for which she received much critical acclaim, and which she has reprised several times.

Both composers had had entries before in the contest. Don Black had been one of the composers of 'Come September' in 1969, while Geoff Stephens had won in 1970 with 'Knock, Knock (Who's There?)' and had the third-placed song in 1976 with 'Queen Of The Mardi Gras'.

| Song Five | 'Just For You' (2'44") | Sung by High Society (Garry Travers, Joy Yates, Jacquie Sullivan and Alex Keenan). | Composed by Ron Roker, Gerry Shury and Biddu. | Backing Vocals: (2). Plus Orchestra. |

1977 UNITED KINGDOM

High Society were an international group. Garry Travers from Sydney, Australia was a graduate of Law. Joy Yates, a New Zealander from Auckland, had been working with Pacific Drum, a jazz and rock band, and had been one of the in-vision backing singers for Polly Brown in the 1976 event. Jacquie Sullivan, from Los Angeles in the USA, had studied classical piano. Alex Keenan, from Dundee in Scotland, had got into pop music after playing euphonium in the Salvation Army. He had been one of the unseen backing singers for Joey Valentine the previous year, and was married to singer Eleanor Keenan. On the demo version of the song, session singer Chas Mills was one of the vocalists.

Ron Roker and Gerry Shury had been two of the composers behind 'Do You Believe In Love At First Sight' in the 1976 contest. The pair had also produced the record version of Lyn Paul's entry, 'If Everybody Loved The Same As You'; and by coincidence that song and their own finished equal in the contest.

Biddu was born in Bangalore and started his career in the '60s as a singer, both as a soloist and as a group member. He decided to widen his horizons and move to London, and started to concentrate on writing and producing. Biddu then met Shury, and one of his first tasks was to provide the soundtrack to the film *Embassy*. This indirectly brought him into contact with vocalist Carl Douglas, whom he decided to use to record a song called 'I Want To Give You My Everything'. While in the studio they came up with the B-side for the single, a track called 'Kung Fu Fighting', which they allegedly recorded within the space of ten minutes. The record company then decided to make the latter track the A-side, against the judgment of Biddu, and the end result was a number one single in August 1974, and a subsequent US number one hit as well. The era of disco music was just beginning, and the influence of Shury, plus the combination of orchestral pop with a latin flavour, led to the creation of the Biddu Orchestra. This resulted in the single 'Summer Of 42', which reached number 14 in the charts in 1975. A follow-up album, *Rainforest*, then produced a top 40 hit with the same title. Biddu received four Ivor Novello awards, including one for 'Rainforest' as best instrumental. Other artists he worked with included Tina Charles and the Real Thing.

For Shury and Biddu, this was the last time either would feature in *A Song for Europe*. Shury was unfortunately

SONGS FOR EUROPE VOLUME TWO

killed in a car accident in 1978. Biddu continued in the music business, producing further albums under the Biddu Orchestra name, before moving into the Bollywood market. He was influential in starting Indi-pop and Hindi dance music, and was much in demand in the last two decades of the 20th Century.

| Song Six | 'A Little Give, A Little Take' (2'45") | Sung by Carl Wayne. | Composed by Roger Greenaway and Tony Macauley. | Backing Vocals: (5). Plus Orchestra. |

Carl Wayne was born in Birmingham in 1943. At 18 he decided on a career in pop music, and one of his first groups was Carl Wayne and the Vikings. In 1966 he teamed up with Roy Wood and formed the Move, with Wayne on vocals and Wood as lead guitarist. The group were renowned for their outrageous stunts and theatrical stage dress. Like the Who, they were infamous for smashing up stage equipment, and even setting light to the stage. For a while the group were banned from every venue in the country. To promote their single 'Flowers In The Rain', they produced a postcard showing Prime Minister Harold Wilson naked in a bathtub with his secretary. Wilson successfully sued for libel, and all royalties from that song ever since have been paid to charity. The group eventually split up and Wayne pursued a solo career while also turning to acting. He sang the theme tune 'You're A Star' for the talent show *New Faces* and appeared in the ITV soap opera *Crossroads*. His wife was actress Susan Hanson, who had played Diane Parker in the latter series.

'A Little Give, A Little Take' was Wayne's only venture into *A Song for Europe*. Subsequently he continued to record, turning out further solo albums and cast recordings for several Andrew Lloyd Webber musicals. He also got the opportunity to represent his country at the *Golden Orpheus Song Festival* in Bulgaria, winning first prize. He sang countless commercial jingles, and was happy to take jobs no matter how big or small. He joined a revised line up of the Hollies and had successful tours with them, before he succumbed to ill health and died in August 2004.

1977 UNITED KINGDOM

'I used Carl Wayne because he was a friend and had sung the theme of *New Faces* for me, and had sung on a lot of demos for me,' reflects composer Tony Macauley, on his final contribution to the contest. 'That song I loved. I thought it was a terrific song, as it wasn't in the typical *Eurovision* style. (In fact I had forgotten I had done so many!) It had a good, rocky rhythm, and everybody said that we were going to win and be the British entry. People like Mickie Most were saying, "Well, you've got it, obviously." But at the eleventh hour there was a strike by the cameramen, so it was just broadcast on radio. I think on the radio "Rock Bottom" just sounded like a total breath of fresh air, whereas had the show been seen live, I think Carl Wayne would have made more of an impact. I think that is the only time where I feel we should have won it. I think that pretty much finished it for Roger and me.'

Macauley went to live in the USA the following year and enjoyed success with Gladys Knight, Glen Campbell and Fifth Dimension, many songs being hits in America that didn't even get released in Britain.

Roger Greenway went on to write the Crystal Gale song 'It's Like We Never Said Goodbye'. In 1983 he became Chairman of the Performing Rights Society, and in 1995 he took charge of the European office for the American Society of Composers, Authors and Publishers.

| Song Seven | 'Rock Bottom' (2'45") | Sung by Lynsey de Paul and Mike Moran. | Composed by Lynsey de Paul and Mike Moran. | Backing Vocals: (4). Plus Orchestra. |

Lynsey de Paul was born in June 1950, her full name being Lynsey Monckton Rubin. She was noted for her keyboard skills, and had her first songwriting success in 1972 with 'Storm In A Teacup', co-composed with Ron Roker, which reached number seven in the charts for the Fortunes. Later that year she was the performer of her own number five hit, 'Sugar Me', and followed this up with the Ivor Novello Award-winning song 'Won't Somebody Dance With Me'. The theme tune to the TV series *No Honestly* won her the same award in 1974, a year in which she also wrote an English lyric for the withdrawn French *Eurovision Song Contest* entry, 'That Old Familiar Feeling'. In addition she wrote the English version of the 1975 French entry as 'Live For Love'.

With all these achievements already, what was her motivation for entering *A Song for Europe*? 'It was more a necessity than a real motivation,' says de Paul. 'Yes, I'd had success, but I had the most awful manager in Don Arden – father of Sharon Osbourne – and he and I had fallen out. He had wanted me to sign a contract for longer than the three years that I was already committed to, because he had sold my services on to third parties for longer than that. I had refused to sign an extension with him, because he owed me at the time around £47,000 – that was what I knew about, not counting what I didn't know about – and in those days that would probably have bought you more than one house in London … So we got into litigation.

'I had a special on London Weekend Television, and one of the musicians in my special was Mike Moran. He told me he was in the group Blue Mink, who were looking for a song with a message, and asked if I'd write it with him. He came over, and I had three pianos in one room, and we started writing "Rock Bottom", not for *Eurovision* but for Blue Mink. At the time, he was published by Chappell Music. We did a demo of the song, and unknown to us, they entered it into *A Song for Europe*, and it got through as one of the 12 songs for the Final. I was very proud to have a song of mine possibly representing the country at *Eurovision*. At no time had I thought of singing it myself, but what happened was that any time a record company approached me for a recording deal, Don Arden would sue them, so they would back off. He didn't have any right to sue them, but of course they didn't know that, and it would have taken two years to get into court to prove my case.'

Polydor records did however approach de Paul. 'They said, "If you sing the song 'Rock Bottom', which we know has got through as one of the 12, we will give you a recording contract," and in that contract there were 30 pages written, just about the law suit. They knew about it, they indemnified me, and they got sued by Don Arden, but they didn't care. Eventually the law suit disappeared after a few years, because Don Arden had no grounds at all to sue me, but it did mess up my life for quite a long time. I had to say to Mike, "The only way I can get a recording contract is to sing 'Rock Bottom', and as it's a duet, would you sing it with me?" He was aghast and said "I don't perform like that," but I said "Do it for me." So that is how I came to sing "Rock Bottom". It was fun, and I was proud of my song getting through, but certainly as an established artist I would not normally have put myself up for it, as it had been several years since any established artist had done it.'

Had 'Rock Bottom' been a reflection of the times? 'Yes, it was about the state of the world and the political times, as it was written as a song with a message for Blue Mink. They had those types of songs, like "Melting Pot", so that is why Mike and I wrote it like that. He and I were on different pianos in my music room. What often happens when you start writing is that you just sing rubbish to begin with, so I'd do "Di da da … rah baba" like scat, and Mike said, "I quite like that. How about 'rah baba' becomes 'rock bottom'?" and that's how it evolved. I think the novelty of having two musicians, sat back to back with 22 feet of grand pianos, worked.'

Whose idea had it been that they should perform the song wearing pin-stripe suits and that de Paul should start off holding a newspaper with the headline 'Rock Bottom'? 'It was mine,' explains de Paul. 'That was my side of it. I was trying to get some kind of image that was going to be very British. I had made up the *Financial Daily* (instead of the *Financial Times*) with the "Rock Bottom" headline, and I asked Dougie Hayward, who was one of the most famous tailors around, if he would make our suits, which he did. In addition, we got the assistance of Lionel Blair to sort of choreograph us. I know we were seated, but he came up with the little touches, the slap of the hands, and made it so that we looked out at the audience at the same time. Originally we had two microphones each – one in front, and one to the side nearest the audience – so that we could lean forward or turn and face the audience and sing into another one, but that all got far too complicated for the BBC, so we were left with the one each. After all this preparation, the rehearsals, the outfits, the choreography, just minutes before going on air, the cameramen went on strike. I felt very sorry for the others, because they had all that time and money wasted – from their own outfits and choreography and preparations – and as it was a live programme, they were stuck with the situation. At least Mike and I got through; but I did feel for them.'

SONGS FOR EUROPE VOLUME TWO

De Paul later had a further attempt at *A Song for Europe*, but the song didn't make it through to the Final.

Mike Moran was born in March 1948 in Leeds. He studied at the Royal College of Music before becoming a session musician, composer and arranger. He had been a member of various groups, including Gillan, Stone the Crows and Blue Mink. He was a highly successful keyboard session player, appearing alongside Paul McCartney, Diana Ross and Shirley Bassey.

Song Eight	'You're My Sweet Sensation' (2'47")	Sung by Sweet Sensation (Vincent James, St Clair Palmer, Seaton Daye and Ricky Patrick).	Composed by Melvyn Taggart and Raymond Roberts.	Backing Vocals: (2). Plus Orchestra.

The four members of Sweet Sensation lived in Manchester, though three of them were originally from the West Indies. Apart from music, their main interests were football and cricket. Ricky Patrick was 17 years old and the youngest singer to participate in the contest.

Songwriters Melvyn Taggart and Raymond Roberts had teamed up about 18 months before the contest. Taggart was from Redcar, Yorkshire and was also interested in football, having formed the Music Business Football League. Roberts had studied at the Royal Academy of Music.

Song Nine	'Swings And Roundabouts' (2'47")	Sung by Val Stokes.	Composed by Richard Crowe and Nicholas Portlock.	Backing Vocals: (5). Plus Orchestra.

1977 UNITED KINGDOM

Val Stokes had been a backing vocalist for Polly Brown in the 1976 contest. She was from Wimbledon, was an established session singer, and had recently finished a season at the London Palladium with Charles Aznavour.

Richard Crowe was from Bromsgrove and was a recording studio manager who had begun his career as a bass player in the Piano Stool Bum Rumble Band. Nicholas Portlock was born in Egypt and played a variety of keyboard instruments; he had a BA in Music and Maths.

Song Ten	'Everybody Knows' (2'53")	Sung by Beano (Freddie Phillips, Ken Smith, Ray Johnson and John Birch).	Composed by Freddie Phillips.	Backing Vocals: (2). Plus Orchestra.

Beano was formed in 1968 in Liverpool, where the group members lived. Freddie Phillips was on lead vocals and rhythm guitar, Ken Smith on lead guitar, Ray Johnson on drums and John Birch on bass.

According to Phillips, he composed the song after watching the 1976 *Eurovision Song Contest* on television: 'The four of us sat down and watched the show, and before it ended, I was at the piano composing "Everybody Knows"'. Phillips' other fondly-remembered compositions include many television themes, including those for the children's programmes *Trumpton*, *Camberwick Green* and *Chigley*.

SONGS FOR EUROPE VOLUME TWO

Song Eleven	'After All This Time' (2'59")	Sung by Wesley, Park and Smith (Steve Womack, Lennie Wesley, Christopher Smith-Eusden and Terence Jenkinson).	Composed by David Mindel and Gary Benson.	Backing Vocals: (1). Plus Orchestra.

The four members of this group all came from Yorkshire. Steve Womack's claim to fame was that he was a local Scrabble champion. Lennie Wesley was the only married member of the group, and had been a member of Foggy Duo, a contemporary folk band based in Sheffield. The group had been together for about four years, and had supported acts like Long John Baldry and Jasper Carrott.

'I had been producing Wesley, Park and Smith,' recalls David Mindel. 'They had wonderful voices. I said to Gary [Benson], "They are not an image group but they play and sing really well, and have been an established act on the northern folk circuit." Lennie Wesley was one of those people who could pick up any instrument and play it.'

This was probably one of the few acts that didn't mind the strike. 'I remember Lennie Wesley saying, "If it gets blacked out, we've got more of a chance!"' adds Mindel. 'You had Lynsey, who looked good, and Carl Wayne, a good looking guy. I didn't know Carl at the time, but we subsequently became very good friends, and he did a lot of sessions for me later. So our group not being seen was an advantage as far as we were concerned.'

Song Twelve	'Promises, Promises' (2'54")	Sung by Rags (Jill Shirley, Nichola Martin and Steve Glen).	Composed by Richard Gillinson and David Hayes.	Plus Orchestra.

1977 UNITED KINGDOM

Originally the group Co-Co, runners-up in the 1976 contest, had been considered to perform this song. Terry Bradford of Co-Co explains: 'I know it sounds awfully cocky, and we didn't have any right to be self-righteous about things, but we just didn't think the song would win. We didn't feel we could do the song justice in a live situation. The line-up we had vocally was very strong, but I felt the way the song was arranged, we couldn't give it the power that the demo had, so we turned it down.'

Rags comprised Jill Shirley, who had previously won the *Knokke Song Festival* in 1975, Nichola Martin, who had won *TV Theme of the Year* with the music for *London Bridge*, and guitarist and pianist Steve Glen.

Martin had always wanted to be a singer, and regularly auditioned for jobs advertised in *The Stage*. 'I met Jill Shirley when we were both doing a summer season in Great Yarmouth in 1968. We were backing singers for Des O'Connor, and also sang and danced in the chorus of the show. I met Steve, who was going out with Jill's flatmate, at a party. He was singing and playing guitar and I joined in singing with him. We became friends and then a few years later we decided to form a five-piece vocal group together, called Love Together. When the original girl, Liz Robertson, left the group, Jill took her place. Then the other two guys left and we became three, i.e. Rags.

'We were approached by the two writers, Richard Gillinson and Dave Most [aka Hayes]. We had been banging on the record company doors trying to get a deal, and someone from the industry suggested us to them. I was very keen to do it; I think all of us were. We liked the song and thought it had a good chance of winning.

'I remember thinking the New London Theatre was a better venue than the BBC Theatre, because it was warm and modern. The contest was very strict about the song not running over three minutes, and "Promises, Promises" was running about 3'05". We were told if it ran over the three minutes, even by five seconds, we would be disqualified, so the conductor Ronnie Hazlehurst speeded it up to make sure it would come in under three minutes, and we all thought the tempo was a bit too fast. Also, during rehearsals, the first time we threw our cloaks of rags off, one of the cloaks landed on Ronnie Hazlehurst's head and nearly knocked him over, which was mildly amusing.

'There were rumblings all day that the cameramen might go on strike, but, as we were extremely optimistic, we didn't think they would. I recall that we were told officially that it would not be transmitted on television about two hours before the start time. We still did a full performance for the invited audience. I think only being heard ruined our chances of winning. I strongly believe that Rags would have won had it gone out on television, because of the visual impact. We wore these cloaks of rags and threw them off on our first chorus to reveal us all in white costumes. I did think that Lynsey de Paul would win, it being sound only, because she had the most recognisable and distinctive voice. Listening to 12 unknown songs without visuals makes it very difficult to judge. To be honest I can't remember what score we got. It really doesn't matter, as you either win or you lose. Second through to last place is all meaningless.'

Fellow group member Jill Shirley provides her version of events: 'We had done *Opportunity Knocks*, five of us as Love Together, which we won for three or four weeks in succession. There was a big fuss in the press about voting scandals, as in those days presenter Hughie Green was known for having favourites, and after this fuss we eventually lost. We then did some odd television here and there, and out of the blue we got a call from Dave Most, asking if we would come up for a meeting. He said he had been watching us, and that he had this song that he wanted to put into *A Song for Europe*, but he wanted the three of us, not five. We used to meet at this place in Mayfair called Rags, which is where the name came from, and then over the next few weeks, between Richard Gillinson, Mickie Most and Dave Most, we rehearsed their song. They had all the ideas of the cloaks that came off and, as I remember, these boiler suits that had Union flags, Welsh, Scottish and Irish flags, so it encompassed everyone. They had spent ages getting this design done, had spent a lot of time and money on us.

'There was so much hype around us at the time that we were real favourites in the studio. Everybody who had spoken to us, including those at RAK records leading up to the contest, had said "This is going to win, you all look good, the cloaks are great." So we were hyped up, to say the least, and didn't really pay much attention to the other songs. We sort of thought we were going to win … and then of course we got blacked out.

'All the artists were very disappointed, obviously, and at one point were refusing to do the show, but then

1977 UNITED KINGDOM

Bill Cotton walked into the green room and got all the artists together, and more or less told us that if this show didn't go ahead … well, I won't say his exact words … but the implication was that everyone's career would be over as far as the BBC was concerned, so we had to go ahead.'

The artists may have been disgruntled, but they weren't the only ones, as Shirley fondly recalls: 'My Mum and Dad came up to watch it, as they lived down in Wiltshire. I know that Dad, who was a redhead like me, had this reputation when he was younger of being a real bruiser, and he was very volatile, especially when he played cricket. When he was older he was a lot quieter, but when I came out of that room, sobbing my heart out, he got one of those cameramen who had gone on strike, and got him by the collar, and threatened him, "You have broken my daughter's heart, you should be hung!" Poor old Dad was even more upset than I was!'

After the contest, Rags went on to win the *World Song Festival* with another Gillinson and Dave Most composition, 'Can't Hide My Love'.

'*The World Song Festival* was amazing,' says Martin. 'It was a tremendous buzz to win, and we did a tour of Japan afterwards, and a lot of television appearances. We stayed in Japan for almost four weeks and came back exhausted. It was compensation to a certain extent for not winning *A Song for Europe*, but it is always nicer to have success in one's own country.'

The group also recorded a Japanese version of 'Can't Hide My Love', which Shirley remembers having to sing phonetically. They also appeared on the Noel Edmonds-presented programme *Lucky Numbers*.

THE CONDUCTOR

Ronnie Hazlehurst was born in 1928. He became a bandsman while doing National Service, and soon became a professional musician. After a brief spell working for Granada, he joined the BBC in 1961, and became its musical director in 1964. Since then he had composed, arranged and conducted for countless variety shows, as well as providing themes and incidental music for many television plays and situation comedies, such as *Some*

SONGS FOR EUROPE VOLUME TWO

Mothers Do 'Ave 'Em and *Last of the Summer Wine*. He had also conducted at several Royal Variety performances and for a number of international stars, such as Bob Hope, Jerry Lewis, Sacha Distel, Ethel Merman, Johnny Mathis, Tom Jones and Eartha Kitt, to name but a few. He was also the Musical Director for the 1974 *Eurovision Song Contest* in Brighton.

THE VOTING

The voting system was the same as had been used in 1976, with 12 points going to the top-placed song, 11 points to the second-paced, and so on down to 1 point for the song in twelfth place. There were 14 regional juries in total.

THE SPOKESPERSONS

Belfast	Michael Baguley
Bristol	Chris Denham
Aberdeen	Gerry Davis
Leeds	Brian Baines
Bangor	Emrys Jones
London	Ray Moore
Birmingham	David Shoot
Cardiff	Frank Lincoln
Glasgow	David Findlay
Manchester	Mike Riddoch
Southampton	Paul Harris
Norwich	Ian Masters
Newcastle	Mike Neville
Plymouth	Kevin Crooks

1977 UNITED KINGDOM

	Belfast	Bristol	Aberdeen	Leeds	Bangor	London	Birmingham	Cardiff	Glasgow	Manchester	Southampton	Norwich	Newcastle	Plymouth	TOTAL	POSITION
'What Do You Say To Love'	7	10	10	10	11	9	12	10	9	7	6	12	10	9	132	2ND
'Where Were You When I Needed Your Love?'	10	11	8	4	10	8	7	7	11	11	7	9	12	10	125	3RD
'Leave A Little Love'	1	7	7	1	4	12	1	3	7	6	2	10	3	2	66	9TH
'If Everybody Loved The Same As You'	4	4	5	6	2	5	5	5	8	9	5	7	6	3	74	6TH=
'Just For You'	11	1	3	8	9	6	2	2	6	4	4	1	9	8	74	6TH=
'A Little Give, A Little Take'	5	6	6	7	7	4	4	4	1	1	9	3	1	4	62	10TH
'Rock Bottom'	12	12	12	12	12	11	8	9	12	3	12	5	11	12	143	1ST
'You're My Sweet Sensation'	2	5	4	2	3	10	3	6	2	8	8	6	7	7	73	8TH
'Swings And Roundabouts'	8	2	2	3	5	1	6	1	5	12	1	2	8	1	57	12TH
'Everybody Knows'	3	3	1	5	1	3	11	12	3	2	3	4	4	5	60	11TH
'After All This Time'	6	8	11	11	6	2	10	11	4	10	11	8	2	6	106	5TH
'Promises, Promises'	9	9	9	9	8	7	9	8	10	5	10	11	5	11	120	4TH

SONGS FOR EUROPE VOLUME TWO

Analysis: It started off as pretty much a one horse race, with 'Rock Bottom' receiving straight top marks from the first five juries. After that it received only three more maximum votes from the remaining nine juries, but it never really looked like being caught. The Manchester jury well and truly bucked the trend by awarding it only three points, and giving their top marks to the song that would finish in last place, 'Swings And Roundabouts'. Norwich didn't do much better, rewarding 'Rock Bottom' with only five points. Six songs in total received at least one set of top marks, with London and Cardiff also awarding top marks to songs that finished near the bottom of the scoring. Only 'If Everybody Loved The Same As You' and 'A Little Give, A Little Take' failed to receive a top three mark from any jury. 'Rock Bottom' received 85.12% of the possible maximum score, with 'What Do You Say To Love' achieving a very respectable 78.57% in second place. The Bangor jury placed the top three in the correct order, and Bristol had the top five pretty close, just switching second and third around.

CREDITS
Producer: Stewart Morris
Designer: Bernard Lloyd-Jones
Sound Supervisor: Chris Holcombe
Lighting: Tommy Thomas
Production Assistants: Marcus Plantin, Lydia Spratt
Musical Director: Ronnie Hazlehurst

A photo call took place on stage for the winning artists at around 21.00.
    Although the show wasn't televised, several of the artists appeared with their entries on other BBC television shows. First up, just one day after the contest was blacked out, were winners Lynsey de Paul and Mike Moran with 'Rock Bottom' on *Top of the Pops* broadcast on 10 March. On Saturday 12 March, Tony Monopoly appeared

on *Ronnie Corbett's Saturday Special* with 'Leave A Little Love'. On Friday 18 March, de Paul and Moran were on that week's edition of *Crackerjack*, and one week later the Foundations were on the same show with 'Where Were You When I Needed Your Love?'. For this latter appearance the Foundations had an extra keyboard player in their line-up compared with the contest. The winning duo also appeared on *Top of the Pops* on 31 March and 21 April, plus *The Val Doonican Show* on Saturday 23 April. Rags appeared on the 28 April edition of *Top of the Pops* with 'Promises, Promises'. All the above appearances exist in the BBC archives.

On ITV, de Paul and Moran performed 'Rock Bottom' on the 20 April edition of *Get It Together*, while Rags performed 'Promises, Promises' on the 11 May edition of the same show. The series exists in the ITV archives.

All the entries were released on 7" singles, but only 'Rock Bottom' achieved chart success, reaching number 19 in the UK.

EUROVISION SONG CONTEST PREVIEWS

The previews had to be available by 12 March, to be broadcast from a central point on 18 March, with national broadcast dates between 22 and 29 March.

The BBC once again jumped the gun slightly in broadcasting the first of its two preview programmes. It decided to stick to its scheduled dates for the programmes, leading up to the 2 April date originally intended for the *Eurovision Song Contest*, although the latter was actually postponed (see next chapter).

Presented by Terry Wogan
Recorded on Saturday 19 March

Part One: Sunday 20 March at 15.55.05 (Duration 28'50"). Audience 5.00% (2.53 million). RI 52.
Part Two: Sunday 27 March at 15.59.48 (Duration 30'42"). Audience 6.80% (3.43 million).

SONGS FOR EUROPE VOLUME TWO

The songs were shown in the same order as drawn in the contest except for the United Kingdom's, which once again was left until the end of Part Two. The preview for 'Rock Bottom' was filmed on board a London double decker bus on Thursday 10 March and Friday 11 March.

CREDIT
Television Presentation: Stanley Appel.

1977 EUROVISION SONG CONTEST

Blackpool, Cardiff and Birmingham were all considered as possible venues for the twenty-second edition of the contest, with a likely date of either 26 March or 2 April 1977. In the end it was the newly built Wembley Conference Centre in Wembley, Middlesex, with seating for around 2,700, that was chosen, with the date fixed for 2 April.

By June 1976 countries were being asked for their views on the language rules, which would be discussed by the Programme Committee at a meeting in Toulouse. At this meeting, it was agreed that countries should have to sing in one of their native languages. However, this was the cause of some confusion, as it hadn't been stipulated to be a mandatory requirement. ARD (Germany) and BRT (Belgium) had gone ahead and commissioned English-language songs on the basis that it was only a recommendation. The BBC was considered to blame for the mix-up, so it was agreed that the Chairman of the Programme Committee could waive this rule if it would embarrass certain television stations. As a consequence, RTP (Portugal) and YLE (Finland) decided to reserve the right to reconsider their participation.

In October 1976, JRT (Yugoslavia) confirmed that it wouldn't be entering the 1977 contest. DR (Denmark) also decided not to enter, but announced that it hoped to enter in 1978. Malta was also considering entering in 1977, on the understanding that this wouldn't set a precedent for the 1978 contest.

By November 1976, SR (Sweden) confirmed it would be returning to the contest, and RTT (Tunisia) also planned to make its debut, while RAI (Italy) was late in confirming its participation. It was beginning to look like another full house of 20 countries, but subsequently Malta decided not to enter after all, which left 19 going into the draw. Tunisia was drawn at number four in the running order.

Two broadcasters had a problem with the planned date of 2 April. ARD (Germany) and ORF (Austria) requested a deferred transmission on that date, due to the planned programme *Am Laufenden Band* being scheduled at the same time. It was decided to allow this, which in effect meant disregarding one of the contest rules at the time. Both broadcasters would comply with all the other rules relating to the juries and the voting. There were concerns that this could set a precedent, especially as Israel had previously requested a deferred transmission due to the contest date falling on the Sabbath, and the BBC regarded this as the thin edge of the wedge.

The rules for 1977 stated that there should be no publication of sheet music or release of records prior to 5 March, and that national finals should be completed by 7 March, which was also the date by which the scores and lyrics should be submitted to the EBU. The BBC however was granted special dispensation to stage *A Song for Europe* on 9 March.

Plans were thrown in chaos when (as described in the previous chapter) the BBC cameramen went on strike, blacking out television coverage of *A Song for Europe*. The ongoing industrial action meant that the BBC could no longer guarantee the staging of the *Eurovision Song Contest*. Over the next few weeks, various discussions were held by the BBC, the ABS (Association of Broadcasting and Allied Staff) union and the EBU. Publically the plan was still to go ahead with the 2 April staging, but privately behind the scenes, alternatives were being discussed.

The BBC held its own meeting on Tuesday 15 March to consider various options. One of the first ideas that had been put forward was that NOS (Netherlands), who had hosted the 1976 contest, could step in and take over the 1977 event, having the experience and the infrastructure needed. However, NOS anticipated that with the short notice the event might cost as much as 1 million Swiss Francs (around £220,000) to stage – plus they needed to clear the union position. By 15 March this option was starting to look a non-starter, as the ABS and Dutch unions had been advised that the contest was 'tainted', and the unions had been asked not to support an NOS production. NOS telephoned the BBC during their meeting and confirmed that, due to their worries about the financing and the unions, they would be withdrawing their offer to stage the contest.

Another EBU idea was to have an international link-up, with each country presenting its own entry. However, there were anxieties over the different production values between countries. For example Greece operated only a black and white television service and could therefore be disadvantaged. An extension of this proposal, to group the countries in perhaps three centres across Europe, was also rejected for similar reasons, i.e. that there would be differing production standards, and that it would still require a considerable effort for each of the hosts to handle.

Even cancelling the event altogether was discussed, but there were fears of possible lawsuits from artists over loss of present and future earnings.

Perhaps one relief for the BBC was that it was established that ITV did not intend to offer its services as alternative hosts, despite having made open bids to stage the contest in 1972 and 1974.

It seemed that there was no way the contest could be held on 2 April as originally planned, and although the proposed alternatives weren't attractive, if an EBU meeting in Geneva on Thursday 17 March decided to go ahead with any one of them, then the BBC would be obliged to go along with it.

Postponing the contest to a date not later than mid-May was another possibility. The BBC would still not be in a position to produce it, as they hadn't resolved the issues with the ABS, but with the benefit of this longer notice another broadcaster might be able to do so at less expense. A postponed contest might also avoid the potential legal problems, although there were still concerns that some artists might not be available on a new date.

The BBC was keen to see the contest continue, and made it known that it was willing to host the 1978 contest in any event. It was also keen that the EBU shouldn't issue any statements aligning itself with management against the unions, even though the dispute had international repercussions; it was a domestic affair.

At its 17 March meeting in Geneva, where Terry Hughes rather than contest producer Stewart Morris represented the BBC, the EBU prepared three possible statements. The first was to be issued in the event of the cancellation altogether of the 1977 *Eurovision Song Contest*, announcing that the EBU was keen to see the contest continue and that the BBC had offered to stage the 1978 event on a date to be decided. The second was to be used if another broadcaster could be found to stage the contest on 2 April, but only at the expense of the BBC withdrawing its entry. The third was prepared in the event that another broadcaster could be found to host a postponed contest. In this draft there was no mention of the BBC withdrawing. None of the above statements was actually issued on 17 March, however, and talks continued to try to find a solution.

On Friday 18 March there was another meeting at the BBC of those involved with the contest. These included Stewart Morris, Terry Hughes, designer Ken Sharp, the set contruction team and other technical personnel. By now the BBC was privately looking at the possibility of a remount on 7 May, and various decisions were made or in some cases deferred.

Ron Copas, who was in charge of the set construction, could see no problem with the 7 May date. As work had been halted in light of events, he was more concerned about the possibility that the programme might be reinstated on 2 April if the industrial action was settled. He noted that although something acceptable could still be constructed in time, including a revolving stage element, this would have an adverse impact on other shows. The possibility was raised of using the unseen *A Song for Europe* set, which was being held in storage. However, it was decided that this wouldn't be suitable for the contest, and approval was given for it to be broken up. It was agreed to recommence work on the set, so that something as close as possible to the original design would be ready in time for 2 April.

It was noted that in light of the possible cancellation of the contest, Brent Council had already authorised the staging of an unrelated concert at the Wembley Conference Centre on Sunday 27 March, and it was probably too late for this to be cancelled. Designer Sharp was concerned that it would be difficult to get the set established on location in time for rehearsals, due to start on Tuesday 29 March. Producer Morris offered to ease matters by giving up one day's rehearsals and to start on Wednesday 30 March instead.

The decision was taken to go ahead with the original transmission dates for the two preview programmes. Other matters discussed included the printing of tickets for security purposes, a decision on which point was deferred for the time being, and the fact that hotel bookings would have to be confirmed as soon as possible if the event was to go ahead on 2 April.

Other discussions were mainly technical, concerning the outside broadcast arrangements and the possibility of having to borrow commentators' equipment from overseas. Alan Millar, who was in charge of studio management, was about the only person who was able to confirm that either 2 April or 7 May would present no problems.

'The problem was that the unions just couldn't give us a guarantee,' says production assistant Lydia Vine. 'They wouldn't say they would hit it, or they wouldn't hit it. In the end it was decided to put the event back until the dispute was settled, which if I remember happened quite quickly.'

On 24 March the BBC confirmed that it could not go ahead with the 2 April date, and announced the information publically. The EBU confirmed that they were looking to stage the contest at a later date in another country. But just a few days later the cameramen agreed to take their dispute to a tribunal, and on 31 March it was officially announced that the contest would go ahead on 7 May.

The edition of *Radio Times* for the week beginning 2 April had already gone to print with a colour cover publicising the contest with a picture of the chosen presenter, Angela Rippon. Inside, there was a four-page feature looking at the preparations and technicalities of staging the contest, along with a score chart for the 1977 entrants. (The edition for 7 May would reprint this score chart.) However, the programme pages warned that the programme was subject to confirmation. As it happened, Rippon was still seen on screen on 2 April, as BBC1 scheduled a repeat of the 1976 *Morecambe and Wise Christmas Show*, in which she was a guest star. This was shown at 21.00 in the slot originally planned for the contest, followed by the film *Kojak's Days*.

According to *Radio Times*, the original plan for this year's postcard inserts was for each act to be filmed in their own country, as in 1976. 'That was an idea that I expect got knocked on the head due to money,' says Vine. 'I could envisage Stewart [Morris] liking that sort of thing, and even possibly asking each country to film their own artist and send it in. So I can see that would have been a germ of an idea. But I don't remember going down that route, and it would have taken a lot of organisation.

'What we couldn't get with the remount was everybody in the same hotel next to the Conference Centre, as the rooms just weren't available. We had people having to be bussed in from hotels at Heathrow, which wasn't a lot of fun for them to get to Wembley. They were stuck out there [and this was before the days of the M25 motorway]. The logistical problems were enormous, and were very embarrassing for the BBC. Actually, the Conference Centre was a pretty horrible venue as well, a bit of a barn of a place, and didn't seem to have much atmosphere.'

Rehearsals for the remounted contest started on Tuesday 3 May. The countries rehearsed in their performance order, with the exception of Austria, who were moved back to be the final country to rehearse. The latter was the only major change from the original rehearsal schedule for the abandoned production. Another, more minor change was to have one more rehearsal on the Tuesday and one fewer on the Thursday, enabling an earlier finish on the Thursday for a party planned for that evening. Each country had an hour allocated for its first rehearsal, with Ireland on stage from 14.00 to 15.00. The first day concluded with Luxembourg, whose act came off stage at 22.15.

Wednesday 4 May started with Portugal at 10.00 until 11.00. Then, after a 30-minute break, it was time for Lynsey de Paul and Mike Moran for the United Kingdom to rehearse between 11.30 and 12.30. Rehearsals continued throughout the day, with Spain being the last country on stage, from 18.15 to 19.15.

Thursday 5 May saw all of the remaining countries rehearse, with Italy starting from 10.00 to 11.00 and Austria concluding the proceedings from 15.45 to 16.45. After a 30-minute break there was a commentators' briefing, which was scheduled for an hour.

In the evening, coaches departed from the Wembley Conference Centre to take all the artists and delegations to the Cockney Restaurant for a dinner and party hosted by the BBC, where cameras recorded the inserts that were planned to be used as the postcards.

Stanley Appel was in charge of the postcards. 'I sat with the editor and he cut the material together and we prepared them all. I was probably editing them all day on the Friday, so it was lot of work to do in a short space of time. They were played in at the rehearsals, and then Bill Cotton said "No!"'

Lydia Vine explains: 'There were a number of delegations that had complained to Bill that it wouldn't look good back home for them to be seen to be enjoying themselves to that extent, wining and dining on expenses. I think it came mainly from those countries that were state funded, and probably even applied to us here, with the licence-payers' money. It was thought it wouldn't go down too well, and Bill made the decision to drop it. I expect Stewart would have fought to keep them in, as it was too late to do anything else. We ended up with endless shots of the audience, but it was all we could do on the day, and Stewart was very disappointed.'

On Friday 6 May rehearsals started at 10.00. Each country had just 20 minutes for its second rehearsal, and all countries now rehearsed in the correct order. The United Kingdom was allocated the 14.40 to 15.00 slot. France finished its rehearsal at 18.25, just before a break for dinner. A full dress rehearsal then took place from 20.00 to 22.00, with commentators expected to be present.

On Saturday 7 May there were technical rehearsals with the presenter and the scoreboard from 10.30 until 12.00, followed by a further hour with the jury spokespersons on sound only. After lunch, at 14.00 there was a technical rehearsal and sound balance until 15.30. Then at 16.00 a full dress rehearsal took place, finishing around 18.00, before a dinner break for all involved.

An hour before the start of the event there was a technical rehearsal and line up, prior to the live transmission at 21.00.

The live transmission was taken by all the competing countries, with the exception of Italy, and also by Denmark, Yugoslavia, Turkey, Jordan, Czechoslovakia, Poland, Hungary, Romania, Bulgaria and Russia. Denmark and Turkey sent their own commentators to the Wembley Conference Centre.

Tunisia, Morocco, Algeria, Iceland, Hong Kong and Italy all recorded the programme for later transmission.

Bookmakers had Belgium 4/1 favourite, United Kingdom 9/2, Germany 5/1, Ireland 6/1, Netherlands 12/1, Italy and Monaco 14/1, Israel and France 16/1.

Angela Rippon was born in Plymouth in 1944. After a spell as a presenter for the BBC in Plymouth she became a regular newsreader on BBC TV's *Nine O'Clock News*. One of her most famous appearances came on the aforementioned 1976 Christmas Day edition of *The Morecambe and Wise Show*, which was produced by Ernest Maxin.

'When I was recording the earlier "Singing In The Rain" number with Eric and Ernie,' recalls Maxin, 'during the lunch break in the studio, I came down the iron staircase from the control room, and I saw Angela there, and she was showing round a friend of hers, or maybe it was a family member of hers from Devon, who had wanted to see the *Morecambe and Wise* set. It was the first time I had seen Angela in a short skirt, and I thought she had lovely legs, and that this might create something in *The Morecambe and Wise Show*. I asked her "Do you dance?" and she said "Yes, I went to dancing school in Devon." So I asked her if she'd like to be in *The Morecambe and Wise Show*, and she said "I'd love to, but I don't know what my boss in current affairs would say." I went to see her boss, and he said "Fine, as long as it's in good taste." So that is how we got her into the show and made her an overnight star.'

'I don't think it would have been Stewart [Morris]'s decision to have Angela as our presenter,' says Vine. 'I think it was Bill Cotton's decision. We had been led to believe that she could speak very good French, but I don't think it was tested.'

Speaking years later about the contest, Angela Rippon had this to say: 'The *Eurovision Song Contest* was probably one of my worst experiences in working in television. There was no autocue, and I literally walked out blind in front of hundreds of millions of people and was told, "Look for the red dot." So I walked out onto the stage, knowing that there were outside broadcast cameras that started somewhere on my right and went all the way round to somewhere on my left, and in the dark, with an audience of a couple of thousand live in the auditorium, I had to find the one that had the red light on top. It looked as if I was trying to be the diva on the night. I literally had to take in the audience and sweep my eyes through the dark until I found the red light … and it went downhill from there really. To be stranded on a programme like that is terrifying. It was a complete nightmare. It was probably one of the worst rehearsed and organised *Eurovision*s that there has ever been.'

Vine refutes that. 'It doesn't ring true to me at all. The end of the contest though is always chaotic. The artists

1977 EUROVISION SONG CONTEST

disappear, and they are overcome with joy, and there is always that hiatus. Apart from that I am sure she had adequate rehearsal, but it would have been a very alien programme for her to do, very different from reading the news.'

The contest had featured in a 7'55" item on *Pebble Mill at One* on Friday 6 May, with presenter Marian Foster interviewing Bill Cotton and Mike Moran on set in the Wembley Conference Centre. The *Tonight* programme on the same day included a discussion on the contest with guests Pearl Carr and Teddy Johnson, and included various clips from past contests. Neither of these programmes still exists in the BBC archives.

Also on 6 May there was a trailer for the contest shown just before that evening's edition of *It's a Knockout*, featuring around 1'00" of 'Rock Bottom' with a voice-over by Astley Jones. Another general trailer broadcast later for Saturday night programmes included 10" of 'Rock Bottom'.

EUROVISION SONG CONTEST 1977
Saturday 7 May at 21.00.00 (Duration 130'00")
From the Concert Hall, Wembley Conference Centre, Wembley, United Kingdom
Presented by Angela Rippon

Pete Murray was the BBC1 commentator, and Terry Wogan was the Radio 2 commentator.

| Ireland | 'It's Nice To Be In Love Again' (2'34") | Sung by the Swarbriggs Plus Two. | Composed by Tommy Swarbrigg and Jimmy Swarbrigg. | Conducted by Noel Kelehan. |

The Swarbriggs had represented Ireland in 1975 with 'That's What Friends Are For' and finished ninth.

SONGS FOR EUROPE VOLUME TWO

| Monaco | 'Une Petite Francaise' (2'52") | Sung by Michèle Torr. | Words by Jean Albertini. Music by Paul de Senneville and Olivier Toussaint. | Conducted by Yvon Rioland. |

In 1966 Michèle Torr had sung for Luxembourg and come tenth with 'Ce Soir Je T'attandais'.

| Netherlands | 'De Mallemolen' (3'00") | Sung by Heddy Lester. | Words by Wim Hogenkamp. Music by Frank Affolter. | Conducted by Harry van Hoof. |

The English version of the song, 'The World Keeps Turning', had a lyric written by Norman Newell. Lester performed this English version on the ITV series *Get It Together* on the edition broadcast on 25 May 1977, which exists in the archives.

| Austria | 'Boom Boom Boomerang' (2'59") | Sung by Schmetterlinge. | Words by E Lukas Resetarits. Music by Georg Hernstadt, Willi Resetarits and Herbert Zöchling-Tampier. | Conducted by Christian Kolonovits. |

1977 EUROVISION SONG CONTEST

Norway	'Casanova' (2'07")	Sung by Anita Skorgan.	Words by Dag Nordtømme. Music by Svein Strugstad.	Conducted by Carsten Klouman.

Jonathan King wrote the English language version of 'Casanova'.

Germany	'Telegram' (2'56")	Sung by Silver Convention.	Words by Michael Kunze. Music by Sylvester Levai.	Conducted by Ronnie Hazlehurst.

Silver Convention had several top 30 UK hits to their credit prior to the contest, including 'Save Me', 'Fly, Robin Fly' and 'Get Up And Boogie'.

Luxembourg	*Frère Jacques* (2'51")	Sung by Anne-Marie B.	Composed by Pierre Cour and Guy Béart.	Conducted by Johnny Arthey.

Johnny Arthey had conducted the United Kingdom entries in 1970 and 1971.

Portugal	*Portugal No Coração* (2'46")	Sung by Os Amigos.	Words by José Carlos Ary dos Santos. Music by Fernando Tordo.	Conducted by José Calvário.

SONGS FOR EUROPE VOLUME TWO

In the line-up of Os Amigos were two former Portuguese entrants: Fernando Tordo, who had sung '*Tourada*' in 1973, and Paulo de Carvalho, who had sung '*E Depois Do Adeus*' in 1974.

| United Kingdom | 'Rock Bottom' (2'51") | Sung by Lynsey de Paul and Mike Moran. | Composed by Lynsey de Paul and Mike Moran. | Conducted by Ronnie Hazlehurst. |

'I always thought the contest would go ahead,' says Lynsey de Paul, 'but I was going through a major lawsuit, and I was doing the contest because I couldn't get a record deal without doing it, and then there was this added complication of the strike. It was a very miserable and stressful time for me.

'It was in an era before videos, so we had to go all over Europe promoting the song, and we would fly into Amsterdam and fly back, or Paris and fly back, and so on, and I got so ill that I actually fainted just before *Eurovision*. After the contest I took myself off on my own to Greece for a week, and then I went to America, where I ended up staying for four years.

'I don't remember any of the other songs now, but at the time I might have made a note on one or two to watch. But when you are in a position like that, all you do is focus on yourself and be the best that you can be, and hope that you win. I think because of how the bookies were going we felt we had a good chance, but you just never know.

'Mike had done the orchestration and the arrangement, and Ronnie Hazlehurst developed it for the full orchestra. We asked Ronnie to wear a bowler hat, the business outfit, and to conduct it with an umbrella, and at first he laughed and thought we were joking, but he was such a good sport that he did it. He was such a well-respected musician, conductor and arranger, and he walked out in front of everyone in full city outfit. I think the orchestra were well amused; we wanted to have fun. The visual was so different from anybody else's act

1977 EUROVISION SONG CONTEST

either before or after, and we tried to make an impression.'

De Paul and Moran also recorded a German version of the song called '*Für Immer*' (lyric: Marianne Rebesky). 'That was quite easy for me, as I speak German,' says de Paul, 'but I'm not so sure it was as easy for Mike. He might have had to do it phonetically.

De Paul concludes: 'I was proud to represent the United Kingdom. I was proud that our song was representing the country. But would I have chosen to be the artist? No; not as an established artist.'

David Wigg, writing in the *Daily Express*, said of 'Rock Bottom': 'One of the few songs to stand out as not having been specially written for *Eurovision*. Stylish performance seated back to back at two grand pianos.'

Speaking to the *Daily Express* after the contest, de Paul said: 'I don't feel we've lost out, because in my opinion the best song didn't win. I really do think the [winning] French entry was unprofessional. The words are mundane. It's a very dated song. It's funny really. She was the only one who didn't bother to do something at all special for the contest. I suppose that's why it stood out. But she was very sweet and good luck to her.'

Greece	'*Mathema Solfege*' (2'48")	Sung by Pascalis, Marianna, Robert and Bessy.	Words Sevy Tilakou. Music by George Hatzinassios.	Conducted by George Hatzinassios.

One of the group members, 26 year old Robert Williams was born in the United Kingdom.

Israel	'*Aa-Haa-Vah Hee Sheer Lish-Naa-Yim*' (2'50")	Sung by Ilanit.	Words by Edna Peleg. Music by Eldad Shrem.	Conducted by Eldad Shrem.

SONGS FOR EUROPE VOLUME TWO

The song was given an English lyric by Stephanie De-Sykes, titled 'I'm No One'. Ilanit had previously sung '*Ey-Sham*' for Israel in 1973, when the country made its debut in the contest.

Sweden	'Beatles' (2'47")	Sung by Forbes.	Words by Sven-Olof Bagge. Music by Claes Bure.	Conducted by Anders Berglund.
Spain	'*Enséñame a Cantar*' (2'52")	Sung by Micky.	Composed by Fernando Arbex.	Conducted by Rafael de Ibarbia.
Italy	'*Libera*' (2'52")	Sung by Mia Martini.	Words by Luigi Albertilli. Music by Salvatore Fabrizio.	Conducted by Maurizio Fabrizio.
Finland	'*Lapponia*' (2'50")	Sung by Monica Aspelund.	Words by Monica Aspelund. Music by Aarno Raninen.	Conducted by Ossi Runne.
Belgium	'A Million In One, Two, Three' (2'46")	Sung by Dream Express.	Composed by Luc Smets.	Conducted by Alyn Ainsworth.

1977 EUROVISION SONG CONTEST

The group Dream Express comprised composer Luc Smets along with Patricia, Stella and Bianca Maessen. The three girls had previously formed the group the Hearts of Soul, which had represented the Netherlands in the 1970 contest, finishing in seventh place with 'Waterman'. Dream Express also performed their entry on the edition of *Seaside Special* broadcast on 9 July, which has been retained in the BBC archives.

Conductor Alyn Ainsworth had conducted the United Kingdom entries in 1975 and 1976.

| France | 'L'Oiseau Et L'Enfant' (2'54") | Sung by Marie Myriam. | Words by Joe Gracy. Music by Jean-Paul Cara. | Conducted by Raymond Donnez. |

Marie Myriam was born Myriam Lopes in May 1957 in Braga, Portugal. The song was given an English lyric by Helen Banks as 'The Bird And The Child' and reached number 42 in the UK charts. The sheet music for this mistakenly titled it as 'The Child And The Bird'.

Marie Myriam appeared on *Top of the Pops* on the edition broadcast on 26 May, performing the English-language version. She also appeared on *The Val Doonican Show* on 14 May and *Seaside Special* on 13 August, but on those occasions she sang the original French-language version. All these programmes still exist in the BBC archives. She also appeared on the London Weekend Television programme *Saturday Scene* broadcast on 21 May.

'I was approached by the British publisher,' says songwriter Stephanie De-Sykes, 'to write an English lyric, and I was delighted. I thought it was a very pretty tune. I don't speak French, but my sister is fluent in it. So I'd be on the phone to her every night, going through the words and getting her to translate the song, to give me a feel for what it was trying to say. She was brilliant. I worked tirelessly on this lyric – which was difficult, considering I didn't speak the language – and I was very proud of what I ended up with. It was titled "Love Is Our Song", and

I recall the opening line was "I am a bird, and you are a dreamer" and the hook was "Love is your song, love is our song". The publisher loved it. On the big night, the song won, and I remember sitting at home watching it, excited to think "I am the writer of the English version of the *Eurovision* winner." I expected a phone call on the Monday morning … except there wasn't one, so by the end of the week I phoned them up, only to be told that the French publishers had decided to get their own English lyric done.'

THE INTERVAL ACT (DURATION 5'20")

Some of the footage shot at the Cockney Restaurant did get used for the interval act, which also featured Acker Bilk and his Paramount Jazz Band entertaining the artists at the restaurant, playing 'Nairobi Knees Up' and 'Strangers On The Shore'

THE VOTING

The voting system was the same as that used the previous year. Colin Berry was the United Kingdom spokesperson. The scoreboard was the first to feature each country's national flag in addition to its name.

There were several errors made on the night that weren't picked up until after the broadcast. Greece managed to award two sets of four points, and France went even better by awarding two sets of three points and two sets of one point, and getting their scores for Portugal and Italy the wrong way round. It meant that nine countries had an incorrect score shown on the scoreboard at the end of the programme. The official correct scores are recorded in this book.

This was the first time for Berry as the United Kingdom spokesperson. He was born in January 1946 and started his career in pirate radio with the ship-based Radio Caroline, initially in an administrative job before gaining the opportunity to be a newsreader, although he suffered from one problem: he couldn't cope very well when there was rough seas. 'I was so ill,' he says, 'death would have been the easy option.' So he did only occasional trips when Radio Caroline were short-staffed, and in the meantime auditioned for other work. He did a lot of commercial voiceovers and some continuity work for HTV, and compèred at discos and clubs. By 1973 he had made enough contacts to join the BBC; and with the launch of Radio London causing a mass exodus from Radio 1 and Radio 2, he found himself with his first job within two days of starting.

'It would have been Tony James, light entertainment organiser, who would have asked me to do the job as spokesperson,' recalls Berry. 'He would probably have asked Ray Moore, who I think had his own Saturday night radio show by this time, if there was anyone he could recommend, and as Ray and I were very good mates, he suggested I do it.

'My role, apart from being the spokesperson, was to be the standby commentator,' adds Berry. 'There is always a lip mic there and a monitor with a direct cue to the television gallery at Television Centre if the line goes. It did actually happen to Pete Murray once, before my time. He accidentally kicked a switch on the floor and it pulled his microphone cable out. I don't know whether or not anyone had to do a standby commentary then. If they did I think it was only for about a minute, and maybe Ray had to jump in before it was sorted out. So you had to constantly listen in to the show; there was no let-up.

'I went down to the Wembley Conference Centre afterwards, and I must admit I got very drunk, and had to be helped into the cab. But the opportunities to do that were very rare. It was just that the venue was so close to Television Centre.'

SONGS FOR EUROPE VOLUME TWO

	Ireland	Monaco	Netherlands	Austria	Norway	Germany	Luxembourg	Portugal	UK	Greece	Israel	Switzerland	Sweden	Spain	Italy	Finland	Belgium	France	TOTAL	POSITION
Ireland		8	1	5	12	5	8	1	12	10	12	8	12	4	8		3	10	119	3RD
Monaco	5			8	1	6	1	6	7	12	2	6	10	8	12	5	2	5	96	4TH
Netherlands	3	3					1	1	1	7		1				10	8		35	12TH
Austria		5			2				3							1			11	17TH
Norway							3	2	2				1		5		5		18	14TH=
Germany	1	1	3	2			2	8	8	8	5		5	5	6			1	55	8TH
Luxembourg	2												7		8				17	16TH
Portugal		2	2			1					4			3			6		18	14TH=
United Kingdom		12	7	12	7	10	12	12		8		8	3	2	4	12	12		121	2ND
Greece		10	10	4	4	4	6	10	5		3	1	7	12	1	6	6	3	92	5TH
Israel	7	7	5	3	5							10	3	6			1	2	49	11TH
Switzerland	6		10	10		5	4	4	6	4				4	10	8			71	6TH

1977 EUROVISION SONG CONTEST

Country																		Total	Place
Sweden						2				▓								02	18TH
Spain			6	1		7	7		3	4		3	▓		7	7	7	52	9TH
Italy	8	6			3		3				2		2	▓	2		7	33	13TH
Finland	12		4	6	8				2	7	5	2			▓		4	50	10TH
Belgium	4		12		6	8	4	7	10	5	6		4			3	▓	69	7TH
France	10	4	8	7	3	12	10	5	6	7	10	12	6	10	10	12	4	136	1ST

Analysis: The early stages of the voting saw the United Kingdom quickly take the lead, despite receiving no votes from Ireland. Also off to a good start were Greece and Israel. However, it was France that would prove to be the strongest challenger. Not for the first time, the strong lead that the United Kingdom had built up in the first half of the voting was eroded in the second half with a succession of low marks. France pulled away into a commanding lead, with Ireland's entry moving into second place, helped in part by the United Kingdom awarding it 12 points.

Two sets of 12 points in the last two rounds lifted the United Kingdom back into second place overall; the tenth time the country had been the runner-up. It meant that for 11 contests in succession the United Kingdom had finished in the top four. No fewer than six countries had voted the United Kingdom's as the top song, easily eclipsing the three countries that placed France's top. However France had scored more consistently, picking up votes from every country. Thus it earned a record fifth victory in the contest. Greece had its best showing to date, finishing in a respectable fifth place.

The awards were presented by the Director-General of the BBC and President of the EBU, Sir Charles

SONGS FOR EUROPE VOLUME TWO

Curran. The previous year's winners, the Brotherhood of Man, hadn't been invited back to present the awards. 'It seems all over Europe they get asked back, but not in Britain,' says group member Martin Lee. 'They don't want to give you too much accolade or too much success.' However, fellow group member Sandra Stevens adds: 'I must be honest and say that every year the contest comes around, the BBC will usually invite us to do something, so they do remember us.'

WINNING REPRISE

France	'L'Oiseau Et L'Enfant' (2'54")	Sung by Marie Myriam.	Words by Joe Gracy. Music by Jean-Paul Cara.	Conducted by Raymond Donnez.

CREDITS
Head of Light Entertainment: Bill Cotton
Executive Producer: Stewart Morris
Designer: Kenneth Sharp
Costume Designer: Peter Shepherd
Graphic Designer: Rosemary Turner
Sound Supervisor: Chris Holcombe
Lighting Supervisor: Tommy Thomas
Engineering Manager: John Wiggins
Producer's Assistant: Lydia Spratt

1977 EUROVISION SONG CONTEST

Production Assistant: Marcus Plantin
Assistants to Head of Light Entertainment: Geoff Jowitt and Queenie Lipyeat
Orchestra Leader: Antony Gilbert
Music Director: Ronnie Hazlehurst
EBU Scrutineer: Clifford Brown

The contest was watched by an audience of 37.90% of the British population (19.14 million) at the start of the programme at 21.00, rising to 45.70% (23.08 million) from 22.00, and scored an RI of 53.

Only a small proportion of the 497 viewers questioned for the Audience Research Report said that they had really enjoyed the contest, and the majority had thought the songs of a low standard, with one or two saying that previous contests had had a better selection of music.

19% of them agreed with the choice of winner, with 56% not entirely agreeing and 25% not agreeing at all. Some thought the French entry had been entirely forgettable and didn't like it. Not many other songs were singled out; those that were included the entries from Belgium, Switzerland, Greece and the United Kingdom.

Angela Rippon had her critics, but the majority had been impressed, and some thought she had handled the tricky moments well when the scoreboard went wrong. A few had disliked her appearance or been irritated by her French, a handful had thought she had been trying to steal the limelight, and a few had compared her unfavourably with Katie Boyle.

A few thought it was a great pity that there had been a problem with the inefficient scoreboard. It was said that this had been an unprofessional touch in an otherwise splendid show and had caused irritation. Some also thought that there had been too many shots of the audience and not enough close-ups of the singers.

The programme as broadcast by the BBC exists in the archives.

The Wembley Conference Centre venue was demolished in 2006.

1978 UNITED KINGDOM

The format that had been so successful in the past two years was retained for 1978. There were 447 entries submitted to the MPA for the Final, which this year would be back at the Royal Albert Hall. These entries were whittled down to 12 by a panel selected from the MPA, the Songwriters' Guild and the BBC.

Rehearsals commenced on Thursday 30 March at 10.00. Each act had a 45 minute slot and rehearsed in costume, in the same order as they would perform on the night. After the first two rehearsals, there was a 15-minute break, before the Fruit Eating Bears took to the stage at 11.45. There was a lunch break from 13.15 to 14.30, before it was time for Sunshine to rehearse, followed by the next two acts. There was a 15-minute break before Co-Co had their opportunity at 17.00. From 18.30 until 19.45 there was a dinner break. Then the final three songs were rehearsed, and everybody finished up at 22.00.

Lydia Vine recalls: 'We used to run it like a mini *Eurovision Song Contest*. Stewart [Morris] was very strict about the rehearsal times allocated to each artist; otherwise you would get terrible complaints.'

Vine would have to type up the camera scripts in preparation for the programme. Apart from showing the rehearsal timetable and the running order for the show, these would include all the lyrics, indicating the number of bars and who would be singing each part if it was a group. Down the left-hand side of each page would be noted each individual camera shot, which camera number was taking the shot, and whether it was a wide, medium or close up shot, or a two shot, group shot or whatever the case may be. There might be some additional directions, such as indicating if there was to be a tracking shot, a mix or a zoom. There would also be a list of the juries and the spokespersons, and the details for the credits for the roller captions at the end of the programme.

On Friday 31 March there was a camera rehearsal from 09.30 for the scoreboard and the interval act, which was a '*Eurovision* Winners Medley'. Following a 15-minute break, all the artists were in place for the first run-through of the day, starting at 11.00, though not in their stage costumes. This took the schedule through to 13.00, when there was a 75-minute break for lunch. Around 14.15, just before a final dress run-through, Terry Wogan recorded a trailer for the programme. Rehearsals then continued until 17.15. The songwriters were then all given a briefing, presumably having a quick run-through of what to do if they were the winners. Dinner break was next until 18.30. With an hour to go before transmission, everything was lined up and tested, and the audience admitted to the Royal Albert Hall in preparation for the live transmission.

A SONG FOR EUROPE 1978
Friday 31 March at 19.30 (Duration 93'17")
Presented by Terry Wogan

The programme opened with Alyn Ainsworth and the orchestra, comprising some 29 musicians, playing *Te Deum* (0.35") over shots of the Royal Albert Hall interior, before a fanfare (0.15") welcomed presenter Terry Wogan on stage. Once his initial introductions were completed, it was time for the songs. After the details of each song were announced, a photograph of the act appeared on screen before they commenced their song.

Song One	'Shine It On' (2'47")	Sung by Christian.	Composed by Bill Martin and Phil Coulter.	Backing Vocals: Eunice Green and Louise Arthurworrey (in vision). Musicians: Cass Richards, Simon Morton and Martin David. Plus Orchestra

SONGS FOR EUROPE VOLUME TWO

Christian was the stage name of Christopher Gill McClure, a well-known singer in Scotland. At the age of 19 he had joined a band called the Fireflies, performing cover versions of Drifters and Buddy Holly songs, and even throwing in a few impressions. In 1971 he heard that Scottish Television was looking for a group for a new programme called *Stramash*, and the band changed its name to the Chris McClure Section. After auditioning, he got a slot on *Opportunity Knocks*, and finished second in the programme. He had the same manager, Frank Lynch, as Billy Connolly, and it was Lynch who suggested he change his name to Christian. He appeared with Dolly Parton at Scotland's *Jubilee Show* in 1977 and supported Connolly on tour, including in an appearance at the London Palladium. Christian had another song up for selection in the 1978 contest, a ballad entitled 'Home', which didn't make it through to the final 12. He continued to work on the club circuit and in pantomimes, and later had the opportunity to appear again at the Royal Albert Hall supporting the Osmonds.

Bill Martin and Phil Coulter had won the 1967 *Eurovision Song Contest* with 'Puppet On A String', and had come second a year later with 'Congratulations'. The pair had returned to the contest in 1975, when they co-composed the Luxembourg entry, finishing in fifth place with '*Toi*'.

Martin says: 'Phil and I had now finished as a team. He had gone off to America to be a film composer. I was friendly with manager Frank Lynch, and he had found this singer called Christian, but I couldn't be bothered going into the studio. I said to Phil, "I've got a chance to record this guy and produce him. Do you want to come back from the States and produce him?" But he didn't fancy doing it either. There was a record chief, another Scotsman, who told me he had an album with a song on it that would be great for Christian, called "Isn't She Lovely", which he would have been great at, but Phil wouldn't do it, so I never did it. When Phil did come back, he said, "We're in *Eurovision*. We'll do that with Christian." But I wasn't interested, and if I'm not interested it just doesn't work out.'

1978 UNITED KINGDOM

Song Two	'Oh, No Look What You've Done' (2'41")	Sung by Brown Sugar (Salli Kamara, Uti Kooffreh and Stellina McCarthy).	Composed by Wayne Bickerton and Tony Waddington.	Backing Vocals: Vicky Brown, Lavinia Rodgers and Liza Strike (OOV). Plus Orchestra.

Brown Sugar had billed themselves as the only Afro-English female group in existence. Salli Kamara had appeared in *The Black Mikado*, and was born into a showbusiness family, as her parents were professional fire eaters. Uti Kooffreh had started out as a journalist before turning to singing. Stellina McCarthy had appeared on stage in productions of *Hair*, *Jesus Christ Superstar* and *The Black Mikado*. The group had previously worked together as session singers.

The songwriting team of Wayne Bickerton and Tony Waddington had previously composed 'A Love For All Seasons', sung by Champagne in the 1976 contest, finishing in eighth place. This was the first of two entries they had in the 1978 Final. Each time, the duo had gone with groups that were already around, rather than creating a group especially for the contest.

'I think it's the tools you work with,' as Bickerton explained. 'If you are working with good singers, with the right attitude, then it doesn't really matter whether they are established or not. I think that is the problem that lots of bands have: they get five people brought together, and you've got one person in there who doesn't see eye to eye with the others. It happens all the time, and that can cause you grief. But I don't think we've ever taken the view that it necessarily has to be an exisiting act. Brown Sugar were available, and we got involved, and I thought we made a good record with them, but it didn't work on the night, and neither did the other one [performed by Sunshine].

SONGS FOR EUROPE VOLUME TWO

'We got more and more involved with control over costumes and choreography though. I don't think most people took that much of an interest initially; they were concentrating on the song, and on how well they could sing it, and if they were interpretating the lyric correctly, or whether they should change this or that. But I think what happened was that Brotherhood of Man had set a precedent, and everyone followed, to a point where, I think, to be candid, that the presentation was more important than the actual music.'

Song Three	'Door In My Face' (2'52")	Sung by Fruit Eating Bears (Neville Crozier, Chris Crash and Gary Croudace).	Composed by Neville Crozier and Chris Crash.	With backing track.

Formed in 1977, the Fruit Eating Bears were described as the first punk group in the contest, but they preferred to be classified as new wave. Songwriters Chris Crash and Neville Crozier were originally from Northampton, and were joined by a Geordie, Gary Croudace. The group, who lived in the Purley area, had built up quite a following.

Song Four	'Moments' (2'56")	Sung by Jacquie Sullivan.	Composed by Jacquie Sullivan.	Plus Orchestra.

Jacquie Sullivan was born in California and had worked as a session singer with artists such as Frank Sinatra,

1978 UNITED KINGDOM

Charles Aznavour and Sammy Davis Jnr. She had been a member of the group High Society that had taken 'Just For You' to sixth place in *A Song for Europe* in 1977.

Song Five	'Too Much In Love' (2'55")	Sung by Sunshine (Stuart Bingham, Rosaline McCerlaine, Bryce Norrie and James Meredith).	Composed by Wayne Bickerton and Tony Waddington.	Backing Vocals; Vicky Brown and Lavinia Rodgers (OOV). Plus Orchestra.

Sunshine was a Belfast-based group that had chalked up six victories on the talent show *Opportunity Knocks*. They had recently released a single, 'Dance With Me', which was a cover version of the original hit by the USA group New Orleans and had done reasonably well in Ireland.

The group members were all from Ulster except for Stuart Bingham, who was born in London but lived in Ulster. They were normally a five-piece, with drummer Arthur Moorhead included in the line-up, but for the contest Moorhead was temporarily dropped in favour of having two backing vocalist performing out of vision. The rules of the contest allowed only a maximum of six performers in total. The group had no connection with the one of the same name that had sung in the 1976 contest. The song though was later covered by the group Champagne, who had sung the Wayne Bickerton and Tony Waddington composition 'A Love For All Seasons' that year.

'Everybody was crazy about routines,' recalls Wayne Bickerton, 'and the whole thing had become a mixture of music and presentation, so I had to go to Belfast to see the group. It was probably one of the most amusing experiences I've had – although my family didn't think so at the time. I ended up being picked up by the manager's driver, who drove me to a pub on the other side of Belfast, and then told me that someone else would be along to pick me up there. It was then I said, "Hang on, am I in the Republican area?" and was told "Yes." "So, where am I going?" I asked, and was informed, "Oh, I don't know, they will tell you."

'I was there for about half an hour, and then another driver came, and he gave me this whole speech that we were going to a club to see the band, and that we might get stopped along the way. I asked where we were going, and I think he said Andersontown, right smack bang in the Republican area. I ended up being stopped by the police, who had searchlights on the car, and then I ended up being stopped by the army. They were adamant that I should get out of the car, and that they should take me back to Belfast, and asked if I realised where I was going. I said, "Yes, I am going to this club." They informed me that the club was run by the IRA.

'When we got there, the priest came out as I got out the car, and he put his arm around me and said to me, "Whatever you do, don't open your mouth." He led me in and there were four guys with balaclavas sitting at this long table, taking the money off people as they were coming in … All very interesting.

'So, I stood there as I watched what the band had rehearsed, and they did it on stage, and that was fine. I then got an invitation to go backstage, but I said to the priest, "Father, if you don't mind, I'd like to get out of here," and he understood, and he walked me past the men in the balaclavas, and I got back in the car, and went back to Belfast. It could have been quite nasty, but I knew that they knew who I was, absolutely knew. It had obviously all been cleared before I went, but when you were actually there it was a bit nerve-wracking.'

James Meredith had joined the group just eight weeks before the contest. Meredith was from Newtonhards, a small market town about ten miles south of Belfast. He recalls: 'As a child, I don't remember having any other interests than listening to Radio Luxembourg and Radio Caroline etc. I got my first guitar, along with Bert Weedon's *Play in a Day* guitar book, when I was about 11 or 12, and started learning the chords and developing the strumming technique. I then started singing along and writing down the lyrics to all my favourites. During my teens I played with quite a lot of local musicians, and eventually switched from guitar to bass. I suppose my first real break was with the local group Tapestry. In 1971 we toured Denmark and Germany for several months, and at that time I knew I would continue with a musical career. So, for several years, I put together many different semi-professional line-ups, all with different degrees of success.

'I was with the Fresh Boogie Band, a five-piece pop, disco-type band, playing mostly weekends around the north west of Ireland. Stuart Bingham and Bryce Norrie, two founder members of Sunshine, whom I already knew, called to see me, and literally offered me a job.

'I thought "Too Much In Love" was the right song for the contest at the right time … but it was always going to be politically sensitive for us in the voting process, due to "the troubles etc" and our regional location at the time. However, during rehearsals, on reflection, I would have picked Co-Co as the winners, followed by the Jarvis Brothers and Midnight.

'The Royal Albert Hall was an awesome venue. Everyone was so professional, and at the same time very friendly, understanding, and at all time courteous.'

However, Meredith adds: 'Sadly the live performance simply wasn't our very best. Too much time was spent on the visuals, and not enough times was given for the song itself, the audio balance etc. It was really disappointing for everyone who had put so much time and effort into it. There can be only one winner, and I believe that the best song won.'

Sunshine though received a good reception on their return to Ulster, and continued to get regular work. Meredith eventually left the group, reformed the Fresh Boogie Band and continued to play in local venues.

'I don't think we ever tried again for the contest,' says Wayne Bickerton. 'Basically we had given it a good shot on a couple of occasions, and it hadn't worked. [Tony Waddington and I] were both involved so much with the music when we were writing and producing that we weren't really taking the time out to be involved with the choreography etc – a role that should be best left with the management.'

SONGS FOR EUROPE VOLUME TWO

Bickerton went on to become an executive of the Performing Rights Society, eventually becoming Chairman and acting Chief Executive. He also became Deputy Chairman of the University of Liverpool Institute of Popular Music and was awarded an honorary doctorate by the University of Liverpool.

Waddington's music has featured in many films, amongst which are *Muriel's Wedding*, *Breakfast On Pluto* and *Resurrection Man*. He has received over 20 gold discs, and has won both an Ivor Novello and a BASCA award as Songwriter of the Year. Recently the songwriting duo has got back together, after a break of over 30 years.

Song Six	'Lonely Nights' (2'50")	Sung by Ronnie France.	Composed by Paul Curtis.	Backing Vocals: Tony Burrows, Neil Lancaster, Jean Hawker, Kay Garner and Clare Torry (OOV). Plus Orchestra.

Veronica France, as this artist was otherwise known, was married at the time to composer Paul Curtis. She had started her career as a dancer, performing in France as a Bluebell Girl. A former Young Generation dancer, she had coincidentally appeared in the edition of *Lulu* that included *A Song for Europe* 1975. She was also a choreographer, actress and model, and had appeared in adverts for jeans and lager.

Paul Curtis from London had previously composed the 1975 UK entry 'Let Me Be The One', sung by the Shadows, and a 1976 entry 'Couldn't Live Without You', performed by Hazel Dean, the latter of which had finished in eighth place. Other artists for whom he had composed songs included Elvis Presley.

1978 UNITED KINGDOM

Song Seven	'One Glance' (3'00")	Sung by the Jarvis Brothers (Tony Jarvis, Anderson Jarvis, Michael Jarvis and Steven Jarvis).	Composed by Paul Curtis.	Backing Vocals: Tony Burrows and Clare Torry (OOV). Plus Orchestra.

The Jarvis Brothers was another act that had to make a compromise for the contest. It normally comprised five brothers, but the youngest, ten year old Ivor Jarvis, was below the minimum age allowed. It was 12 year old Tony Jarvis who took lead vocals. The oldest member was 19 year old Anderson Jarvis. The brothers were from north London and had been coached in music by their father, who was a bus driver.

This was the second of two songs that Paul Curtis had in the 1978 contest.

Song Eight	'The Bad Old Days' (2'35")	Sung by Co-Co (Terry Bradford, Keith Hasler, Cheryl Baker, Paul Rodgers, Josie Andrews and Charles Brennan).	Composed by Stephanie De-Sykes and Stuart Slater.	Plus Orchestra and backing track.

SONGS FOR EUROPE VOLUME TWO

Co-Co had previously finished a very close second to the Brotherhood of Man in the 1976 *A Song for Europe* with the song 'Wake Up', but had turned down the chance to perform 'Promises, Promises' in the 1977 contest.

There had been some changes to the group by 1978, with only Terry Bradford, Cheryl Baker and Keith Hassler remaining from the 1976 line-up. Paul Rogers had joined, having previously been in a comedy act called High Estate. Josie Andrews, another new member, had done some cabaret with a group called Flair and had won the *New Faces* talent show. Drummer Charlie Brennan from Scotland completed the new line-up.

Lead singer Bradford takes up the story: 'We had recorded an album, which was finished and all ready to go, and had got a record deal with Hansa, when we were offered "The Bad Old Days". We realised straight away that we stood a chance of winning.

'We knew from the first time round what we had done wrong. One of the things we had done was to be too interested in what everyone else was doing. I believe you should focus on what you do, and use your strengths, so I took charge of the whole thing. We never even told the record company, we kept it totally in house, and just got three or four very good professionals in who knew the business, a great costume designer in David Terry and a really good choreographer in Irving Davies – not that there was too much choreography, but at least he could tell us how to present it well. We spoke to them and told them how we wanted to develop ourselves, what we wanted to do and how we wanted to come across. So when we walked out there with those garish, crazy costumes on, we knew that people would actually take notice. Over the top as they were, it did make people realise we had put a lot of effort into it. It didn't matter if they thought the look was horrible. Nobody saw it until we walked out in the dress rehearsal. We said to leave the music to us. We could at least cope with the music and focus on doing a good job singing on the night. We felt quite comfortable with the orchestra, because we knew a lot of them, having worked with them in sessions and on jingles, so we weren't overawed by those wonderful string players and the rest. We had learned from two years earlier, and I'm a bit of a perfectionist, so we knew that as long as we did it correctly, we had a very good chance on the night.'

In a contemporary interview in *Look-In* magazine, Bradford also noted: 'Irving Davies was absolutely invaluable. He kept an eye on the monitors during rehearsals, checking who the cameras were on and when. Then he made sure that the person was doing something while they were in the picture, and we didn't have anyone not doing something being picked up by the cameras. But he kept it very simple, because we didn't want to look like a bunch of dancers.'

How had Bradford felt during the voting? 'I have to be honest, I sat in the dressing room under the Royal Albert Hall and I didn't listen to the voting, because it had been so close in 1976. I'll never forget how, that first time, the floor manager had come up to us with one round of voting to go and said, "Get your guitars; there's no chance you are going to get beaten." So we had got our guitars, thinking we'd won it, and then of course Brotherhood of Man went and won. In 1978, I wasn't going to go through that again, so I stayed down in the dressing room, and it was only when they came down and told me that I knew we had won.'

Bradford, along with fellow singer Josie Andrews, told *Look-In* of an incident that had almost caused some embarrassment. 'We were trying to untangle ourselves,' grinned Bradford. 'On my costume I have glitter down the side of my trousers, and I don't know how it happened, we passed too close or something, but it got caught on Josie's tights and we were locked together.'

'Yes,' agreed Andrews. 'They were gold fish-net tights and somehow, I don't know how, they got wound around the glitter. Anyway, it was 30 seconds before we were due to go on stage and there we were – caught. We ripped the tights in freeing ourselves and I just had to pull them up hard and go on and do the song.'

'The thinking behind it, to come up with the very flamboyant costumes, was great,' adds fellow group member Cheryl Baker. 'You never expect to win *A Song for Europe*. The more you hear the other songs, and the more familiar they become, the better you think they are. Christian was good, and I loved Labi Siffre.'

Stephanie De-Sykes, born in July 1947, had had her first hit single as a singer with the group Rain in 1974. That was 'Born With A Smile On My Face', written by fellow group member Simon May, which reached number two in the charts. A year later she had had a further hit, this time as a solo artist, with 'We'll Find Our Day', which had featured in the ITV soap opera *Crossroads* – a show in which she had played the character Holly Brown. With Chas Mills, another member of Rain, she had tried entering songs in the contest several times before, but they hadn't made it through to the final stages. She had sung out-of-vision backing vocals on the 1976 entry 'Love, Kiss And Run', performed by Sweet Dreams.

Stuart Slater, born in July 1945 in Liverpool, had been a lead singer with the group the Mojos. He and De-Sykes had been living together, and the couple naturally drifted into songwriting together.

'We didn't intend to write together, it was sort of symbiotic,' says De-Sykes. 'When it came down to finishing off the loose ends, I'd tie up the lyrics and Stuart the music. But I was equally capable of writing the music, and Stuart was the same with the lyrics. I'm probably more of a wordsmith than Stuart, and he had an instantaneous natural outpouring of musical ideas.

'What would happen was that your publisher would say, "Right it's November, the date of *A Song for Europe* has been announced … The closing date is … Get writing, or bring your songs to us, and those that we like, we will demo them." That was if you hadn't already demoed them. They would pay for the demos of those that they liked. I would always put in a song that I really thought was my best shot. I would write a song specifically tailored to *Eurovision*, which I would think is the least recommended way to do it, but I'd also put in a wild card, an off the wall thing. Your publisher could only submit so many songs, so it was then down to them, but you could be in a position where they'd submit maybe three of your songs. What we did in 1977/78 with "The Bad Old Days" was we approached Robin Blanchflower, who was running the Ariola record label, and told him that we had this song that ATV Music were putting in for *A Song for Europe*, and he said, "I have this band called Co-Co, who I think would be good for it." I had sung the demo version, but we struck a deal whereby if the song ended up in the contest, Co-Co would do it, so we put the name Co-Co on it.

'I remember well the day when it was announced the song had been selected for the Final. I'd being doing

1978 UNITED KINGDOM

session work at either Advision or Nova studios in the morning, and then gone off to the MPA Christmas lunch afterwards. I was so nervous throughout the lunch, as I knew "The Bad Old Days" was on the shortlist. In the afternoon, at around 4 pm, I had another session, and arrived there with my feet hardly touching the ground, still shaking. I just couldn't believe it when I heard we had got through. It was such a huge event back then.

'At that point the whole production of the piece was wrested from us. This was our first experience of the contest, and suddenly the group and their producer were changing the arrangement and putting on these ludicrous costumes. I remember thinking, "This wasn't what we had in mind at all." As a result, of all the songs we ever submitted, "The Bad Old Days" wasn't the one that we would have liked to represent us. It was a song we'd written for Demis Roussos in the first place, as a plaintive song, really slow and heart-wrenching, but we beefed it up for the contest, and did a really good demo. I felt what Co-Co did with it went over the top, and down the other side. I don't blame them, because there were people involved in their image and in their production. But we decided that next time we would just put a made-up name for the artist against the song, so we could retain control.'

Song Nine	'We Got It Bad' (2'53")	Sung by Bob James.	Composed by Bob James and Labi Siffre.	Backing Vocals: Dave Christopher, Stu Calver and Teresa Christopher (in vision). Plus Orchestra.

Composer and singer Bob James started his musical career at 14 with the guitar. He later learned to play the

SONGS FOR EUROPE VOLUME TWO

flute and alto sax. He had been a member of a band called Skin Alley, which had produced four albums. It was his songwriting partner Labi Siffre who had discovered him as a singer. This was the first of two songs that Siffre had in the 1978 event.

Song Ten	'Don't Bother To Knock' (2'45")	Sung by Midnight (Tony Stackton (aka Tony Jackson), Jimmy Chambers and Ruby James).	Composed by Kenny Lynch, Steve O'Donnell and Colin Horton-Jennings.	Backing Vocals: Sylvia James, George Chandler and Colin Young (OOV). Plus Orchestra.

Midnight comprised three ex-session singers who had backed the likes of Rod Stewart and Elkie Brooks. Tony Stackton was from Barbados, Jimmy Chambers was from Trinidad and Ruby James was from Jamaica. Tony Stackton (as Tony Jackson) had been one half of the duo Sweet Dreams, who had sung 'Love, Kiss and Run' in *A Song for Europe* 1976, finishing in fourth place. Since then Jackson had sung the theme song to the film *The Cassandra Crossing*, released in 1977.

Composer Kenny Lynch had previously sung in *A Song for Europe* in 1962 with 'There's Never Been A Girl', which finished in sixth place. Since then he had achieved two top ten hits, 'Up On The Roof' and 'You Can Never Stop Me Loving You', and some further top 40 songs, including the winner of *The British Song Festival* in 1965, 'I'll Stay By You'. He had also written songs, most notably for the Small Faces, including in collaboration with Mort Shuman their number three hit 'Sha-La-La-La-Lee' in 1966. He had also written for the Hollies and had some acting parts in programmes including *Z Cars, Till Death Us Do Part* and *The Sweeney* and films

1978 UNITED KINGDOM

including *The Plank* and *Carry On Loving*.

The songwriting team of Lynch, Steve O'Donnell and Colin Horton-Jennings had written tracks for Cilla Black. O'Donnell and Horton-Jennings had also worked together on a number of soul, disco and funk tracks. In 1986, under the name Cognac, O'Donnell and Horton-Jennings re-recorded and released 'Don't Bother To Knock' as a dance mix, which appeared on both 7" and 12" singles with extended and instrumental versions.

Song Eleven	'Don't Let Me Stand In Your Way' (2'51")	Sung by Babe Rainbow (Patricia Henry, Cheryl Augustine, Ellen Warren and Nikki Wright).	Composed by Irving Martin and Peter Morris.	Plus Orchestra.

This four-member group had been known as the Ramelles until 1977, then along came manager Justin De Villeneuve to give them a fresh start, renaming them Babe Rainbow.

In the '60s, Irving Martin had been best known as a producer, with a number of pop beat and harmony vocal tracks to his credit. One of the hits he produced was 'I've Been Hurt' by Guy Darrell in 1973. He co-composed the theme music for the TV show *The Return of the Saint* in 1978. Songwriter and arranger Peter Morris wrote the song 'Sunday, Monday, Tuesday', which made the charts in several countries.

SONGS FOR EUROPE VOLUME TWO

| Song Twelve | 'Solid Love' (3'00") | Sung by Labi Siffre. | Composed by Labi Siffre. | Backing Vocals: Vicky Brown, Lavinia Rodgers and Mary Partington (in vision). Plus Orchestra. |

Singer and composer Labi Siffre was probably the best-known name in the 1978 line-up. He was born in June 1945 in London. Amongst his hits were 'It Must Be Love' in 1971 and 'Crying, Laughing, Loving, Lying' in 1972. He had six albums released between 1970 and 1975 and toured the UK and Europe supporting acts like the Hollies, Ike and Tina Turner and the Carpenters before moving to Los Angeles in 1977. Although he had two songs in *A Song for Europe* 1978, this was the only time he participated in the event. In 1983 he enjoyed his first success in the USA, when Madness covered his song 'It Must Be Love' and it made the Billboard Top 100. He appeared in the group's music video of the song. He later wrote and performed '(Something Inside) So Strong', an anti-apartheid anthem, which was a number four chart hit in 1987 and won an Ivor Novello Award for Best Song Musically and Lyrically. He has had a poetry book published, and in 2006 an album was released entitled *The Last Songs*.

THE INTERVAL ACT
For the interval act, Alyn Ainsworth and the orchestra played a medley of past *Eurovision* winners over stock film footage of scenes from the respective countries.

1978 UNITED KINGDOM

Netherlands 1975	'Ding Dinge Dong'	Music by Dick Bakker.	0.55"
Ireland 1970	'All Kinds Of Everything'	Music by Derry Lindsay and Jackie Smith.	1.00"
Sweden 1974	'Waterloo'	Music by Benny Andersson and Björn Ulvaeus	0.50"
Monaco 1971	*Un Banc, Un Arbre, Une Rue*	Music by Jean Paul Bourtayre.	0.45"
Spain 1968	'La,La,La'	Music by Manuel De La Calva and Ramón Arcusa.	0.40"
France 1977	*L'Oiseau Et L'Enfant*	Music by Jean-Paul Cara.	1.10"

THE VOTING

The same voting system was used as in *A Song for Europe* 1976. There were 14 regional juries in total.

THE SPOKESPERSONS

Aberdeen	Gerry Davis
Norwich	Chris Denham
Manchester	Mike Riddoch
Bangor	Gwyn Llewelyn
Southampton	Peter McCann

SONGS FOR EUROPE VOLUME TWO

Leeds	Brian Baines
Belfast	Michael Baguley
Bristol	Derek Jones
Glasgow	Kenneth Bruce
Birmingham	Tom Coyne
London	Ray Moore
Cardiff	Frank Lincoln
Newcastle	Mike Neville
Plymouth	Donald Heighway

Ken Bruce, the spokesperson for the Glasgow jury, recalls: 'When I joined the BBC, as a newsreader, I was actually known as Kenny Bruce, but they decided that I couldn't read the news with a name like that, so it had to be Kenneth. Then later the BBC shortened it to Ken when I was put into programmes, without ever asking me – though often these decisions were better than the ones I would have made myself.'

The banter between Terry Wogan and the spokespersons was always spontaneous, as Bruce explains: 'Sometimes you would do a rehearsal, but it was never the same as it would be on broadcast. It was for technical reasons, and if you exchanged some banter, it would be completely different from what happened on the night. Everybody doing it in those days was a professional broadcaster, because things could go wrong, and did frequently, and you had to be able to fill and pad if necessary. It was actually the first time I did any work with Terry Wogan, albeit 450 miles apart.'

1978 UNITED KINGDOM

THE RESULTS

	Aberdeen	Norwich	Manchester	Bangor	Southampton	Leeds	Belfast	Bristol	Glasgow	Birmingham	London	Cardiff	Newcastle	Plymouth	TOTAL	POSITION
'Shine It On'	12	11	9	10	5	4	11	12	12	7	9	3	5	4	114	3RD=
'Oh, No, Look What You've Done'	7	2	2	1	3	2	2	9	5	2	3	1	4	6	49	11TH=
'Door In My Face'	2	1	7	2	1	7	3	3	2	3	1	2	10	5	49	11TH=
'Moments'	8	8	11	7	8	3	9	6	10	8	10	6	3	9	106	6TH
'Too Much In Love'	9	3	5	4	2	6	10	7	9	5	6	7	6	2	81	8TH
'Lonely Nights'	1	4	1	8	4	5	1	2	1	10	7	11	12	1	68	9TH
'One Glance'	6	7	3	5	9	12	6	11	11	9	12	4	11	8	114	3RD=
'The Bad Old Days'	11	12	12	11	10	11	7	4	3	11	11	12	8	12	135	1ST
'We Got it Bad'	3	6	10	3	12	1	4	1	8	1	4	5	1	7	66	10TH
'Don't Bother To Knock'	4	9	8	6	11	10	8	5	7	12	8	10	7	11	116	2ND
'Don't Let Me Stand In Your Way'	5	5	4	9	7	8	5	10	6	6	5	9	2	3	84	7TH
'Solid Love'	10	10	6	12	6	9	12	8	4	4	2	8	9	10	110	5TH

SONGS FOR EUROPE VOLUME TWO

Analysis: The initial rounds of voting saw 'The Bad Old Days' edge into the lead, chased by 'Shine It On' and 'Solid Love'. When Southampton and then Leeds both gave low marks to 'Shine It On' and high marks to 'The Bad Old Days', it looked as if the latter was going to run away with it, with 'Solid Love' in second place following the Leeds vote. Then came a reversal of fortunes, with Belfast, Bristol and Glasgow all giving low points to 'The Bad Old Days' and high points to 'Shine It On', providing 'Shine It On' with a clear five point lead.

The next couple of rounds were the most exciting. 'The Bad Old Days' cut the deficit back to a single point and then, after London's contribution, turned that around to a one point lead. With three juries to go it looked as if it was going to be another thrilling climax for a contest held in the Royal Albert Hall. However, the challenge of 'Shine It On' quickly faded after the Cardiff vote, and 'The Bad Old Days' romped home. The eventual runner-up, 'Don't Bother To Knock', had been nowhere for much of the first half of the voting, eventually climbing to fourth place following Birmingham's vote, and then to third after Cardiff's, reaching second place only in the last round of voting. Similarly, 'One Glance' managed to achieve joint third place in the final round of voting despite having been not much of a contender earlier on.

A total of seven songs received at least one set of maximum 12 points, and four regions – Norwich, Manchester, Cardiff and Plymouth – placed 'The Bad Old Days' as the winner. Of these, only Plymouth placed 'Don't Bother To Knock' in second place. The Norwich jury though showed pretty good judgement, getting the top six in the top six places, albeit in a slightly different order. 'The Bad Old Days' scored 80.36% of the maximum vote it could have obtained, while 'Don't Bother To Knock' achieved 69.05%.

The awards were presented by the BBC TV Head of Light Entertainment, James Gilbert. Stephanie De-Sykes and Stuart Slater both came on stage to receive their awards, and Terry Bradford accepted the award on behalf of Co-Co.

Co-Co reprised 'The Bad Old Days' with the end credits playing over the song.

1978 UNITED KINGDOM

CREDITS
Producer: Stewart Morris
Designer: Victor Meredith
Assistant Designers: Jim Hatchard and Debby Knight
Costume Designer: Barbara Lane
Make-Up Designer: Judy Cain
Sound Supervisor: Chris Holcombe
Lighting Supervisor: Bert Robinson
Vision Mixer: Mike Turner
Senior Communications: Roy Carpenter
Engineering Planner: John Wiggins
Show Working Supervisors: Les Runham and Reg Smoothey
Assistant Floor Manager: Annie Ogden
Production Assistants: Martin Shardlow and Lydia Spratt
Floor Assistants: Ian Pleeth, Michael Leggo and Carmella Milne
Musical Director: Alyn Ainsworth
Scrutineer: Jim Heywood
Scoreboard Production Assistant: Joe Austin
House Manager: Les De Souza

The contest had an audience of 25.70% of the population (12.98 million) from the start of the programme at 19.30, rising to 29.00% (14.65 million) from 20.15, and scored an RI of 56. A copy of the programme has been retained in the BBC archives.

SONGS FOR EUROPE VOLUME TWO

All the songs were released on 7" singles. Only the winner, 'The Bad Old Days', made the charts, reaching number 13. The initial release had a picture sleeve cover, and curiously noted the B-side as being a song called 'Keep Singing Those Love Songs', although it was actually one called 'Get You Out Of My Life'. A USA promo single features both mono and stereo versions of 'The Bad Old Days'.

Co-Co performed 'The Bad Old Days' on *Miss England 1978* on 5 April, the editions of *Top of the Pops* broadcast on 6 and 20 April, *Pebble Mill at One* on 12 April, *The Val Doonican Show* on 15 April and *Cheggers Plays Pop* on 17 April. All five members of the Jarvis Brothers also appeared on *Cheggers Plays Pop* with 'One Glance' on the edition broadcast on 10 April. All these programmes have been retained in the BBC archives.

Co-Co also performed their song on ITV, on the edition of *Tiswas* broadcast on 8 April, which is not known to exist, and in an item on *Magpie* broadcast on 14 April, a copy of which is held in the archives of the British Film Instute.

A live version of 'The Bad Old Days' also appears in a Brian Matthew-presented programme on the BBC *Top of the Pops* transcription disc number 705, an LP that was sent out for use by overseas radio stations.

EUROVISION SONG CONTEST PREVIEWS
Presented by Terry Wogan.
Recorded on Saturday 8 April

The previews, which were once more co-ordinated by the BBC, had to be ready by 1 April, and were transmitted over the Eurovision Network on 7 April, for broadcast between 10 and 18 April. As usual, the rules allowed for them to be shown only once. Also as usual, BBC1 transmitted the first programme earlier than was technically allowed.

1978 UNITED KINGDOM

Part One: Sunday 9 April at 16.12.24 (Duration 32'00"). Audience 7.10% (3.59 million). RI 57.
Part Two: Sunday 16 April at 16.44.32 (Duration 31'35"). Audience 4.30% (2.17 million). RI 59.

Each of the two preview programmes was publicised by way of a trailer after the previous evening's edition of *The Val Doonican Show*. These trailers ran for 32" and 23" respectively and featured Terry Wogan. A copy of the one used for Part Two is known to exist on audio.

The songs were previewed in the order in which they would be performed in the contest, except for the United Kingdom's, which as usual was shown at the end of Part Two. The preview for 'The Bad Old Days' was shot around the Tower Bridge area in London.

CREDIT
Television Presentation: Marcus Plantin

The BBC Audience Research Report on the *Eurovision Song Contest* 1978 would later ask its sample of 490 viewers whether or not they had watched the preview programmes beforehand. 13% had watched Part One only, 13% had watched Part Two only, and 19% had watched both. However, 52% had seen neither, and 6% weren't sure if they had seen them.[2]

---

2 Total comes to more than 100% due to rounding.

1978 EUROVISION SONG CONTEST

Two countries returned to the line-up this year: Denmark, who had been absent since as long ago as 1966, and Turkey, who made only their second appearance, having debuted in 1975. This made it the first time that Turkey and Greece had appeared in the same contest, and brought the total number of entrants up to a new record of 20 – the maximum allowed.

The Grand Amphitheatre in the Palais des Congrès was the venue chosen by French hosts TF1 (Télévision Française 1). This could seat an audience of around 3,700. In addition to the participating countries, the programme was shown in Yugoslavia, Tunisia, Algeria, Morocco, Jordan, Iceland, Hungary, Czechoslovakia, Soviet Union, East Germany, Poland, Japan and Hong Kong (who took it live by satellite for the first time).

In December 1977, Dubai Radio and Colour Television in the United Arab Emirates had written to the EBU (of which they were an associate member) to enquire if they would be eligible to enter the 1979 *Eurovision Song Contest*, indicating that, if so, they would be prepared to hold a national selection for it. In January 1978 they were informed that only active members of the EBU could participate, but that they could broadcast the forthcoming edition live (or by deferred transmission) if they paid the passive participant fee. They decided to pay the fee, and therefore the event was broadcast for the first time in the United Arab Emirates also.

Overall the contest was expected to be seen by a total audience of some 500 million – the largest to date.

For the first time, the contest had two presenters, Denis Fabre and Léon Zitrone. The latter did most of the English announcements, and was the first male presenter since Lohengrin Filipello in the first contest in 1956.

After the confusion in 1977, the rules had been strengthened to enforce the use of a native language from each country.

The budget for the contest was divided up as follows: 50% of the total came from France, the United

1978 EUROVISION SONG CONTEST

Kingdom, Germany, Italy and Spain, each contributing 31,157 Swiss Francs; 33% came from Belgium, the Netherlands, Austria, Switzerland, Denmark, Sweden, Norway, Turkey, Finland and Greece, each contributing 10,281 Swiss Francs; and the remaining 17% came from Portugal, Ireland, Luxembourg, Monaco and Israel, with 6,231 Swiss Francs each.

On Monday 17 April rehearsals started in the Palais des Congrès with the orchestra between 17.00 and 20.00.

The first full rehearsals with the artists commenced on Tuesday 18 April at 13.00. They had 40 minutes each and rehearsed in order, starting with Ireland. The United Kingdom's slot was from 20.30 to 21.10. Belgium concluded the first day, finishing at the rather late time of 22.50.

Rehearsals also started at 13.00 on Wednesday 19 April and followed the same pattern as the first day, from the Netherlands through to Sweden.

The second round of rehearsals started on Thursday 20 April at 13.30 with Ireland. This time each country had just 20 minutes on stage. The United Kingdom was scheduled between 16.10 and 16.30, with Belgium finishing at 17.10. The commentators' briefing followed at 18.00, and then there was a rehearsal of the voting from 19.00.

The countries in the second half of the draw had their second rehearsal on Friday 21 April from 13.30, again following the same pattern as the previous day. The first full dress rehearsal with dummy voting came later that evening, from 20.30 to 23.30.

Saturday 22 April saw a further rehearsal with the scoreboard from 14.30, followed by a final dress rehearsal from 14.30 until around 16.30 or 16.45. The live broadcast was at 21.30 local time.

Bookmakers had the United Kingdom 7/2 favourite, France and Luxembourg 4/1, Ireland 6/1, Belgium 8/1, Netherlands 10/1, Spain 12/1 and Monaco 14/1.

Radio Times promoted the contest with a four-page feature on the French pop scene, including an article written by Paul Gambaccini. This edition of the magazine was publicised from Wednesday 19 to Friday 21 April by way of trailers broadcast each evening on BBC1, featuring 20" of 'The Bad Old Days' and 25" of the French entry *Il Y Aura Toujours Des Violons*.

Also on the evening of Friday 21 April, BBC1 broadcast a 1'10" trailer for the contest itself. This featured Terry Wogan and concluded with 20" of 'The Bad Old Days'. A copy of this trailer exists on audio.

The same evening's edition of BBC1's *Tonight* programme had an extensive *Eurovision* feature, which included interviews with Bryan Johnson, Ronnie Carroll, Caline and Olivier Toussaint, Co-Co, Bill Martin and Frank Naef and featured clips from some of the contests previously held in United Kingdom, specifically those of 1960, 1963, 1974 and 1977. In addition there were a couple of extracts, of 19" and 31" duration respectively, of Co-Co performing their entry, this time taken from the 20 April edition of *Top of the Pops*. There were also audio extracts of 'Puppet On A String' and 'Congratulations'. This programme is still retained in the BBC's archives.

There were a couple of trailers on BBC1 on Saturday 22 April. One used 15" of 'The Bad Old Days' as part of a general Saturday evening programmes trailer; the other, shown just after *Rolf on Saturday OK!*, was specifically devoted to the contest and used 1'09" from 'The Bad Old Days'.

EUROVISION SONG CONTEST 1978
Saturday 22 April 1978 at 20.30.01 (Duration 146' 16")
From the Palais des Congrès, Paris, France
Presented by Denis Fabre and Léon Zitrone

Terry Wogan provided the commentary for BBC1, and Ray Moore for Radio 2.

1978 EUROVISION SONG CONTEST

Ireland	'Born To Sing' (2'56")	Sung by Colm C T Wilkinson.	Composed by Colm C T Wilkinson.	Conducted by Noel Kelehan.

Norway	*'Mil Etter Mil'* (2'38")	Sung by Jahn Teigen.	Composed by Kai Eide.	Conducted by Carsten Klouman.

Italy	*'Questo Amore'* (2'56")	Sung by I Ricchi E Poveri.	Words by Sergio Bardotti. Music by Dario Farina and Mauro Lusini.	Conducted by Nicola Samale.

Finland	*'Anna Rakkaudelle Tiliaisuus'* (2'26")	Sung by Seija Simola.	Words by Reijo Karvonen and Seija Simola. Music by Reijo Karvonen.	Conducted by Ossi Runne.

Portugal	*'Dai Li Dou'* (2'23")	Sung by Gemini.	Words by Carlos Quintas. Music by Vitor Mamede.	Conducted by Thilo Krassman.

SONGS FOR EUROPE VOLUME TWO

France	'Il Y Aura Toujours Des Violons' (2'53")	Sung by Joël Prévost.	Words by Didier Barbelivien. Music by Gérard Stern.	Conducted by Alain Goraguer.

Spain	'Bailemos Un Vals' (2'52")	Sung by Jose Véléz.	Composed by Ramón Arcusa and Manuel de la Calva.	Conducted by Ramón Arcusa.

United Kingdom	'The Bad Old Days' (2'34")	Sung by Co-Co (Terry Bradford, Keith Hasler, Cheryl Baker, Paul Rodgers, Josie Andrews and Charles Brennan).	Composed by Stephanie De-Sykes and Stuart Slater.	Conducted by Alyn Ainsworth.

'To do the *Eurovision* was absolutely fantastic,' is the opinion of lead singer Terry Bradford. 'It was a phenomenal thing to do. We didn't know how the song would do in the contest itself, had no idea. Everyone was telling us we were the favourites, but it was down to us to do the best we could. Looking back, the sound balance was pretty awful, but to be fair they had got about a 30-second turnaround from one song to the next. There is one thing that stands out in my mind: as we walked onto the stage, all the microphones were in the wrong places, and at

1978 EUROVISION SONG CONTEST

the wrong heights. The bit you don't see is me shouting across to the guys, and us just grabbing the microphones and putting them where they were supposed to be. So we'd gone from being pretty calm, to sheer panic.

'We thought we had done all right, because our performance got a huge reaction in the hall; absolutely enormous. But of course that's not the feed that is going down the line to people's televisions. The feed in the hall is basically just a PA. We thought we had done the best we could, and with the tremendous reaction, we thought we had a chance. I remember reading some newspaper articles afterwards saying how bad the sound balance had been. I'm not making excuses, it was just what happened. I know now from my years in a recording studio just how difficult it can be, and the pressure on the sound engineer on a live show with that huge audience was enormous.

'When the votes came in, we thought we couldn't have been as good as we had thought, and it was disappointing. But we had achieved a hit record, had appeared on *Top of the Pops* and had gained a lot of television work – everything you dream of as a young musician – and no-one can take that away from you.

'There were some good songs in the contest, and I did have a feeling that Israel would win. The juries went for a good hook and chorus, and it was a strong song. We had a fantastic time, we had a ball, it's something I loved doing and it was hugely enjoyable.'

'The *Eurovision* really wasn't a nice experience at all,' states Cheryl Baker by contrast. 'When everyone else came off stage all the other artists applauded. When we came off stage no-one did. I think the United Kingdom always used to be the favourites, and there seemed to be a bit of animosity. The countries were segregated, and the only time you were all together was at formal functions, where you would meet the mayor etc, and it was all very staid. Then to lose so badly, coming eleventh, the worst the UK had done at that time, was just awful.'

'I hoped we would do creditably well, and I was surprised we did so badly,' says composer Stephanie De-Sykes. 'I couldn't understand it, because we almost got a standing ovation in the hall, it was amazing. When we got home, I saw the replay – it was the early day of video recorders – and I thought someone must have thrown a switch [to mute the sound]. It didn't bear any relation to what had happened in the hall. It was the best performance they'd done … So I was confused. Something went wrong somewhere.'

Greek singer Demis Roussos told the *Daily Express*: 'Their voices didn't come over strongly enough because the sound balance of the microphones wasn't high enough.' Turkish officials also criticised the French TV coverage: 'The microphones were weak and they often filmed the group from the back at important moments in the song, missing their effective moments. Co-Co should never have been eleventh. Their song was good as well as their choreography and clothes.'

Before the contest, the *Daily Mail* opined: 'Already shaping up to be a hit in Britain, the song itself is unremarkable, except that it contains all the tested ingredients that market researchers feel necessary for success. It could well win and will certainly be highly placed.'

Brian Wesley of the *Sun* said: 'It could win, thanks mainly to a lack of opposition. I think it's trite, but then I said the Bee Gees were finished! Rating 7/10.'

Another, unknown reviewer wrote: 'If Co-Co don't win, it won't be through lack of trying. They prepared for *Eurovision* like six athletes going for the Olympics. An easy-on-the-ear foot tapper. The Continentals see us as their biggest rival.'

Switzerland	*'Vivre'* (2'49")	Sung by Carole Vinci.	Words by Pierre Alain. Music by Alain Morisod.	Conducted by Daniel Janin.
Belgium	*'L'Amour Ça Fait Chanter La Vie'* (2'56")	Sung by Jean Vallée.	Composed by Jean Vallée.	Conducted by Jean Musy.

1978 EUROVISION SONG CONTEST

Jean Vallée had sung for Belgium in 1970, finishing in joint eighth position with '*Viens L'oublier*'. He recorded an English version of his 1978 entry as 'Goodbye', with lyrics by Bill Martin and Phil Coulter.

Netherlands	"T Is Ok' (2'33")	Sung by Harmony.	Words by Toon Gispen and Dick Kooiman. Music by Eddy Ouwens.	Conducted by Harry van Hoof.
Turkey	'*Sevince*' (2'44")	Sung by Nazar.	Words by Huli Aktunç. Music by Dağhan Baydur and Onno Tunç.	Conducted by Onno Tunç.
Germany	'*Feur*' (2'48")	Sung by Ireen Sheer.	Words by John Möring. Music by Jean Frankfurter.	Conducted by Jean Frankfurter.

In 1974 Ireen Sheer had sung for Luxembourg, finishing joint fourth with 'Bye, Bye, I Love You'.

SONGS FOR EUROPE VOLUME TWO

Monaco	*Les Jardins De Monaco* (2'36")	Sung by Caline and Olivier Toussaint.	Words by Didier Barbelivien and Jean Albertini. Music by Olivier Toussaint and Paul de Senneville.	Conducted by Yvon Rioland.

The English version of the song, 'The Garden Of Monaco', had a lyric written by Paul Greedus.

Greece	'Charlie Chaplin' (2'40")	Sung by Tania Tsanaclidou.	Words by Yannis Xanthulis. Music by Sakis Tsilikis.	Conducted by Charis Andreadis.

Denmark	'Boom-Boom' (2'58")	Sung by Mabel.	Composed by Michael Trempenau, Andy Kulmbak Christian Have and Peter Nielsen.	Conducted by Helmer Olesen.

1978 EUROVISION SONG CONTEST

Luxembourg	'Parlez-Vous Français?' (2'53")	Sung by Baccara.	Words by Frank Dostal and Péter Zentner. Music by Rolf Soja.	Conducted by Rolf Soja.

The duo Baccara from Spain had already achieved two hits in the British charts. 'Yes Sir, I Can Boogie' had been a number one hit in October 1977, and 'Sorry, I'm A Lady' had reached number eight in February 1978. Their self-titled album reached number 26 in the album charts in March 1978.

Despite finishing only seventh in the contest, this song was one of the biggest hits, charting in Sweden, Austria, Germany and the Netherlands.

Israel	'A-Ba-Ni-Bi' (2'52")	Sung by Izhar Cohen and the Alphabeta.	Words Ehud Manor. Music by Nurit Hirsh.	Conducted by Nurit Hirsh.

Izhar Cohen was born in March 1951 in Giv'atayim in Israel. He joined the army aged 18, entertaining fellow soldiers in organised shows, and within two months had his first hit record. The backing group Alphabeta comprised Reuven Erez, Lisa Gold-Rubin, Itzhak Okev, Nehama Shutan and Ester Tzuberi. Nurit Hirsh became the only woman to conduct a winning song in the contest.

The song had narrowly won the Israeli national final after an inital tie, beating *Belev Echad* sung by Chedva Armani and Pilpel Lavan. 'The hard part was winning the Israeli contest and figuring out how to present the song,' Cohen was quoted as saying in a later *Radio Times* article by Paul Gambaccini. 'What we were to wear, how we were to act, that was hard. Winning *Eurovision* was easy.'

The Israeli victory proved a problem for the Arabic countries taking the broadcast; several had opted out of the original performance, going to a commercial break instead. When it became obvious during the voting that Israel was going to win, they ended the transmission early. Jordanian television notoriously showed a picture of a bunch of flowers on screen and announced that Belgium had won the contest instead.

The winning song, 'A-Ba-Ni-Bi', was released with an English verse and Hebrew chorus. It eventually reached number 20 in the charts. Prior to that, though, there was an objection from the union Equity when it was proposed that Cohen and the Alphabeta should perform the song on *Top of the Pops*, as agreements stated that foreign artists had to have a top 30 hit before appearing on the show. Even pressure from the Israeli embassy failed to change the union's minds. However, video performances were permitted to be shown. Therefore an appearance by the act on the 11 May edition of *Top of the Pops* came from the *Eurovision Song Contest* itself, with the end credits played over it, and one on the 25 May edition was supplied by a foreign broadcaster and featured the English/Hebrew mix version. Both of these editions of *Top of the Pops* still exist in the BBC archives.

| Austria | 'Mrs Caroline Robinson' (2'27") | Sung by Springtime. | Words by Norbert Niedermayer, Gerhard Markel and Walter Markel. Music by Gerhard Markel and Walter Markel. | Conducted by Richard Österreicher. |

1978 EUROVISION SONG CONTEST

| Sweden | 'Det Blir Alltid Värre Framåt Natten' (2'52") | Sung by Björn Skifs. | Composed by Peter Himmelstrand. | Conducted by Bengt Palmers. |

Björn Skifs had wanted to perform the song in English as 'When The Night Comes', and up until moments before he was due to go on stage had every intention of doing so. However, the Swedish delegation was warned that this would mean instant disqualification. When he got on stage, Skifs said, 'Sorry we kept you waiting, but here's the top of the bill,' and some of the first lyrics he delivered were nonsense, as he was unprepared to sing the Swedish version. However, he slipped into Swedish after a few lines for the rest of the performance.

THE VOTING
The voting system used was again the one adopted in 1975. Colin Berry announced the United Kingdom jury's points. The scoreboard was in French.

SONGS FOR EUROPE VOLUME TWO

	Ireland	Norway	Italy	Finland	Portugal	France	Spain	UK	Switzerland	Belgium	Netherlands	Turkey	Germany	Monaco	Greece	Denmark	Luxembourg	Israel	Austria	Sweden	TOTAL	POSITION
Ireland		12		3		5		7	10		10	5		10		10			6	8	86	5TH
Norway																					00	20TH
Italy	10	6			1	4	8	6	1	1		1	2	8	2		3				53	12TH
Finland		2																			02	18TH=
Portugal			4				1														05	17TH
France	6	3	10	2	2		5	8	6	8	6	4	10	5	8	8	1	5	12	10	119	3RD
Spain			7					8	2	4	7		4	6	12	2		6	7		65	9TH=
United Kingdom	3				6	2	3		2	4	2	6	8	7	3		5	2	5	3	61	11TH
Switzerland		5	1	1		7	4	2		7	8		6	2		3	8	1	10		65	9TH=
Belgium	12	7	6	6	4	12	2	12	10		5		3	12	12		7	7	4	4	125	2ND
Netherlands			5					3				4	1		5	6	12		1		37	13TH

1978 EUROVISION SONG CONTEST

Country																					Total	Place
Turkey		1				1		▨													02	18TH=
Germany	1		3	12	7		10		3	5	7	8	▨	10	7	1		3		7	84	6TH
Monaco	4	4	7	8	5	1		10	5	6	10	5	7	▨	4	10		8	1	12	107	4TH
Greece	7		2	5	8	10	7		4					▨	4	4	10	3		2	66	8TH
Denmark						6				1					▨		4	2			13	16TH
Luxembourg	2		12		12		12	7		3	3	2		6	1	7	▨			6	73	7TH
Israel	8	8	8	10	10	8	6	5	12	12	12	12	12	3	5	6	12	▨	8		157	1ST
Austria				3						3	1				2				▨	5	14	15TH
Sweden	5	10		4		3		4												▨	26	14TH

Analysis: For the first half of the voting there were two clear front-runners, Belgium and Israel, with the latter taking the lead in the fourth round. Unusually for what turned out to be the winner, Israel's entry didn't receive its first set of 12 points until as late as the ninth round of voting. After Belgium, the tenth country to vote, also gave its 12 points to Israel, the result never looked in doubt. Only Sweden, the final country to vote, awarded the Israeli song no points at all, but by then it didn't matter.

    The United Kingdom awarded the winner a modest five points, one of the lowest scores it received, and showed a remarkable preference for the French-language entries, distributing its top four votes to Belgium, Monaco, France and Luxembourg. It ignored the only other English-language entry, from Ireland. For the first time since 1966, the United Kingdom had finished outside the top four, eleventh place being a considerable come-down. It was also the first time under the new scoring system that the United Kingdom had failed to get a 12 point score from any jury, the best being an eight points from Germany.

It was the first ever win for Israel, and the best result to date for Belgium, while Norway became the first country to achieve zero points under the new scoring system.

WINNING REPRISE

| Israel | 'A-Ba-Ni-Bi' (2'46") | Sung by Izhar Cohen and the Alphabeta. | Words Ehud Manor. Music by Nurit Hirsh. | Conducted by Nurit Hirsh. |

CREDITS

Director: Bernard Lion
Music Director: François Rauber
EBU Scrutineer: Frank Naef

The contest was watched by 28.70% of the British population (14.49 million) at the start of the programme from 20.30, falling slightly to 28.00% (14.14 million) by 21.15, before rising to 37.10% (18.74 million) by 22.00. It scored an RI of 49.

1978 EUROVISION SONG CONTEST

The BBC's Audience Research Report indicated that the majority of the viewers sampled had enjoyed the programme, though some had had difficulty in reading the scores, and a large number did not agree with the result. Several said they had not enjoyed the United Kingdom's entry and that the songs hadn't been as good as in previous years. A third thought that the artists had been good and made the best of the material, and a few noted that the performers had seemed to concentrate more on bizarre dress and not on the vocals and tunes.

Viewers had enjoyed Terry Wogan's humorous and light-hearted comments, and some thought him the best part of the programme. A few considered him too critical, but most thought he was the right person to hold this type of programme together. Some thought he ran the risk of being over-exposed.

The BBC has retained a copy of its broadcast version in its archives.

1979 UNITED KINGDOM

603 songs were submitted for the 1979 competition, with the final 12 being revealed on Tuesday 18 December 1978, at the same time the date and venue of the Final were announced: 8 March 1979 at the Royal Albert Hall.

Martin Pursey of the MPA told the press: 'In previous years there has been criticism that the method of choosing the song was unfair. So we have tried to devise a foolproof system. We've had some pretty duff stuff to sift through. But there are some really good numbers left in this year's batch of songs.'

There had been ten panels, each with ten judges, to sort out the entries. Each panel was played exactly two minutes of each of 60 songs, on the basis of which the judges awarded them points out of ten. Then all the panels got together to vote for a shortlist of 30 songs. After that the BBC took over, with Head of Light Entertainment James Gilbert, Radio 1 Controller Dennis Chinnery and members of the MPA, to decide the final 12.

Two of the songs that didn't get through were 'Back In The Air Again', composed by Harold Spiro and sung by Tim Clark, and 'Don't Shine Your Light', composed by John Howard and sung by Tenth and Parker. The latter reached the shortlist of 30, but not the final 12.

Just as in 1977, however, the contest was hit by industrial action. A strike was called by the Association of Broadcasting Staff in protest over the dismissal of rigger-driver Terry Ryan, who had allegedly been involved in an incident with his boss outside the BBC Club in Acton, west London, which led to his boss being taken to hospital for treatment. The BBC refused to reinstate Ryan, so his workmates walked out.

In this instance, the strike meant that the event had to be abandoned altogether. Consequently the songs were judged on the basis of the record versions instead – with 'Mary Ann', performed by Black Lace, coming out the winner. The cancellation of the programme was estimated to have cost the BBC £50,000.

Alan Barton, lead singer of Black Lace, said at the time: 'All the entrants knew by five minutes to six at the

1979 UNITED KINGDOM

Royal Albert Hall that the show was definitely off. The trouble had been brewing all afternoon, so no-one was surprised. We all assumed the contest would go out on radio at least, but it seemed they'd left the radio side of things too late and it was impossible to slot it in.'

Singer Eleanor Keenan was having her make-up done when she heard the news: 'Composer Roger Whitaker had organised a great designer to do my beautiful dress and a choreographer for the presentation, and he'd said that he didn't want the BBC to do my make-up, so he'd got a suite in a hotel nearby and had a make-up artist come in. About half-way through having my make-up done, a phone call came through to say it was cancelled. It must have been around four or five in the afternoon. We were all told to go to the Royal Garden Hotel, where the winner would be announced. My family had flown over from Ireland to be there, and my boyfriend had flown in from Scandinavia, and Roger said, "We are not going anywhere, and not to the Royal Garden Hotel unless you have won." So we all went to Soho to have a meal!'

Nola York, composer of the entry due to be performed by the group Ipswich, recollects: 'We were told quite early on that it might be cancelled, so we sat all afternoon waiting to hear. About five o'clock we heard it was off. Obviously the group were upset, as I think it would have been their first television appearance. I just took it on the chin – that's showbusiness – but I felt sad for Ipswich. I was also disappointed for my friend Ray, who had hired a lot of Muppet costumes for the performance. All my friends had seats in a box, so win or lose it would have been great fun. Even my accountant and my bank manager and his wife were going to be there.'

Paul Griggs of the group Guys 'n' Dolls wrote in his book *Diary of a Musician* (extract reproduced here with permission):

> Thursday 8 March: It was our second day at the Royal Albert Hall rehearsing for tonight's *A Song for Europe* contest, which was due to be broadcast live. Around five o'clock everything seemed to stop and there were small groups of technicians and staff having discussions. At six o'clock it was announced that

an unofficial strike had been called by technicians and the contest was cancelled. There was mayhem, as some of the four thousand people who were going to make up the audience started to gather outside. All of the contestants had friends and family turning up and were frantically trying to find them to break the news that the show was off.

On BBC1's *Nationwide* news magazine programme that evening, presenter Bob Wellings had to make an apology on behalf of the BBC and request that those with tickets should not make their way to the Royal Albert Hall.

Because the show was never broadcast, research paperwork is minimal. Details such as the expected duration of the songs and the names of group members and backing vocalists are incomplete. Such information is included here only where known, and some spellings could be inaccurate. The names of the producers and/or arrangers of the record versions are given where known.

A SONG FOR EUROPE 1979
Thursday 8 March (Scheduled for 19.20) (Scheduled duration: 100'00")
Presented by Terry Wogan (Scheduled)

| Song One | 'Mary Ann' | Sung by Black Lace (Alan Barton, Colin Routh (aka Colin Gibb) Terry Dobson and Steven Scholey). | Composed by Peter Morris. |

1979 UNITED KINGDOM

Black Lace was a four-piece band from Wakefield, Yorkshire. Terry Dobson (drums and percussion) and Alan Barton (lead singer and guitar) had met in the early '70s at a music centre in Wakefield, and initially formed a five-piece group. This first group split up, but after a few months Dobson and Barton decided to try again with another one. This was when Steve Scholey (bass guitar and vocals) joined. Their first gig, playing at a local club, was for a fee of £2.50 … between them! After years of gigging semi-pro, they decided to take the gamble and turn professional, giving up their day jobs to concentrate on a music career. Barton had been a riveter, Dobson a joiner and Scholey a plater. However, a fourth group member at that time didn't want to take the risk, so at that point Colin Routh (lead guitar and vocals), a former lift engineer, was brought in as a replacement.

The name Black Lace was adopted by the group after an agent suggested it. 'This was way before the time of the similarly-named Paper Lace,' Barton informed journalist Gerry Fallon. 'Mind you, just as we were getting our own name known around the club circuit, Paper Lace had their first hit single ["Billy Don't Be A Hero"]. It got to a point where people kept mistaking us for them. We've even been called Bootlaces.'

Black Lace had already gained a couple of awards by 1979, one for being Radio Leeds Group of the Year and one for winning a National Talent Contest organised by the *Cabaret and Variety* newspaper.

Dobson, the drummer in the group, celebrated his twenty-seventh birthday on the day of the abandoned *A Song for Europe* event.

Composer Peter Morris had apparently approached the band after seeing a promotional video they had made in order to try to obtain more work. He felt they were ideal for his song, 'Mary Ann', which he wanted to have a sound similar to that of the group Smokie. It was decided that Barton's voice would suit the song best on the lead vocal, although Scholey had previously been the main vocalist, and allegedly there was some tension within the group over the decision.

The band made a demo of the song, which was sent to EMI Records and favourably received. After being signed up, Black Lace then recorded the final version of the song. The single's B-side, 'Drivin'', was composed by

SONGS FOR EUROPE VOLUME TWO

group members Barton and Routh.

There were some allegations at the time that 'Mary Ann' plagiarised the song 'Oh Carol', coincidentally recorded by Smokie, and legal action was considered. The publishers of 'Mary Ann', ATV Music, insisted that any similarity was purely coincidental. They proved that the notation of the two songs was different, and the case was dropped. Composer Morris said: 'My song is nothing like "Oh Carol", and I am naturally very upset at some of the suggestions.'

About the event being hit by industrial action, Routh told the *London Evening Standard*: 'The contest is all about the songs, and that's how the winner was picked.' Barton agreed: '[It] is a songwriters' contest, and it was a fairer way to pick the best song. But we were very disappointed at not going on television; it would have been our first time. We were really glad we won. We have a good song and we were lucky to go on first. But we don't want to get into a slanging match about the way the winner was chosen.'

Morris had co-composed the 1978 *A Song for Europe* entry 'Don't Let Me Stand In Your Way', which had finished seventh for the group Babe Rainbow. He produced the record version of 'Mary Ann'.

| Song Two | 'You Are My Life' | Sung by Lynda Virtu. | Words by Tony Colton. Music by Jean Roussel. |

Lynda Virtu had started her career in a group called 5,000 volts, working in pubs and clubs, where she was spotted by the brother of popular singer-songwriter Cat Stevens.

Tony Colton had begun his career working in small bands and eventually progressed to backing bands with Eddie Cochran and Gene Vincent. He had gone to the USA and written and produced mainly country music for Johnny Cash, Deniece Williams and Joe Cocker amongst others.

1979 UNITED KINGDOM

Jean Alain Roussel was born in Port Louis, Mauritius in 1951. He had started to learn piano on a boat from Mauritius to Britain in 1954 with musician Robert White. He had studied at the Trinity College of Music, London, on piano from the age of seven and cello from the age of 12. Under the guidance of American jazz lyricist and singer Jon Hendricks he worked on jazz and blues music. In 1969 he started playing on various records, mainly on keyboards, and working as an arranger, with artists like Cat Stevens, Donovan, Elkie Brooks and Thin Lizzy.

Colton and Roussel produced the record version of 'You Are My Life'.

Song Three	'Who Put The Shine On Your Shoes?'	Sung by Ipswich (Wendy Chapman, Chris Connolly, Jean Perry, Richard Croome, Tim Moore and David Nelson).	Composed by Nola York.

Ipswich was formed in 1977 and took its name from the home town of two of the members. As with Black Lace, this would have been the group's first appearance on television.

Nola York had sung with a girl trio called the Chantelles and had written the music for the musical *The Lady or the Tiger*, which had transferred to the Fortune Theatre in London, making her the first woman to write a complete musical score for the West End. 'Who Put The Shine On Your Shoes?' was her first and only entry into the contest. York recalls: 'I wrote a lot of songs that I recorded in Decca Studios, and they asked me if they could put a group together and use one of my songs, "Who Put The Shine On Your Shoes?", and enter it in the contest.

SONGS FOR EUROPE VOLUME TWO

I thought I had as much chance as anybody else, but I did like Terry Bradford's song sung by the Nolans. When the show was cancelled we all went back to a friend's house in Chiswick and had a terrific party, and we got the results later on that evening.'

York adds: 'Would I enter again? I don't think so, but I would never say no, and I do still watch it. I think it's great fun, and much the same as it always was, but with perhaps more emphasis on the performance.'

York later wrote and sang the disco track 'Hi Fantasy', which was released in the Netherlands and got to number four in the United Kingdom Dance Chart in 1985. She also wrote the music for another West End musical, *Wild, Wild Women* at the Astoria. Today, she continues performing, singing, playing the piano and composing songs and musicals.

| Song Four | 'Mr Moonlight' | Sung by Herbie Flowers and the Daisies (Doreen Chanter, Irene Chanter, George Fenton, Barry de Souza and Ken Freeman). | Composed by Herbie Flowers and Doreen Chanter. |

Herbie Flowers (born Brian Keith Flowers in 1938) is a musician specialising in bass guitar, double bass and tuba. He had been a member of the Johnny Harris Orchestra, and played in the orchestra accompanying Lulu in the 1969 *A Song for Europe*. He had worked with Elton John and David Bowie. In 1969 he co-founded the highly successful group Blue Mink, and in the mid-'70s featured in the line-up of T Rex. Amongst his songwriting credits he is probably best remembered for the novelty hit 'Grandad' for Clive Dunn. Shortly after the contest he founded the group Sky, together with classical guitarist John Williams and Francis Monkman.

There were five people in the backing group the Daisies, including the co-composer Doreen Chanter and her sister Irene. The pair had started in a group called the Chanters in 1967 along with their five brothers. A year later they had formed a duo, Birds of a Feather, and recorded four singles and an album. Later they had changed their name to the Chanter Sisters.

The sisters have performed backing vocals for many big name stars, including Elton John, John Miles, Chris Farlowe and Long John Baldry, and for many *A Song for Europe* entries over the years, quite often out of vision. Amongst the songs that Doreen Chanter has composed are 'Star' and 'Midnight Flyer' for Kiki Dee, the latter with her sister Irene. Doreen Chanter went on to tour with the likes of Meatloaf, Joe Cocker and Van Morrison.

Ken Freeman was one of the pioneers of electronic music, and worked with Mike Oldfield. He went on to write the theme music for the BBC's dramatisation of John Wyndham's *The Tripods* and both *Casualty* and *Holby City*.

George Fenton is best known as a composer and has written over 70 film and television scores, including for *Ghandi*, *The Madness of King George*, *Bergerac* and *The Blue Planet*.

Barry de Souza was one of the country's leading session drummers and worked with the likes of Rick Wakeman. He died in March 2009.

Jeff Wayne produced and arranged the record version of this entry.

| Song Five | 'Miss Caroline Newley' | Sung by M Squad (Adrian Baker, Brian Hudson, Tom Marshall, Steve ? and Colin ?). | Composed by Adrian Baker. |

SONGS FOR EUROPE VOLUME TWO

The five performers had all played in other groups in the past, but about a year earlier had decided to renew their schoolboy acquaintance and formed M Squad.

Composer Adrian Baker, born in 1951, was known more as a singer, having had his first solo album released in 1975 under the title 'Into A Dream'. He had had a hit single, 'Sherry', which reached number ten and stayed in the charts for eight weeks, and had performed several times on *Top of the Pops*. Baker had also written, arranged and produced for the group Liquid Gold, with the songs 'Anyway You Do It' and 'My Baby's Baby'.

Drummer Brian Hudson went on to become the Nolan Sisters' tour manager, and married Linda Nolan in 1981. He died in September 2007.

The strings on the record version of this entry were arranged by Lynton Naiff.

| Song Six | 'Call My Name' | Sung by Eleanor Keenan plus five backing vocalists (including Lavinia Rodgers, Louis Rodgers and Jan Mercedes). | Composed by Roger Whittaker. |

Eleanor Keenan had been part of the all-girl vocal group Three's A Crowd, which had had hits with the songs 'Dance In The Old Fashioned Way' and 'Cry Baby'. She had also worked as a vocalist with the Syd Lawrence orchestra and as a backing singer for the likes of Vince Hill, Matt Monro and Lulu. She had appeared in *A Song for Europe* 1976 as one of the backing singers on stage for Tony Christie's entry 'Queen Of The Mardi Gras'.

Keenan explains how her 1979 appearance came about: 'I was a backing singer for Roger Whittaker for

1979 UNITED KINGDOM

about a year before the contest, and we travelled everywhere. Roger was huge in Canada, Scandinavia, Germany and all over the place. I didn't really want to be a backing singer, but this was a way of seeing the world and not having to pay for it! It was a very nice job and he was a nice guy. One day when we were touring in Canada I was doing the sound check – in fact I don't think I have sung through a better PA system since. On occasions like that we used to have a little play around with songs while we had the chance. Roger wasn't always at the sound check, so I used to sing some of my own songs. That day, he came in and actually heard me doing some solos of my own. He collared me at the end of the evening and said, "Look, the *Eurovision* is coming up. I'm going to write some songs, would you be interested in singing them?" I said "I'd love to." He came up with a couple of songs, and we went into a studio in Toronto and put them down. Money was no object to him, as he was doing so well, so he paid for a full orchestra, producer, everything; it was amazing. I'd thought I'd died and gone to heaven. So we recorded two songs, and he sent them off, and then a few months later, he came into the gig one night and said, "We've got in. It's 'Call My Name'; they have chosen that one." We were over the moon.'

However, the good times weren't to last, as Keenan reveals: 'Running up to the contest, Roger kept saying to me on the gigs, "Get yourself a lawyer, because if you win, you'll need to sort out contracts. If you win, I'd like to manage you, and I would like you to do the first half of my show. But if you don't win, I'd still like you to be my backing singer, and I'll give you a spot in the show." I sought advice from someone and they said, "Don't sign anything until *A Song for Europe* is over, and then see where you stand." I took their advice, which I don't think was good advice, and right up to the day, I hadn't signed anything. Roger's manager was Irene Collins, and she kept getting her people to call me, and I would put them off by saying I hadn't signed anything yet, as I had been told that I shouldn't, and what was the point; "Roger trusts me, and I trust him, and we'll go along with whatever happens when it's over." So I didn't sign anything, and there was a big tour coming up with Roger after *A Song for Europe*; we were going off to Germany again. Roger came into the Royal Albert Hall that night and didn't speak to me, and it was all very awkward. The very next day after the contest I got the sack, because I hadn't signed anything. I got a telegram from Irene Collins saying, "As you haven't signed anything we have decided to dispense with your services. You are not even required as a backing singer." It was very, very disappointing.'

Decca Records rang Keenan, as they had heard the song and wanted to bring it out as a single, but she had already signed to CBS records some years earlier, and they wouldn't let her out of her contract to allow this. Eventually CBS released the single themselves, but by then the *A Song for Europe* momentum had gone, plus Whittaker had released his own version.

I asked Keenan why she thought that Whittaker hadn't entered the contest himself singing the song. She told me: 'I think at the time he was too big to do it. He was earning mega money, and I don't think he would have done it, as there were a lot of unknowns. He was travelling all over the place anyway; he could fill stadiums with thousands of people. I don't think he had even tried before as a composer.'

The whole experience still stands out for Keenan. Her memories are a little upsetting, owing to the Royal Albert Hall concert being cancelled and her then getting the sack, but she remembers liking the Guys 'n' Dolls entry. However, she adds: 'I never thought the song that won would have done so, ever … I remember we kept getting phone calls coming in, telling us what was happening, and the votes were coming in and it looked as if we were going to win, right up until about ten minutes before the end. It was a great song, and I really do believe that if it had been seen and heard, as it was quite dynamic, then it would have won. It had a really strong hook.'

For a brief while Keenan was out of work, but she then rejoined the Syd Lawrence Orchestra and is currently still with them. Although the big band music scene was very different from *A Song for Europe*, she would have loved to have done the contest again had the opportunity come her way, but it never did.

Whittaker was born in Nairobi in 1936 and arrived in the UK in 1959 to study at Bangor University. In the final year of his course he got involved with the student rag week and composed some demo songs for the rag show. One of these demos found its way to a music publisher, and within weeks Whittaker was recording his first single. Since then many big hits have followed, including 'Durham Town', 'New World In The Morning' and

1979 UNITED KINGDOM

'The Last Farewell', the latter helping him break into the US market.

Germany has always been a strong market for Whittaker, and he has recorded many songs in German, despite by his own admission being unable to speak a word of the language and having to deliver the lyrics phonetically. He is still working and touring at the time of this book's publication.

| Song Seven | 'How Do You Mend A Broken Heart?' | Sung by Guys 'n' Dolls (Julie Forsyth, Martine Howard, Dominic Grant and Paul Griggs). | Composed by Ben Findon and Michael Myers. |

The group Guys 'n' Dolls was formed in November 1974, originally with six members. They had a huge hit with 'There's A Whole Lot Of Loving' in January 1975, reaching number two in the UK charts. Several other singles followed, including 'You Don't Have To Say You Love Me', which was a number five hit. In 1977 two of the members, David Van Day and Thereza Bazar, left to form their own duo, Dollar.

Paul Griggs' book *Diary of a Musician* reveals more of the story behind their entry to *A Song for Europe* (extracts reproduced with permission):

> Tuesday 5 September 1978: The *Eurovision Song Contest* was often considered as a possible vehicle for resurrecting a flagging recording career, and this year, much to our dismay, Michael Levy (founder of Magnet Records) had this in mind for Guys 'n' Dolls. Today we were back in the studio with Ben Findon and Mike Myers, recording their overly dramatic ballad 'How Do You Mend A Broken Heart'. The idea was that this would be entered into *A Song for Europe* and hopefully reach the final 12 from which the British entry would be chosen.

SONGS FOR EUROPE VOLUME TWO

Tuesday 19 December, 1978: I had a call from Michael Levy to say we were in the final 12 for *A Song for Europe*. I think he expected me to be jumping around with joy, but I wasn't.

Monday 5 March: 'The *A Song for Europe* competition was looming and none of us was very enthusiastic, but today we visited the BBC rehearsal studios in Acton for the first get-together of contestants. With the exception of Guys 'n' Dolls and the Nolans, all the others were unknown.

Speaking to the press the day before the contest, group member Julie Forsyth said: 'We had reservations about entering, because no-one likes to lose in a song contest. But we know we have a good song and that, if we win, we could have another enormous hit on our hands.'

Paul Griggs takes up the story again in his diary, recalling what happened after the cancellation of the contest was announced:

Thursday 8 March: I managed to find Mum, Dad and [my wife] Lynne and got them inside the Royal Albert Hall while we pondered our next move. Michael Levy suggested we all go back to the Magnet office and await the result. He laid on food and drink and it turned into a bit of a party. At 21.20 the party came to an abrupt halt when we received a phone call to say that the then unknown Black Lace had won with a song called "Mary Ann" and Guys 'n' Dolls placed a lowly tenth out of 12. The atmosphere became subdued and everybody drifted off home. Despite having not really wanted to be in the contest I felt deflated, but I [also] felt very sorry for the unknown acts that had missed out on a chance of performing on stage at the Royal Albert Hall and appearing on television; an opportunity that might not come their way again. Michael Levy said that he would still release our record, but the reality was that failed *A Song for Europe* entries have no chance of chart success.

1979 UNITED KINGDOM

Composer Ben Findon had had a couple of songs before in the contest. In 1974 his and Geoff Wilkins' composition 'Hands Across The Sea' had finished third, while a year later his and Michael Myers' song 'Stand Up Like A Man' had finished second to 'Let Me Be The One'. He also co-composed the big Billy Ocean hit 'Love Really Hurts Without You'. Findon produced the record version of 'How Do You Mend A Broken Heart'; the musical director was Tom Parker.

Song Eight	'All I Needed Was Your Love'	Sung by Linda Kendrick (plus two backing vocalists).	Composed by Doug Taylor.

Linda Kendrick had been recording since the age of 14 and had worked with several pop acts, including Kiki Dee, the Kinks and Hot Chocolate. Amongst the singles she released were 'I Will See You There' (1969) and 'Sympathy For The Devil' (1974). Kendrick died in 2010.

This was the only entry by composer Doug Taylor to make it into the Final of *A Song for Europe*. He had a degree in law and had been writing songs since 1971.

The record version was produced by Norman Kurban.

Song Nine	'Home Again (Living With You)'	Sung by Monte Carlo (Barry Wortley, Paul Wortley, David Knowles and Michael Pearce).	Composed by David Knowles.

SONGS FOR EUROPE VOLUME TWO

Monte Carlo was a four-man working band from East Anglia, with Barry Wortley on drums, Paul Wortley on bass guitar, Michael Pearce on lead guitar and composer David Knowles on rhythm guitar.

The orchestra arrangement for the record version was conducted by Gerry Shury.

Song Ten	'Let It All Go'	Sung by Sal Davis plus backing vocalists (Val Stokes, Tony Jackson, Ruby James, Tracy Miller and John Clark).	Composed by Paul Curtis.

Sal Davis (aka Salim Abdullah) was born in Kenya and had toured with the Three Degrees, Boney M and Manhattan Transfer. He sang 'Back In Dubai', also written by Paul Curtis, which became very popular in the Gulf States.

Amongst the backing singers were Val Stokes, who had sung 'Swings And Roundabouts' in the 1977 contest; Ruby James, who had been a member of Midnight in 1978; and Tony Jackson, who had been a member of Sweet Dreams in 1976 and Midnight in 1978. Jackson died of a heart attack in 2001.

This was composer Paul Curtis's fifth entry to reach a Final of *A Song for Europe*. He had won the contest in 1975 with 'Let Me Be The One'. He also produced the record version of 'Let It All Go'; it was arranged by Colin Frechter, a distinguished arranger, conductor and composer.

Song Eleven	'Harry My Honolulu Lover'	Sung by the Nolan Sisters (Maureen Nolan, Anne Nolan, Bernie Nolan and Linda Nolan).	Composed by Terry Bradford.

The Nolan Sisters were an all-Irish female band. They had started out as the Singing Nolans when their family moved from Dublin to Blackpool in 1962. Originally the group comprised parents Tommy and Maureen, brothers Tommy and Brian and sister Denise and performed mainly on the northern club circuit. In 1974 the five daughters began performing as the Nolan Sisters and appearing on programmes like *It's Cliff Richard*, *Summertime Special*, *The Two Ronnies* and *The Morecambe and Wise Show*. In 1975 they supported Frank Sinatra on tour. In 1978 Denise left the group to pursue a solo career, leaving them at the time of the contest as a four-piece.

They were one of the favourites to win the contest and broke down and wept at the news of the cancellation. Anne Nolan told the press: 'The whole thing was a fiasco. We had worked for weeks on a special dance routine, which had to be seen.'

The group had already been pre-booked to appear on a special programme to mark the twenty-fifth anniversary of the Eurovision Network, in Montreux, Switzerland in April 1979, leading to speculation that it had been assumed they would win. They also had one of their biggest hits later that year with 'I'm In The Mood For Dancing', reaching number three in the charts.

The group has had line-up changes over the years, with younger sister Coleen joining and several of the members having pursued solo careers in singing, acting and presenting. There have also been some family splits and rows, but four of the sisters – Coleen, Bernie, Linda and Maureen – got back together for a tour in 2009. Bernie Nolan died of cancer in 2013.

Composer Terry Bradford had already been in the competition twice as a singer, as lead vocalist and guitarist with the group Co-Co, who had won the contest in 1978 with 'The Bad Old Days'. This year however he entered as a songwriter and, as he explains, he turned to one of his colleagues from Co-Co for assistance:

'I wrote the song and I got Cheryl Baker to sing on the demo. I thought her voice was absolutely right for the demo, and I asked her if she would do it as a favour. The one thing I learned from Co-Co and the nature of the music industry is that we had a limited shelf-life. If it had happened for us in 1976, we would have had a few more years out of it, but because punk and new wave came along in 1977, we were sort of old-fashioned before we had even started. As a boy/girl group we had achieved what we wanted, and we were quite happy with that. We had travelled everywhere, done shows and had a great time. Out of it had come a lot of great music-business experience as well, and it had opened a huge number of doors for me as a producer and a writer. I knew the Nolan Sisters' manager at the time, a guy known as Ray Scott, and I said to him that Co-Co couldn't really do the contest, because we had done it the year before, and we were still on the road as Co-Co, and it wouldn't have been ethically right to do it. So I asked if the Nolan Sisters would be interested in doing the song, because we were getting a very good reaction to it, and it was a quirky number.'

However, Bradford still wanted to be very much involved: 'The Nolans were in the studio at the time with Ben Findon, making their first album. I used to know the CBS records guy, Nicky Graham, and when this opportunity came along, almost as a bit of a bonus for them, I pushed like mad to be allowed to produce the record, as I knew the sort of style we could make it in, I'd done the demo, and I knew how we could make it really good. I had absolutely no chance, but I was invited to the recording studio, and the one thing I did say to them was that there was talk of the BBC having a strike, and if that happened, the songs would be judged on the records, so if they wanted to win it – and the girls were desperate to win it – then it was crucial that it was a really good record. I probably made myself very unpopular by pushing to produce it, but I wanted to get it absolutely right. To my horror, when we arrived in the studio, the girls didn't even know they were going to sing it on the day, so it was a case of "Get Bernie to try it," or "Get Linda to try it," and "Okay, that'll do," and the record was just sort of put together.

'I realise why. They had their album ready to go, and this was just a case of "Get it on, get it done, keep everybody happy and sing." I was obviously a bit disappointed that they'd not put the effort in, because although it came out okay, it could have been a really good record. At that point I had a little bit of a sinking feeling that if the judging was going to go to records, then they would not win it. They had a great routine and were well-choreographed, they looked great and they were a nice warm act to look at, all very good-looking girls. They would have stood a huge chance had it

1979 UNITED KINGDOM

been done and seen live, and they were huge favourites to win it. If the record had been stronger, then they might still have won. They were absolutely devastated when they came fourth, and I was disappointed as I knew that was my strongest chance of doing something as a songwriter in the contest. I thought Black Lace had a good pop song and a good record, but sometimes songs that are good records are not necessarily the best songs. With the Nolan Sisters, it was all going to be about the visual, and with Black Lace it was the better record.'

The record version of the sisters' entry was ultimately produced by Mike Hurst.

| Song Twelve | Fantasy | Sung by Kim Clark. | Composed by Richard Gillinson. |

Kim Clark from Glasgow was the youngest contestant of the night at the age of 18; she was also probably the shortest, at just four feet ten inches. She shared the same manager as Christian, who had come third the previous year.

'It's the most exciting thing that has happened so far in my singing career,' Clark told the *Daily Record*. She had fronted her own band when she was just 15, and had already appeared with other *Eurovision* artists such as ABBA, Cliff Richard and Lulu.

Composer Richard Gillinson must have thought he was cursed, as the previous time he had had a song in the Final, in 1977, the show was also hit by industrial action. His entry that year was 'Promises, Promises', co-written with David Hayes, which had finished fourth sung by Rags. Coincidentally it too had been the last song in the running order. Gillinson had won the *World Song Festival* in Toyko with 'Can't Hide My Love', also performed by Rags. He also produced the record version of 'Fantasy'.

THE VOTING

Though the show was blacked out, a song still had to be chosen to represent the United Kingdom at the forthcoming *Eurovision Song Contest*, so the 14 regional juries that were already assembled up and down the country still had to judge the songs. The usual procedure was for the jury members to hear the songs first on tape, then go off and have a meal, and then return to watch and vote upon the live performance. The only difference this time was that on their return after the meal, they simply listened again to the tapes of the songs and voted upon these versions. The voting system was the same as had been used since 1976.

Amongst the Glasgow jury was the author of this book, Gordon Roxburgh, who had been selected via a postcard quiz on BBC Radio Scotland. Other jury members were Tom Ferrie, a DJ with Radio Scotland; Winnie Lees, a TV critic for the *Sunday Mail*; and James Carson, who was still at school at the time. Writing in the fan club magazine *Eurovision Network News*, Carson reported on his evening: 'We were all really disappointed [by the cancellation of the concert], but we were told we would still get our chance to vote. Kim Clark, a Glasgow girl, did well in the Glasgow poll. In spite of the cancellation, I enjoyed my night as a juror, if only because it gave me celebrity status for a few days at school.'

My own memories of the experience are as follows. Our spokesperson (who may well have been Ken Bruce) did his own version of Terry Wogan between the songs, told us which entry was coming up next and tried to give us a bit of background information about the artist. After the final song was played and the marks were added up, I recall that we had a tie for one of the positions. We weren't told at the time which positions we were determining, but I think the song 'Miss Caroline Newley' was one of the songs involved, as I quite liked it and voted for it in the tie. There was a bit of a wait and then we heard a voice via the speakers from London informing us that they were ready to receive the votes – which according to later press reports were all called in by BBC Light Entertainment Head James Gilbert. I quickly grabbed some paper to write down the various juries' votes, which were intended to be taken in alphabetical order. Some were very faint and hard to hear, but our spokesperson kept a running tally to keep us informed of which entry was leading. We had no idea how our own jury had voted until the votes were announced, and I remember most of us looking surprised when it turned out that Black Lace had received our top points. No-one would admit to having placed it top, so my own theory was that it had just scored a good average mark all round, probably helped by it having been the first song, as it had been hard to pitch the marks at the beginning. So I suspect that it got a lot of three votes out of five.

I also remember that several of the regional juries proved hard to contact and had to be skipped over and returned to later, meaning that ultimately they were taken out of alphabetical order. Consequently I can't be sure of the exact order they came in towards the end. Two juries were particularly slow, one of them being Manchester. By this stage we were literally sitting waiting for the final two juries. The BBC staff were hinting it was time for us to go, but one or two of us were still keen to find out the result, as although Black Lace were in a good lead, mathematically they could still have been caught. Then at long last the penultimate jury came through and their marks meant that Black Lace could not now be overtaken. By this time we were obviously outstaying our welcome and were politely asked to leave.

Unfortunately, the votes of that final Manchester jury currently remain unknown. It is only thanks to the notes I took at the time that information about the other juries' votes survives to this day. This has since circulated in magazines and on the internet and has been generally been adopted as the official result. The official top five placings are included below.

Terry Wogan appeared on BBC1 at 21.26.28, following that evening's *Nine O'Clock News*, in a 1'55" item to announce who had won *A Song for Europe*. Winning group Black Lace had their first live interview on Radio 2 later in the evening, on Brian Matthew's *Midnight Ride* show, when the song 'Mary Ann' received its first airplay in full.

SONGS FOR EUROPE VOLUME TWO

	Aberdeen	Bangor	Belfast	Birmingham	Bristol	Cardiff	Glasgow	Leeds	London	Manchester	Newcastle	Norwich	Plymouth	Southampton	SUBTOTAL	POSITION
'Mary Ann'	5	5	11	9	11	12	12	12	11		9	11	12	12	132	1ST
'You Are My Life'	4	6	7	10	1	9	4	4	6		10	10	6	5	82	
'Who Put The Shine On Your Shoes?'	6	11	5	5	7	10	2	8	4		12	9	2	9	90	5TH
'Mr Moonlight'	7	10	8	2	9	6	5	6	3		6	8	10	10	90	
'Miss Caroline Newley'	1	2	6	1	3	3	7	5	7		3	1	1	4	44	11TH=
'Call My Name'	11	12	12	8	10	11	8	1	8		8	4	8	8	109	2ND=
'How Do You Mend A Broken Heart?'	3	1	3	12	8	2	3	3	5		7	3	5	1	56	10TH
'All I Needed Was Your Love'	2	7	1	3	2	1	1	2	1		1	2	4	6	33	12TH=
'Home Again'	12	4	4	4	6	4	9	9	10		4	12	3	2	83	
'Let It All Go'	10	3	2	6	5	5	6	7	12		5	6	7	3	77	
'Harry My Honolulu Lover'	9	9	10	7	4	8	10	10	2		11	5	9	7	101	4TH
'Fantasy'	8	8	9	11	12	7	11	11	9		2	7	11	11	117	2ND=

Analysis: Although 'Home Again' scored the first top mark, it was 'Call My Name' that stormed into an early lead, having achieved 35 out of a possible 36 points by the end of the third round of voting. In these early stages

1979 UNITED KINGDOM

it was being chased by 'Fantasy'. By contrast the eventual winner, 'Mary Ann', got off to a slow start, certainly by comparison with most previous winners. The first two juries, from Aberdeen and Bangor, both awarded it just five points, the lowest it would receive. It didn't achieve its first top mark until the sixth jury, and didn't rise to share the lead until the eighth, from Leeds, also awared it the maximum 12 points while giving 'Call My Name' just one point. After a few more rounds it surged into a runaway lead, and even the missing votes from Manchester weren't going to change things at the top of the board. No fewer than seven of the 12 songs received at least one set of maximum points.

It was the first time since the final of the *Festival of British Popular Songs* in 1956 that a song had won from position number one in the running order. It was the first time since 1971 that there had been a tie for second place.

CREDITS (Scheduled)
Producer: David G Hillier
Executive Producer: Robin Nash
Designer: John Hurst
Lighting: Barry Thomas
Sound: Chris Holcombe
Musical Director: Alyn Ainsworth

The programme was replaced in the BBC1 schedule with the movie *Hannibal Brooks*.

On Friday 9 March, Terry Wogan played all the entries on his morning Radio 2 programme, and had a short interview with Black Lace, recorded the previous evening. He also announced which songs had finished in the top four. An audio copy exists of most of this show.

Later that evening on BBC1, *Nationwide* covered the results, playing brief excerpts of the top five songs and a short interview with Black Lace. This edition of *Nationwide* is not in the BBC archives.

Nearly all of the songs were released as 7" singles, but only the winner, 'Mary Ann', was to make the charts, reaching number 42, one of the lowest positions for a United Kingdom entry to date. However Black Lace still made two appearances on *Top of the Pops*, on the editions of 15 and 29 March, the latter of which featured just a 1'04" extract of the song. These programmes both exist in the archives. Black Lace also appeared on *Multi-Coloured Swap Shop* on 10 March.

Roger Whittaker recorded his own composition, 'Call My Name', and released it on a single; he also recorded a German language version as '*Ruf Nach Mir*' (with lyrics by Klaus Munro).

The Nolans Sisters appeared on *The Val Doonican Show* on 21 April performing 'Harry, My Honolulu Lover', while Sal Davis was seen on *The Shirley Bassey Show* several months later, on 29 September, with 'Let It All Go'. Both shows exist in the BBC archives.

M Squad performed 'Miss Caroline Newley' on the edition of ITV's *Tiswas* broadcast on 31 March. This programme is currently not known to exist.

Although Guys 'n' Dolls had a disappointing result in the contest, their song 'How Do You Mend A Broken Heart' reached number 16 in the Belgian charts and number 15 in the Dutch charts. A video performance of the song was recorded on 21 August 1979 for the Dutch programme *TopPop*. This was not broadcast at the time, but has subsequently appeared on DVD.

EUROVISION SONG CONTEST PREVIEWS

Once again the BBC coordinated the preview programmes. All broadcasters had to submit their videos by Saturday 10 March, and they were to be transmitted by the BBC over the Eurovision Network on Friday 16 March.
Presented by Terry Wogan
Recorded: Saturday 17 March

1979 UNITED KINGDOM

Part One: Sunday 18 March at 16.12.38 (Duration 31'54"). Audience 6.50% (3.39 million), RI 58.
Part Two: Sunday 25 March at 16.47.16 (Duration 34'04"). Audience 5.40% (2.82 million), RI 59.

(The audience statistics exclude Wales, as the programmes were shown at different times in Wales.)

The following countries' entries were shown in this order in Part One: Portugal, Italy, Denmark, Ireland, Finland, Monaco, Greece, Switzerland and Israel. The following countries' entries were shown in this order in Part Two: Belgium, France, Germany, Luxembourg, Netherlands, Sweden, Norway, Austria, Spain and the United Kingdom.

The preview video of the United Kingdom entry was shot on Friday 9 March on a boat cruising down the River Thames, taking in various London landmarks. The four members of Black Lace were dressed in brightly-coloured sou'westers, and were seen larking about and having fun on board the boat.

The German song wasn't available at the time the preview programmes were recorded, as the German Final for the contest was actually staged on the evening of that day, 17 March. Thus when Terry Wogan introduced this entry he was unable to make any reference to the title or artist. The German video was edited into Part Two later on, shortly before broadcast. ARD had to transmit their preview video via Frankfurt on Monday 19 March between 14.30 and 14.45. This is one of the reasons why the running order of the entries in the previews had to be different from that in the *Eurovision Song Contest* itself.

CREDIT
Television Presentation by Dave Perrottet

1979 EUROVISION SONG CONTEST

For the first time, the *Eurovision Song Contest* would be broadcast from somewhere outwith the geographical confines of Europe – specifically, from the Israeli capital, Jerusalem. Colour television was still in its infancy in the country; there had been some colour transmissions in November 1977 of the historic visit by Egyptian President Anwar Sadat, but the 1979 contest was the next major event to be broadcast in colour by the IBA (Israel Broadcasting Authority).

Originally the countries that registered for the 1979 contest were the same 20 as had participated the previous year. However Turkey – whose entry, '*Seviyorum*', sung by Maria Rita Epik and 21 Peron, had been drawn at number 11 in the running order – were pressurised to withdraw from the event by Arab countries, leaving 19 in the line-up.

For the first time since 1961, Yugoslavia didn't broadcast the event. This was because it had no diplomatic relations with Israel and regarded Jerusalem as an occupied city. The country had been absent from the contest since 1977, a state of affairs that had been far from popular there, especially with composers and artists, who felt deprived of the opportunity to compete at an international level. In 1978 a major music magazine in the country initiated a survey as to whether Yugoslavia should participate, and more than 100,000 respondents agreed, with just 2,600 disagreeing.

Not surprisingly, the Arab nations didn't take the programme. However, it was broadcast in Romania, Iceland and Hong Kong.

The event was staged in the Menahem Ussiskin auditorium of the Binyaney Haouma Centre. This could normally seat around 3,100 spectators, but seven rows of seats were removed to accommodate the set for the contest, and further rows were removed for the commentators' boxes, reducing the capacity to around 2,000.

1979 EUROVISION SONG CONTEST

News footage shows that, when the scoreboard was being constructed, 'Norway' was unfortunately misspelt 'Norwey'. But by the time of rehearsals this error had been corrected.

The five largest financial contributors, United Kingdom, France, Germany, Italy and Spain, each contributed 32,500 Swiss Francs to the budget, making up 50% in total. 42% came from Belgium, Austria, Switzerland, Denmark, Sweden, Netherlands, Norway, Finland, Turkey, Greece and Portugal, contributing a maximum of 5% – 16,250 Swiss Francs – each. Finally 8% came from Ireland, Luxembourg, Monaco and Israel, contributing a maximum of 2% – 6,500 Swiss Francs – each. There was a small surplus carried forward from the 1978 contest by the EBU, therefore the BBC's contribution actually ended up being 32,029.50 Swiss Francs. The contribution of all the other countries also fell in proportion. Turkey was still liable for its share of the budget despite its late withdrawal.

Black Lace flew out to Jerusalem on Monday 26 March, the same day that rehearsals commenced at 10.00 in the contest venue. Each country had a first rehearsal of 40 minutes, with Portugal through to Israel rehearsing on the first day. All artists were required to be in their stage costumes. This was for lighting purposes, and also for the benefit of the photographers who would be present on the first two days to take the pictures that would be used in the official souvenir programme.

On Tuesday 27 March rehearsals took place with those countries in the second half of the draw. The United Kingdom act had been originally timetabled between 17.40 and 18.20, but as the schedule had still included the now-absent Turkey it is possible they were pulled forward to the earlier slot of 16.30 to 17.10.

Wednesday 28 March saw the second rehearsals take place, with each country now having just 20 minutes of rehearsal time. The scheduled finish time was 18.20. Luxembourg was due to be the final country on stage, but with the absence of Turkey, the Netherlands may have been slotted in at the end.

The remaining countries in the running order had their 20-minute second rehearsal on Thursday 29 March. Black Lace were due on stage from 11.50 until 12.10, but again may have rehearsed in the earlier slot of 11.00 until 11.20.

SONGS FOR EUROPE VOLUME TWO

A full general rehearsal took place the same afternoon, from 15.15 until 17.45, and this was followed by the commentators' briefing from 18.00 until 20.00.

On Friday 30 March there was a general rehearsal at 13.30 with an audience present.

On the morning of Saturday 31 March the two presenters had a rehearsal from 10.30 until 12.15. A full rehearsal with dummy voting then took place from 15.00. For this the artists weren't required to be in their stage costumes. The live transmission would take place at 22.00 local time.

Bookmakers had Italy 9/2 favourite, United Kingdom 6/1, France, Ireland and Sweden 7/1, Israel 10/1, and Germany, Luxembourg and Spain 12/1.

Radio Times had a colour artwork cover promoting the contest. This depicted a musical note representing a map of the world, with a bright shining St David's star above Israel. Inside there was a five-page feature written by Paul Gambaccini on the music scene in Israel, including colour photos of Milk & Honey and Izhar Cohen, plus a score chart for the contest.

A BBC1 trailer broadcast on Friday 30 March at 22.53.31 included 58" of the record version of 'Mary Ann' dubbed onto the videotape. This was shown again on the Saturday, just after that evening's edition of *Rolf on Saturday*.

BBC1's early evening news bulletin on 31 March included a 1'16" item on the contest, covering the security aspect and showing Black Lace rehearsing their entry. This item has been retained in the BBC archives.

EUROVISION SONG CONTEST 1979
Saturday 31 March at 21.00.00 (Duration 177'03")
From the Binyaney Haouma Centre, Jerusalem, Israel
Presented by Daniel Peer and Yardena Arazi

Terry Wogan opted not to go to Israel, having made unfavourable comments on the 1978 winner '*A-Ba-Ni-Bi*',

1979 EUROVISION SONG CONTEST

suggesting that part of the lyric sounded like ... 'I wanna be a polar bear'! Another Radio 2 presenter, John Dunn, instead made his one and only contribution as the commentator on the contest for BBC1. Born in Glasgow in 1934, Dunn had started his broadcasting career in the RAF before joining the BBC in 1956, initially as a studio manager and then as an announcer. He was the regular early evening drive-time presenter on Radio 2. At six foot seven, he was probably the tallest *Eurovision* commentator ever. He retired from his early evening programme in 1998, but still presented the occasional programme after that. Dunn died in November 2004 after suffering from cancer.

Ray Moore once again provided the commentary on Radio 2 and on Radio 1 VHF.

Portugal	'*Sobe, Sobe Balão Sobe*' (2'49")	Sung by Manuela Bravo.	Composed by Carlos Nóbrega e Sousa.	Conducted by Thilo Krassman.

Italy	'*Raggio Di Luna*' (2'59")	Sung by Matia Bazar.	Words by Salvatore Stellita and Giancarlo Golzi. Music by Antonello Ruggiero, Piero Cassano and Carlo Marrale.

The Italian entry was the first ever to rely entirely on a backing track, without the orchestra.

SONGS FOR EUROPE VOLUME TWO

Denmark	'Disco Tango' (2'48")	Sung by Tommy Seebach.	Words by Keld Heick. Music by Tommy Seebach.	Conducted by Allan Botchinsky.

Ireland	'Happy Man' (2'58")	Sung by Cathal Dunne.	Composed by Cathal Dunne.	Conducted by Pronsias O'Duinn.

Finland	*Katso Sineen Taivaan* (2'53")	Sung by Katri Helena.	Words by Veikko Salmi. Music by Matti Kalevi Siitonen.	Conducted by Ossi Runne.

Monaco	*Notre Vie C'est La Musique* (2'53")	Sung by Laurent Vaguener (Jean Baudlot).	Words by Jean Albertini and Didier Barbelivien. Music by Paul de Senneville and Jean Baudlot.	Conducted by Gérard Salesse.

1979 EUROVISION SONG CONTEST

Greece	'Socrates' (3'01")	Sung by Elpida.	Words by Sofia Tsotu. Music by Doros Georgiadis.	Conducted by Lefteris Halkiadakis.

Switzerland	*Trödler Und Co* (2'43")	Sung by Peter, Sue and Marc, Pfuri, Gorps and Kniri.	Composed by Peter Reber.	Conducted by Rolf Zuckowski.

Peter, Sue and Marc had previously represented Switzerland in the 1971 and 1976 contests.

Germany	'Dschinghis Khan' (2'56")	Sung by Dschinghis Khan.	Words by Bernd Meinunger. Music by Ralph Siegel.	Conducted by Norbert Daum.

Israel	'Hallelujah' (3'02")	Sung by Gali Atari and Milk & Honey.	Words by Shimrit Orr. Music by Kobi Oshrat.	Conducted by Kobi Oshrat.

The song 'Hallelujah' had originally been offered to the group Habibi, but they had turned it down. They would though end up representing their country in the 1981 contest.

SONGS FOR EUROPE VOLUME TWO

Gali Atari, born in December 1953, was an actress as well as a singer. She had entered the Israeli heat for the *Eurovision Song Contest* in 1978 and finished third behind Izhar Cohen. Milk & Honey were a three-man group comprising Re'uven Gvitrz, Shmulik Bilu and Yehuda Tamir.

'Hallelujah' reached number five in the UK charts, and the group performed the song in the *Top of the Pops* studio for the edition broadcast on 5 April. A repeat of this was then included in the edition broadcast on 19 April. Both editions exist in the BBC archives. The group also appeared on *The Val Doonican Music Show* broadcast on 7 April, which has likewise been retained in the archives.

A follow-up single, 'Goodbye New York', failed to make much international impact, and Atari split from the rest of the group not long afterwards and returned to a solo career. Milk & Honey had a couple of unsuccessful attempts at representing Israel again, in 1981 and 1989, on both occasions joined by female vocalist Lea Lupatin. In the 1988 contest, two members of the group, Gvitrz and Tamir, were backing vocalists for Yardena Arazi, coincidentally the presenter of the 1979 contest.

Turkey (Withdrawn)	'*Seviyorum*'	Sung by Maria Rita Epik & 21 Peron.	Composed by Maria Rita Epik.

France	'*Je Suis L'Enfant-Soleil*' (2'54")	Sung by Anne-Marie David.	Words by Hubert Giraud. Music by Eddy Marnay.	Conducted by Guy Mattéoni.

Anne-Marie David had won the 1973 contest for Luxembourg with '*Tu Te Reconnaîtras*'.

1979 EUROVISION SONG CONTEST

Belgium	'Hey Nana' (2'56")	Sung by Micha Mara.	Words by Guy Beyers. Music by Charles Dumolin.	Conducted by Francis Bay.

Luxembourg	*J'ai Déjà Vu Ça Dans Tes Yeux* (2'52")	Sung by Jeane Manson.	Composed by Jean Renard.	Conducted by Hervé Roy.

Netherlands	'Colorado' (2'49")	Sung by Xandra.	Words by Gerard Cox and Ferdi Bolland. Music by Rob Bolland.	Conducted by Harry van Hoof.

Xandra (Sandra Reemer) had twice before represented the Netherlands, in 1972 and in 1976.

Sweden	*Satellit* (2'51")	Sung by Ted Gärdestad.	Words by Kenneth Gärdestad. Music by Ted Gärdestad.	Conducted by Lars Samuelson.

SONGS FOR EUROPE VOLUME TWO

| Norway | 'Oliver' (2'38") | Sung by Anita Skorgan. | Words by Philip Kruse. Music by Anita Skorgan. | Conducted by Sigurd Jansen. |

Anita Skorgan had previously represented Norway in 1977 with 'Casanova', finishing in fifteenth place.

| United Kingdom | 'Mary Ann' (2'56") | Sung by Black Lace (Alan Barton, Colin Routh, Terry Dobson and Steven Scholey). With two backing vocalists. | Composed by Peter Morris. | Conducted by Ken Jones. |

In a contemporary interview, lead singer Alan Barton said: 'After years of struggling, playing some grotty northern clubs, the contest is the big break we've been waiting for. There are a thousand bands back home who dream every night of having the chance we've got. If we win, we're made. If we can have the same success as groups like Brotherhood of Man, we'll be more than satisfied.'

The *Daily Express* said of 'Mary Ann': 'Zestful tune, cheeky lyrics and excellent arrangement.' The *Sun* meanwhile opined: 'A song with plenty of beat. This is their big break and they'll give it all they've got. My rating: 7/10'. 'The only song not to rely on a big band or orchestra,' remarked Charles Catchpole in the *Daily Mail*, 'and its boozy, good-natured, pub singalong simplicity may just prove a winner, coming after all the flash and oompah of the preceding songs. But it sounds like Mungo Jerry circa 1970 to me.' Regular commentator

1979 EUROVISION SONG CONTEST

Terry Wogan stated bluntly: 'I don't think Britain is going to make it this year. I think Italy could win.'

The usual procedure was that whoever had produced *A Song for Europe* would go on to represent the BBC at that year's *Eurovision Song Contest*. In 1979, this would have been David Hiller, but he was unable to go, so Tony James, a manager in the BBC's Light Entertainment Department, did the job instead.

'It was extraordinary,' says James, 'because it so happened that as we were *en route*, literally in mid-air, a peace treaty was signed between Egypt and Israel. As we were flying on the Israeli airline El-Al, I had a word with the captain, and with his permission Black Lace sang some peace songs on the flight. When we got to Israel there was this colossal atmosphere of peace.

'I think when you are out in another country for the contest, apart from being involved in presenting our act, one of the benefits is the chance to see something of the host nation. One of the things we did while in Jerusalem was to visit Yad Vashem, the museum dedicated to the Holocaust and the six million people who died. It is actually quite horrific what you see on display, with the photographs, and details of the numbers killed; it's all very harrowing. What was interesting was that the Chief Rabbi of Yad Vashem took only the United Kingdom delegation around, but only because we were the only ones who had asked.'

James recalls that, wiping away a tear at the time, he got talking to the Rabbi. 'I had noticed that on either side of the Eternal Flame, there were flowers, and I asked about them. He said, "These ones are from President Carter and these ones are from President Sadat … and those ones are from Marks and Spencer." So I said, "Does that mean anyone can place flowers there?" and he replied, "Absolutely." So we discussed it further, and we decided we would have a little service. All of us went – Black Lace, Bill Cotton, James Gilbert – and we took our own flowers on behalf of the BBC, and paid our respects to the state and those who were murdered.'

In the aftermath of the contest, a follow-up single by Black Lace failed to make any impact, but the group continued to make appearances across Europe, including at festivals in Poland and Bulgaria. They toured in Denmark and worked alongside Tommy Seebach, the artist who had represented that country in Jerusalem.

SONGS FOR EUROPE VOLUME TWO

By 1981 both Dobson and Scholey had left the group, leaving Barton and Routh to carry on the name as a duo. However it was then that they had their biggest successes, with the singles 'Superman', 'Agadoo' and 'Do The Conga' all making the top ten in the charts between 1982 and 1984. Further singles in 1985 and 1986 made the top 75. The albums *Party, Party* and *Party, Party 2* reached the top 20 in 1984.

In the following years there were periodic changes in the line-up. Barton eventually left to join the group Smokie, and was on tour with them in 1995 when he was killed in a coach crash.

In 1999, to mark their twentieth anniversary since the contest, former drummer Dobson organised a charity reunion concert, appearing alongside Routh and Dean Barton, son of the late Alan Barton.

By 2002, Routh had semi-retired and emigrated to Tenerife, where he still performs in occasional Black Lace shows.

Austria	'Heute In Jerusalem' (3'12")	Sung by Christine Simon.	Words by André Heller. Music by Peter Wolf.	Conducted by Richard Österreicher.

Spain	'Su Canción' (2'51")	Sung by Betty Missiego.	Composed by Fernando Moreno.	Conducted by José Luis Navarro.

THE VOTING

The voting system was again the same as had been used since 1975. On the British jury were Stewart Barker, Mrs M Bartel, Mrs C Carmichael, Mr A Charlton, Mr B Crisp, Miss L Gilchrist, Miss A Knight, Mr I Jones, Mr S Noel, Miss J Parker and Canon E Young. Colin Berry was the United Kingdom spokesperson.

1979 EUROVISION SONG CONTEST

One award of points from Spain were misheard on the transmission as 'Portugal dix points', when it was in fact 'six points', so the correct figure is shown here.

	Portugal	Italy	Denmark	Ireland	Finland	Monaco	Greece	Switzerland	Germany	Israel	France	Belgium	Luxembourg	Netherlands	Sweden	Norway	UK	Austria	Spain	TOTAL	POSITION
Portugal		6			2	5		4	4		10	5	3	3	3	6		7	6	64	9TH
Italy	8				8										3				8	27	15TH
Denmark				2		3	12	1	10	12	6	7	4	8	1		3	3	4	76	6TH
Ireland	5	5	5		6		10	6	6	3		10	7		8	5	4			80	5TH
Finland		7					7	8	5		5		6							38	14TH
Monaco	1	2	4								3								2	12	16TH
Greece	10		1	4		7		7	2	10	4	1	5	7	2			2	7	69	8TH
Switzerland			7	1	10	2	2		7	4	7				8			12		60	10TH
Germany	2	1	12	5	3	12				6	12	4	1	2	6		8		12	86	4TH
Israel	12		6	12	12	8	4	5			1	2	8	1	12	12	12	8	10	125	1ST

SONGS FOR EUROPE VOLUME TWO

France	6	10			1	10	8	10		5	▓	6	12	12	5	7	6	5	3	106	3RD
Belgium			2					1				▓					2			05	18TH=
Luxembourg	7			3	4	4	5	3		2			▓	4		2	10			44	13TH
Netherlands			8	10	5		3		3	7		3		▓	4	4		4		51	12TH
Sweden				6			1			1					▓					08	17TH
Norway	3	3		8		6			2		8	2	6	10		▓	7	1	1	57	11TH
United Kingdom	4	8	10	7	7	1		2	8				5		10		▓	6	5	73	7TH
Austria		4														1		▓		05	18TH=
Spain		12	3			6	12	12	8	8	12	10	10	7	1	5	10		▓	116	2ND

Analysis: The early rounds of voting saw Israel and the United Kingdom as the main contenders, with the eventual runners-up Spain not figuring at all. Israel then surged ahead, while the United Kingdom dropped down the leader board. It was looking good for the host nation, but they then had a few low-scoring rounds and Spain overtook them and went into the lead. France was also scoring well, and was lying in second place. Israel then had a good run of maximum marks, including one from the United Kingdom, to move back into second place. Going into the final round, Spain had a one point lead over Israel, but it was Spain to vote, and of course they could not vote for themselves. By awarding Israel ten points they handed them the title for the second year

1979 EUROVISION SONG CONTEST

in succession.

Israel joined Luxembourg and Spain as the only countries to have won two contests in a row. It was also the first entry to win from being drawn tenth in the running order, meaning that only positions two, four and – curiously – 16 had yet to yield a winner (although not all contests had had 16 or more entrants). The United Kingdom received its highest scores of ten points from Denmark and Norway, and although its final position was an improvement on the previous year, it was still one of the poorest results up to this point.

WINNING REPRISE

| Israel | 'Hallelujah' (3'14") | Sung by Gali Atari and Milk & Honey. | Words by Shimrit Orr. Music by Kobi Oshrat. | Conducted by Kobi Oshrat. |

CREDITS
Producer: Alex Giladi
Director: Yossi Zemach
Designer: Dov Ben-David
Music Director: Itzhak Graziani
EBU Scrutineer: Frank Naef

The contest was watched by 32.50% of the British population (16.90 million) at the start of the programme from 21.00, falling slightly to 32.20% (16.80 million) from 22.00 and then increasing to 36.80% (19.20 million) from 22.45. It scored an RI of 59. The BBC has retained a copy of the broadcast version in its archives.

AFTERWORD

As the 1970s came to a close, the contest was still highly popular with the British public, although it had started to take a slight dip in the audience figures. Part of this dip could perhaps be attributed to the increased network coverage by BBC2, and to whatever programmes ITV decided to screen in opposition each year. However, more significantly, toward the end of the decade there also came the introduction of affordable domestic video recorders, and video film rentals, meaning that viewers were no longer restricted to watching just the network broadcasts. (It was estimated in 1978/1979 that 75% of video film rentals were for X-rated films, not often seen on BBC1 or ITV.)

At the beginning of the decade, well-known artists were being recruited to represent the United Kingdom in the contest, but despite achieving respectable results, none of them was able to take the coveted top place. The music press and music professionals were also picking up on the fact that the British public had an uncanny knack of choosing the same type of song each year, perhaps in an attempt to find another 'Puppet On A String' or 'Boom Bang-A-Bang'. Top artists thus became increasingly reluctant to enter the contest, not wishing to risk their reputations by losing or being associated with a song that they actively disliked. Top songwriters may also have become unwilling to submit their best material in case it was rejected in favour of a throwaway pop number.

The industrial action that had affected *A Song for Europe* in 1977 and 1979 may also have had an impact on the programme's popularity, taking the United Kingdom's entry briefly out of the public eye and giving it a weaker launch than it would have received had the programme been broadcast. This was particularly the case in 1979, when the unknown group Black Lace won, and the lack of exposure probably had an impact on their chart position as well.

However, it wasn't just the British entries toward the end of the decade that were failing to reach the top ten

AFTERWORD

in the UK charts. The same was pretty much the case with the *Eurovision Song Contest*'s winning songs as well. Fortunately, the 1979 winner 'Hallelujah' managed to buck the trend, showing that a big *Eurovision* hit was still possible and giving the contest a much-needed boost as it headed toward its twenty-fifth anniversary.

There was however one major stumbling block … which broadcaster would take responsibility for staging the 1980 contest?

The next volume will cover what happened in the 1980s, when there would be some further highs and lows for the United Kingdom in the contest, and a then-unknown French-Canadian singer would triumph for Switzerland and go onto become an international superstar …

ERRATA

Despite my best efforts to ensure that everything contained within these books is accurate, a few errors slipped through in Volume One. This section details those that I have since spotted or had pointed out to me. It also contains some previously-missing facts that have since come to light.

1956 UNITED KINGDOM
Page 91 Credits: George Melachrino should appear under Musical Directors and not under Technical Operations Manager.
Page 369: In the scorechart, the three songs finishing in 7TH position should be marked 7TH=.

1957 UNITED KINGDOM
Page 104: An additional detail is that the song 'Rainbow Island' was recorded by Andy Cole as a single, released in 1962. 'Simple Waltz' was composed by William Henmore (not 'Helmore').

1958 EUROVISION SONG CONTEST
The BBC was the first choice of broadcaster to host the 1958 contest, however it had problems reaching agreement with the various artistic unions, and by 22 July 1957 it formally withdrew its offer, allowing the Dutch broadcaster NTS to take over.

Initially the BBC was going to submit an entry for the contest, but ultimately withdrew. Monaco likewise intended to submit an entry (as they had also planned to do in 1957) but withdrew.

The BBC was still prepared to take the live broadcast of the 1958 Final on Wednesday 12 March. However,

ERRATA

live coverage of a sports event on the same date meant that the broadcast had to be deferred until 16 March.

1961 UNITED KINGDOM

Results: A more complete breakdown of the voting has now been discovered, thanks to one viewer who wrote down the cumulative scores at the time of transmission. Unfortunately either their taking down of the votes was rushed at the start, or else perhaps there were actually some errors made on the scoreboard at the time, so the votes of the first four juries are still 'best guesses' taken from their scorechart (shown in *italics*). The rest of the information however would appear to be 100% correct.

	Aberdeen	Glasgow	Belfast	Leeds	Bangor	Manchester	Norwich	Birmingham	Cardiff	London	Bristol	Southampton	TOTAL	POSITION
'Dream Girl'	*4*	*2*			2	2			2		3	1	16	4TH
'The Girl Next Door'				*1*	1	1							03	7TH
'Why Can't We?'	*4*		*6*		2	1	3	4	1		1	2	24	3RD
'A Place In The Country'				*3*					2		1		06	5TH
'I Will Light A Candle'			*1*	*2*								1	04	6TH
'Suddenly I'm In Love'		*8*			2	1	5	1		7	3	3	30	2ND

SONGS FOR EUROPE VOLUME TWO

'Too Late For Tears'					1			1		1			03	7TH
'Tommy'						2			1				03	7TH
'Are You Sure?'	2			7	3	2	2	5	3	3	1	3	31	1ST

Analysis: Very quickly several songs surged away in the voting, and by the half-way stage there were four – 'Dream Girl', 'Are You Sure', 'Why Can't We?' and 'Suddenly I'm In Love' – that looked to be in contention, repeatedly swapping the lead. When Norwich voted, three of them were sharing the top spot, with 'Dream Girl' starting to fall behind the others. By the time Cardiff voted, it looked as if 'Are You Sure' was starting to open up a small lead over 'Why Can't We?' and that 'Suddenly I'm In Love' was falling behind. However the London jury delivered a large vote for the eventual runner-up, and the contest was heading for a thrilling conclusion – especially when Bristol reduced the gap between the top two to a single vote. Although 'Why Can't We?', which had been in strong contention for much of the voting, faded towards the end, it could still mathematically have won in the final round of voting. However, it was really down to either 'Are You Sure?' or 'Suddenly I'm In Love'. The Southampton jury kept the tension going to the end, and it went right down to the wire, the final vote from the final jury giving 'Are You Sure?' the narrowest of wins.

1964 EUROVISION SONG CONTEST
Page 348: Ian Fenner provided commentary for British Forces Radio.

1965 EUROVISION SONG CONTEST
Page 370: Ian Fenner provided commentary for British Forces Radio.

ERRATA

1966 UNITED KINGDOM
Due to the songs being previewed in a different order from that of the Final, the Audience Figures and RI were transposed in error as a result. The relevant entries should have read as follows:

Page 400: 'Country Girl'
The 6 January edition in which 'Country Girl' was previewed was watched by 20.6% of the population (10.30 million) and scored an RI of 65.

Page 401: 'As Long As The Sun Shines'
The 13 January edition in which 'As Long As The Sun Shines' was previewed was watched by 19.0% of the population (9.50 million) and scored an RI of 68.

Page 402: 'Comes The Time'
The 30 December edition in which 'Comes The Time' was previewed was watched by 22.30% of the population (11.15 million) and scored an RI of 65.

Page 403: 'A Touch Of The Tartan'
The 23 December edition in which 'A Touch Of The Tartan' was previewed was watched by 20.5% of the population (10.25 million) and scored an RI of 73.

1966 EUROVISION SONG CONTEST
Page 407: Ian Fenner provided commentary for British Forces Radio.

SONGS FOR EUROPE VOLUME TWO

1967 UNITED KINGDOM
Page 425. The third paragraph should read: 'As mentioned by Mitch Murray …' (and not 'by Peter Callander').

1967 EUROVISION SONG CONTEST
Page 434: Thurston Holland provided commentary for British Forces Radio.

1968 UNITED KINGDOM
Page 453: Richard also recorded a German-language version of the third-placed song, 'Wonderful World', also titled 'Wonderful World' (lyric: Günter Loose).

1968 EUROVISION SONG CONTEST
Page 459: Thurston Holland provided commentary for British Forces Radio.

1969 EUROVISION SONG CONTEST
Page 483: John Russell provided commentary for British Forces Radio.

Page 487: In the entry for Germany, Siw Malmkvist's first name is misspelt as 'Sim'.

Songs for Europe: The United Kingdom at the Eurovision Song Contest: Volume One: The 1950s and 1960s by Gordon Roxburgh

Every year since 1956 millions of people around Europe and beyond have tuned in to watch the annual Eurovision Song Contest. It has become compulsive viewing, as viewers support their favourite song or country, and eagerly watch the performances and anticipate the excitement of the international voting as the show heads towards its climax.

Through examination of surviving archive material and documentation, plus interviews with those involved both behind and front of the camera, this series of books charts the history of the United Kingdom in the contest. Find out more about how the songs were selected to represent the country, and details on the all important voting each year.

This first volume looks at how the contest was created, and how important the BBC were in influencing its development. There is in depth coverage of those contests staged in the United Kingdom, and interviews with artists, composers and production personnel who took part in both the domestic and international competitions.

A detailed and exhaustive work of reference which fans of music and television history will find invaluable and fascinating.

500pp approx. A5 paperback book in landscape format. ISBN 978-1-84583-065-6 (pb). Paperback @ £16.99 + p&p.